Progressively Worse

The burden of bad ideas in British schools

Robert Peal

CIVITAS
INSTITUTE FOR THE STUDY
OF CIVIL SOCIETY · LONDON

First Published May 2014

55 Tufton Street
London SW1P 3QL

email: books@civitas.org.uk

ISBN 978-1-906837-62-4

Independence: Civitas: Institute for the Study of Civil Society is a registered educational charity (No. 1085494) and a company limited by guarantee (No. 04023541). Civitas is financed from a variety of private sources to avoid over-reliance on any single or small group of donors.

All publications are independently refereed. All the Institute's publications seek to further its objective of promoting the advancement of learning. The views expressed are those of the authors, not of the Institute.

Designed and typeset by
Richard Kelly

Printed in Great Britain by
Berforts Group Ltd
Stevenage, SG1 2BH

Upon the education of the people of this country the fate of this country depends.

Benjamin Disraeli, 1874

Dare any call Permissiveness
An educational success?
Saner those class-rooms which I sat in,
Compelled to study Greek and Latin.

W. H. Auden, 1972

I would label myself a political liberal and an educational conservative, or perhaps more accurately, an educational pragmatist. Political liberals really ought to oppose progressive educational ideas because they have led to practical failure and greater social inequity.

E. D. Hirsch, 1999

Contents

Author

Robert Peal is a history teacher and education research fellow at the think-tank Civitas. He taught for two years at an inner-city secondary school in Birmingham through Teach First and will be returning to the classroom in September 2014 to teach at a free school. He is a regular contributor to *Standpoint* magazine and keeps a blog on education. Until recently, he wrote under the pseudonym Matthew Hunter, described by Michael Gove as 'one of the brightest young voices in the education debate'.

Robert graduated in 2010 with a starred first in history from Sidney Sussex College, Cambridge and gained a Thouron Scholarship to the University of Pennsylvania. He lived in West Philadelphia for a year, before moving to the West Midlands. He now lives in London.

Acknowledgements

This book benefited from emerging at a time when a community of teachers has been challenging the dominant ideas in British schools. I am indebted to Katharine Birbalsingh, Daisy Christodoulou and Joe Kirby for their knowledge of the education debate, and to Katie Ashford, Kristopher Boulton and Bodil Isaken for some spirited conversations. In particular, thank you to Andrew Old, the titan of teacher-bloggers, who took time from his blog 'Scenes from the Battleground' to write the foreword for this book.

Another observer of the education scene, Toby Young, introduced me to *Standpoint* magazine, where the editor, Daniel Johnson, published my first stabs at education commentary. My old friend Laura Freeman kindly thought to put me in touch with Civitas. Thank you to all three for making this book a possibility. At Civitas, thank you to David Green for guiding me through the project, to Daniel Bentley for his thoughtful advice during its later stages and to the referees whose comments on an earlier version of this book were so helpful.

Thank you to all my friends and family who have kept me company through the lonely business of writing a book, in particular Rob Orme – almost all the arguments in this book have originated in our conversations. Thank you to the Bakers for their hospitality, and to Georgie for being wonderful throughout. Lastly, thank you to my parents for their continual guidance and support, and also for their proofing: had it not been for this, my first draft would have been an embarrassing verification of declining education standards in Britain.

Acknowledgements

Foreword

Few publications can claim to be subversive, but that is a fitting description for what Robert Peal has written here. He has related a piece of educational history and described a debate that many educationalists, managers and inspectors will not want teachers to be aware of. It is not simply that his arguments against the influence that progressive education has on our education system will challenge many of those in a position of undeserved power and authority; he also provides the context that is lacking for so many of those who are, or soon will be, a part of our education system.

While academics and journalists (or even bloggers like myself) might talk of an ongoing and established debate over education methods between progressives and traditionalists, it is not something that one can expect to hear much of when one becomes a teacher. It is entirely possible to be trained as a teacher in a university and in schools and teach for several years without ever hearing that there is any doubt over whether teacher talk is harmful; discovery learning is effective; or knowledge is less important than skills. To inform teachers that these disputes exist is to cast doubt on the expertise of most of those who train teachers; many of those who run schools; and also those with the greatest power in education: the schools inspectorate – Ofsted. For at least some readers, this will be the first time they have heard that certain orthodoxies have been, or can be, challenged.

Of course, for the informed reader this may not be the first time such challenges to the progressive consensus have been encountered in print. The last few years have seen the publication of titles such as Daisy Christodoulou's *Seven Myths About Education,* Tom Bennett's *Teacher Proof* and Katharine Birbalsingh's *To Miss With Love,* which have demonstrated the existence of influential voices in education expressing views many teachers have never heard before. This has been supplemented further by many, many bloggers who have been hostile to the ideological status quo. Additionally, it has also been informed by influential books from the United States by individuals such as Daniel Willingham, Doug Lemov and E.D. Hirsch. These writers, while not necessarily writing polemical or ideological tracts, have nevertheless confidently explored ideas about the curriculum, teaching methods and the psychology of learning that fell far outside the comfort zone of the English education system.

However, I believe Robert Peal is now making a unique and essential contribution to this debate by providing the political and historical context of the arguments. Neither progressives nor traditionalists can claim to represent a new development in education. With the possible exception of some of the latest evidence from cognitive psychology for the effectiveness of traditional teaching, almost all the arguments described here have been part of the history of our education system for more than five decades. Generations have fought these battles, proved their points and bucked the system, only to be airbrushed from history by an educational establishment only too keen to recycle ideas from 1967's Plowden Report as the latest innovation. The historical chapters here analyse and present the history of those arguments in a way which perhaps most closely resembles *Left Back,* Diane Ravitch's magisterial recounting of the 'education wars' in the United States. If this causes teachers to realise that they can find ideas and inspiration, not just in the contemporary critics of progressive education, but in the writings of Michael Oakshott or R.S. Peters, then the educational discussion will be thoroughly enriched. The debate on education is not one limited to the present generation; it is not a scrap between, for example, Sir Ken Robinson and Michael Gove. It is a conversation that dates back, at least to the nineteenth century, in which figures such as Matthew Arnold, Charles Dickens, G.K. Chesterton, D.H. Lawrence, George Orwell, Dorothy L. Sayers and C.S. Lewis have had something to say on one side or the other. We should not let the latest iteration of the disagreement, with its talk of '21st Century Skills' and 'flipped classrooms', blind us to that wider perspective.

A historical perspective should also save us from being convinced that this row is one conducted along narrow party political lines. While their efforts to stem the tide of progressivism may have faltered in office, it is impossible to miss the extent to which some of the voices speaking out against the education establishment were those of Labour politicians such as Callaghan, Blunkett and Blair. While the influence of progressive education seems to have been greater on the left than the right, the case against it can be made on egalitarian grounds as easily as conservative ones. Robert Tressell, the undoubtedly working-class political activist and author, wrote in *The Ragged Trousered Philanthropists*:

> What we call civilisation – the accumulation of knowledge which has come down to us from our forefathers – is the fruit of thousands of years of human thought and toil. It is not the result of the labour of the ancestors of any separate class of people who exist today, and therefore it is by right the common heritage of all. Every little child that is born into the world, no matter whether he is clever or dull, whether he is physically perfect or lame, or blind; no matter how much he may excel or fall short of his fellows in other respects, in one thing at least he is their equal – he is one of the heirs of all the ages that have gone before.

If this point is then accepted, education, in the sense of the full entitlement to the best of our society's culture and knowledge, is not a relic of a discredited tradition, but wealth that should be distributed to all. Comprehensive education, when viewed as an academic education for all, might represent a core principle of the left. By contrast, progressive education, with its contempt for the accumulated knowledge of mankind, is likely to work only to deprive the disadvantaged and excluded of an asset that will remain the exclusive property of the privileged and powerful. Middle-class partisans of both right and left would happily misrepresent the education debate as a mere reflection of wider political disagreements. However, many of us who identify our politics most closely with the aspirational, working-class tradition within the Labour Party are happy to campaign as firmly against the excesses of progressive education as we do against the excesses of free-market capitalism. This is for fundamentally the same reason; it increases the deprivation of the less fortunate for the sake of an ideological experiment conducted at their expense by those with little to lose personally.

So with this in mind, I welcome what Robert Peal has achieved here. He has provided a much needed perspective on a debate that has been at best narrowed, and at worst hidden. It should be essential reading for anyone who wishes to engage with an argument that has raged for over a century, and shows every sign of continuing. For those unfamiliar with educational politics, appropriately it will be an education. For those who have only seen the disagreements over education described from the perspective of progressive educationalists, it will be a shock. For those within the education system who are already sympathetic to his cause, it will be a call for subversion.

Andrew Old

Introduction

How should children learn? For many this may seem like an obvious question, but for those involved in education it has been the subject of fifty years of furious debate.

Should children learn from the wisdom of an authoritative teacher, or should they learn independently and discover things for themselves? Should children learn an academic curriculum, or is this just filling their heads with 'mere knowledge' where 'skills' would be more useful? Should children be driven by the structure of rewards and examinations, or should they be motivated by lessons that are 'relevant' and 'fun'? Should children be sanctioned for misbehaving and not working, or is such a practice cruel and authoritarian?

For the moderate minded observer, it would seem that the obvious path lies through the middle of each of these statements. However, this would be to ignore the status quo in the contemporary 'thoughtworld' of British state education. Over the past half century, the education establishment has become firmly wedded to the latter statement in each of these dichotomies. These ideas can be grouped together under the term 'progressive education'. It is the thesis of this book that if any significant improvement is to take place in British schools, we must move away from this damaging doctrine.

In October 1996, Tony Blair made his keynote speech at the Labour Party Conference in Blackpool. The audience roared with approval as he declared: 'Ask me my three main priorities for government and I tell you: education, education, education.'[1] In financial terms, Blair certainly fulfilled his pledge. Over the 13 years of New Labour government, education spending saw an unprecedented rise. Total public expenditure on education rose from £39 billion in 1997-98 to £89 billion in 2009-10, going from 4.5 per cent to 6.2 per cent of Britain's total GDP.[2] There was a bewildering flurry of building projects, new initiatives and human activity, but by 2010 few would claim that Britain's schools had been transformed. Above all else, New Labour's exuberant spending demonstrated that a lack of funding is not the root cause of Britain's education problem.

The view that there is a fundamental problem in British education is often ridiculed as sensationalist panic, but the bare figures are hard to ignore:

- The 2012 Programme for International Student Assessment (PISA) ranked the UK 23rd in the world for reading, 26th for maths and 21st for science out of 65 countries or regions.[3]
- According to a 2013 OECD survey of adult skills, England/N.Ireland is the *only country in the developed world* where literacy and numeracy levels amongst 16-24-year-olds are no better than amongst 55-65-year-olds.[4]
- Amongst British employers, 55 per cent report problems in English and 51 per cent problems in numeracy with their employees.[5]
- More than one in five English children is identified as having Special Educational Needs (SEN), five times the EU average.[6]
- A 2010 Teacher Support Network survey reported that 92 per cent of respondents said pupil behaviour had worsened during their career. In 2010, attacks from pupils hospitalised 44 teachers.[7]
- 43 per cent of graduates who begin teacher

training leave the profession within five years.[8]

- One in 17 sixth form students from independent schools, and one in 29 sixth form students from grammar schools, go to Oxbridge. Only one in 125 pupils do so from state comprehensive sixth forms.[9]

If one takes a historical view, this is a longstanding problem. A thorough report into comparable, long-term statistics on numeracy and literacy in the UK published in 2010 concluded that British reading scores steadily improved from 1948 to 1960. There was no improvement between the years 1960 to 1988. A gentle rise from 1997 to 2004 was then followed by another plateau. Due to decades of inadequacy, the total number of British people of all ages thought to be functionally illiterate is estimated to be seven million. Functional illiteracy has stayed remarkably consistent since World War II, hovering just under 20 per cent.[10] This has endured despite government spending on education increasing by almost nine times, in real terms, between 1953 and 2009.[11]

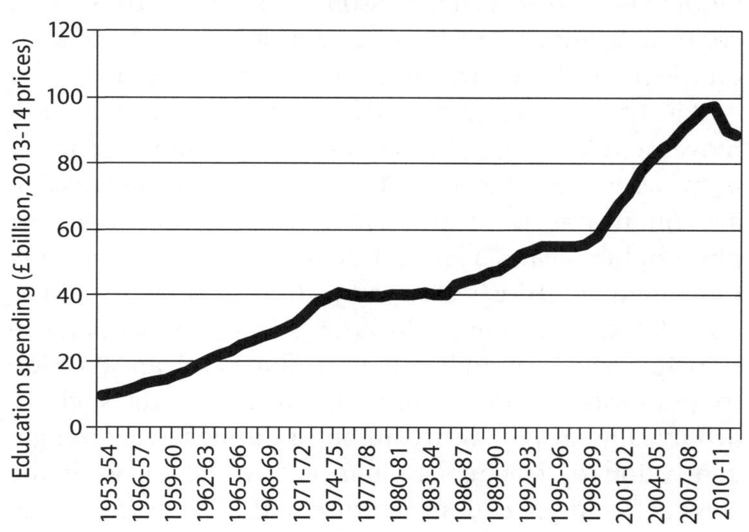

For such an enormous increase in education expenditure to be matched with so little change in this basic marker of pupil success suggests that something has gone very wrong in Britain's classrooms over the past half century.

The question of Britain's enduring educational failure was on my mind when I began working at a challenging, inner-city school in 2011. Such schools are often described as 'deprived', but as the months moved on I began to question what exactly was depriving this school. Funding was higher than ever, members of staff were bright and hard-working, and we were housed in an immaculate, new, multi-million pound building. Yet, the school was unruly and pupils were underachieving.

I realised that more important than any material deprivation was a deprivation of ideas. Many features of the school struck me as inimical to good schooling, and its prevailing philosophy left me deeply confused. Sanctions were not enforced. Nothing was done about the high levels of illiteracy. The subject that I taught, history, had been emptied of content and replaced with a series of bogus 'skills'. I was criticised in observations for conducting whole-class, teacher-led lessons. Lastly, excuses were continually made for the under-performance of 'our kids' on the basis of their socio-economic background.

All these strange features could be traced to a movement known, with a certain irony of nomenclature, as 'progressive' education. The origins of this movement are often traced to the eighteenth-century and the philosopher Jean-Jacques Rousseau, although it only took hold in British state education during the 1960s and 1970s. Progressive education seeks to apply political principles such as individual freedom and an aversion to authority to the realm of education. As such, it achieved great popularity amongst an idealistic younger generation of teachers influenced by the ideas of the New Left and the counter-culture of the 1960s. Although often associated with the political left, it is wrong to see progressive education as its direct corollary. Many within the British Labour movement forcefully opposed progressive education during the 1960s and 1970s, and again during the 1990s.

The idealism of progressive education had, and continues to have, a strong emotional appeal to modern sympathies. Freeing pupils from the overbearing authority of teachers, allowing them to follow their own interests, and making learning fun as opposed to coercive, all appear as sensible measures to the enlightened, liberal-minded onlooker. However, as I hope to show, such an approach has had a devastating effect on pupils' education. There are four core themes that constitute progressive education, which have been increasingly influential on state education since the 1960s. They require some prior discussion.

1 **Education should be child-centred.** Perhaps the most important of progressive education's themes, child-centred learning states that pupils should direct their own learning. Set against a more traditional vision of 'teacher-led' or 'whole-class' teaching, child-centred learning relegates the role of the teacher from being a 'sage on the stage' to a 'guide on the side'. It states that learning is superior when pupils find things out for themselves, and are not simply told information by a knowledgeable authority. To achieve this, teachers should play the role of 'facilitators', designing lessons that are active, relevant or fun in an environment where pupils can learn for themselves. Child-centred advocates typically have an aversion to practices 'imposed' upon the pupils by the teacher, such as discrete subject divisions, homework, examinations, note-taking or rote-learning, preferring to organise

lessons around topics, group work, activities and extended projects. The analogy of a child with a growing plant is popularly used, suggesting that no external input is needed to nurture a child's education, but simply the provision of the right environment in which they can flower.

2 **Knowledge is not central to education.** This theme is set against the more traditional idea of education as the transfer of knowledge. Progressive educators parody this as 'rote-learning' or 'filling buckets' – a reference to the aphorism 'Education is not the filling of a vessel, but the lighting of a fire', often attributed to W. B. Yeats but actually from Plutarch. Knowledge is re-characterised as a transitory component of education, only necessary for the ultimate aim of developing certain abilities or traits. These could be 'critical thinking', 'creativity' or 'a love of learning'. More recently, educationists have challenged the knowledge that the teacher seeks to impart as being politically or culturally partisan, for example promoting the work of 'dead white men' in the canon of English literature. Also, this aversion to knowledge has fused with the modern, managerial language of 'skills'. Subjects now seek to equip pupils not with knowledge but with certain 'transferable skills', which will aid them in later life.

3 **Strict discipline and moral education are oppressive.** Whilst the previous two themes challenge the teacher's role as an authority in their subject, this theme challenges the teacher's role as a moral authority. Strongly influenced by romantic idealism, which proclaims the innate good of a child, this theme leads to a greater leniency in dealing with poor pupil behaviour. The root of bad

behaviour is seen not as the fault of the child, but the fault of the teacher or institution. Therefore, the pupil should not be punished, but the teacher or institution should amend their ways to become more aligned with the needs of the child. As such, this theme is related to the first theme, as there is an assumption that if a teacher makes a lesson sufficiently 'child-centred', the pupils will be willing to learn and coercion will become unnecessary. In addition, progressive educationists do not believe that schools have the moral authority to influence the character formation of the pupil. Instead, they take a rationalist view of a child's moral formation, which suggests the school should give pupils the requisite information to reach moral conclusions independently, a change summed up by the mantra 'teach, don't preach'.

4 **Socio-economic background dictates success.** This theme is really an addendum to the previous three. Whilst the other themes are concerned with a pupil's education at school, this theme is aimed at explaining their subsequent academic performance. It is heavily influenced by the work of Basil Bernstein, a professor of Educational Sociology. In 1970, Bernstein wrote a seminal essay for *New Society* entitled 'Education cannot compensate for society'. Such thinking caused generations of teachers to believe that schools can do little to change a pupil's academic performance, as the overriding determinant of their success is their home background. This 'sociological view' links with the first theme as many educationists have concluded that, instead of expecting working-class pupils to access curriculum content designed by middle-class interests, they should have schooling tailored to their own interests and

> needs. In America the 'sociological view' has led to the popularity of the saying 'you cannot solve education until you solve poverty'. This theme has formed a convenient alliance with the previous three themes as a means of excusing, or deflecting attention away from, the problems they have caused.

These four themes have become an orthodoxy within British state education over the past half a century. They may have been watered down at classroom level, but their underlying principles still govern the behaviour of many British teachers. This surrender of worldly knowledge to the existing interests of the child, and the dethroning of the teacher as both a moral and subject authority, have led to a profound dumbing down in our schools. As such, it is reasonable to conclude that progressive education is as close as one can get to the root cause of educational failure in Britain.

It has become unfashionable to pose the ideas of progressive education against those of, for want of a better term, 'traditional' education. Education commentators are likely to say that such 'polarising rhetoric' establishes 'false dichotomies', when in reality a sensible mixture of the two approaches is required. This is true. No one in education should be an absolutist, and the best 'traditionalist' teacher will still pay heed to the existing interests of their pupils, and know how to combine authority with friendliness. Such dichotomies (skills/knowledge, child-centred/teacher-led) are perhaps better thought of as sitting at opposite ends of a spectrum. If we are to decide what constitutes a sensible position on each spectrum, we need to appreciate better how far British schools currently gravitate towards the progressive ends. Whilst a wholesale move towards traditionalist modes of education would be harmful, a corrective shift in that direction is desperately needed.

Some may protest that British teachers in the twenty-first century are not wedded to such 'ideological' thinking as progressive education. Indeed, many within the profession may not even be familiar with the term 'progressive education'. However, this merely goes to show how comprehensive its diffusion into the educational landscape has been. For many, progressive ideas are simply the received wisdom of how to teach, the very definition of best practice. To paraphrase J. M. Keynes, teachers who believe themselves to be quite exempt from any intellectual influence are usually the slaves of some defunct educationist.

In a speech to the Social Market Foundation in February 2013, Michael Gove described the influence of an educational movement, which he claimed has been termed 'progressive' with 'tragic inappropriateness'.[12] Four days later, Gove was contradicted in the leader of the *Observer*, which stated:

> At heart, the problem is that Gove is trying to make an education system fashioned out of his own education experiences, while holding up as straw man a caricature of a 1970s progressive education movement, which, while it did tragically ruin the lives of some, does not grip huge swaths of the modern state education system, as he would have us believe.[13]

If only this were the case. Progressive education was not a passing fad of the 1970s; its principles have endured and are now woven into the fabric of state education. Today's teachers are surrounded by the vestiges of progressive education, from the design of textbooks to examination content, from school architecture to teaching methods, from teacher-training workshops to the 'gurus' of the education conference circuit. Many teachers who entered the profession during the idealistic 1960s and 1970s have captured the commanding heights of the profession, and the education establishment – made up of teacher-training colleges, teaching unions, government agencies and local authorities – is largely defined by its attachment to progressive education. Until recently, it has been very hard for schools to stray from this orthodoxy.

Within education, there will always be debate over issues such as length of holidays, teacher pay and school admissions – all important issues, but all unlikely to provoke fundamental change. It is the underlying philosophy of our state education system, the ideas that govern the teaching style of nearly half a million teachers and the curriculums of 24,000 schools across the country, which needs to change. It is not of ultimate importance whether a school is an academy, a free school, a comprehensive or a voluntary aided faith school: if they have a misguided pedagogical philosophy, they will underachieve regardless of their categorisation. Parliamentary legislation and changes in bureaucracy alone cannot triumph in what is essentially a culture war in the classroom.

This book is made up of two parts. Part I will tell the story of teaching methods and school organisation from the early 1960s to today, and explains how progressive education became an orthodoxy within the education establishment. Part II will take each of the four themes of progressive education, describe their genealogy and suggest why they have had such a damaging effect. In the conclusion, I will look at the changes happening within state education today, as reforms designed to weaken the intellectual hegemony of the education establishment are already being felt. Many schools now have the freedom to demonstrate that educational renewal in the twenty-first century invariably involves overturning the shibboleths inherited from the twentieth century.

Critics of progressive education are frequently accused of nostalgia, seeking a return to the prelapsarian educational landscape of the 1950s. This book is not a call to return to some distant glory, and the world of blackboards, canes and the 11+ is not the future that it proposes. To claim that education took a wrong turn during the 1960s is not to imply that schools were previously travelling in the right direction. To have a sensible debate about education, we must move beyond chronological caricatures. A good education system combines the technology, imagination and funding of the present, whilst relinquishing soft discipline and excessively child-centred teaching methods by which it need not necessarily be accompanied.

I frequently hear colleagues working in education grumble about the 'madness' of what surrounds them. However, there is insufficient understanding that much of this madness is the product of a defined movement. Progressive education has been in the ascendency for nearly half a century, and has directly coincided with a prolonged crisis of poor behaviour and academic underachievement in British schools. It is high time we held it accountable for the effect it has had, and freed our schools from this burden of bad ideas.

Those who claim that British education is failing are often labelled as pessimists, but this is inaccurate. The true pessimists are those who look around at the state of our schools and are willing to call what they see a success. Critics are optimists, because within such criticism lies the knowledge that our schools could do so much better.

I

HISTORY

1

Radicalism: 1960-1969

The 'do-as-you-please' school

During the early 1960s, a small independent boarding school about 100 miles from London began to attract visitors from around the world. Its founder and headmaster was an elderly Scot named Alexander Sutherland Neill. Born the son of a village schoolmaster, A. S. Neill rebelled against his Calvinist upbringing and founded his own school in 1921. It would turn him into the leading prophet of Britain's progressive education movement, and was called Summerhill. By the 1960s, Summerhill catered for around forty pupils, all educated in an environment of total freedom. Pupils could wake and go to bed when they pleased, with days spent attending a series of optional lessons and activities. As Neill wrote, 'We set out to make a school in which we should allow children freedom to be themselves. In order to do this, we had to renounce all discipline, all direction, all suggestion, all moral training, all religious instruction.'

The school was run through a system of self-government, with rules and decisions made democratically at the weekly General School Meeting. Neill enjoyed hosting individual lessons with pupils, which would begin with him offering them a cigarette to 'break the ice'. Nude swimming amongst staff and pupils in the school duck pond was encouraged, and Neill once satisfied the curiosity of a pupil who had a 'sense of sin about nakedness' by stripping off in front of him, and encouraging a female member of staff to do the same. His solution to pupil theft was to reward the pupil, and if a pupil was caught smashing windows in the school, Neill joined them in their vandalism.

Guiding Neill's educational philosophy was a blend of romanticism and a radical view of child-psychology, influenced by Sigmund Freud but more importantly the counter-cultural psychoanalyst Wilhelm Reich. Neill believed that children must be freed from adult authority, claiming: 'My view is that a child is innately wise and realistic. If left to himself without adult suggestion of any kind, he will develop as far as he is capable of developing.' He rejected any of the traditional apparatus of schooling, as he believed that: 'Children, like adults, learn what they want to learn. All prize-giving and marks and exams sidetrack proper personality development. Only pedants claim that learning from books is education.'[1]

This vision was laid out most completely in Neill's 1962 book *Summerhill*, which became an international sensation. It was republished by Pelican in 1968, reprinted ten times between 1970 and 1980, and sold over two million copies worldwide.[2] Neill lectured trainee teachers across the country, and many teachers who fell under his spell during the 1960s went on to reach the highest echelons of British state education. In 2007, *Summerhill* was voted the ninth most inspiring book published on education by a joint NUT and Teachers TV poll.[3] Tim Brighouse, who until 2007 was the Schools Commissioner for London, is one prominent admirer. Writing an introduction to a book about Summerhill in 2006, he recalled:

> There can be very few teachers in education in the UK and trained during the period 1945-1990 who have not heard of A. S. Neill... Neill represented, especially to teacher educators in the colleges of education and the university departments of education, a noble alternative.[4]

Summerhill failed on any normal measure of what makes a good school. It never achieved high academic standards and Neill always had a stated disdain for public examinations. Neither did it produce any remarkable pupils in non-academic fields, as Neill himself admitted: 'No, so far no geniuses; perhaps a few creators, not famous as yet.'[5] Neither did the 'do-as-you-please school' result in a community of harmonious co-existence, and it is clear even from Neill's own writing that Summerhill was an unruly place. Though many contemporaries admired the school, few were willing to place their children in Neill's care, and the school was only saved from financial ruin in 1961 with an influx of foreign, mostly American, students.[6]

So how did this school, with its chaotic environment, falling roll and academic underperformance, become an inspiration for the future of British education? The answer lies in the temper of the times. Neill had been running his school since 1921, but his ideas only gained widespread admiration in the 1960s. Whilst it is a mistake to see this decade as a caricature of personal liberation and revolutionary enthusiasm, the counter-culture was undoubtedly influential amongst the young graduates who became teachers. In this atmosphere of social and cultural upheaval, when university students adopted the slogan 'trust no one over thirty', the old certainties of Britain's schools seemed redundant. New alternatives were enthusiastically embraced.

Early developments

Progressive education has a long history, stretching back to the Romantic Swiss philosopher Jean-Jacques Rousseau and his 1762 book *Émile, or On Education*. Rousseau offered a philosophy remarkably similar to that of the 1960s progressive primary school teacher, advising you should 'give your scholar no verbal lessons; he should be taught by experience alone'.[7] Rousseau believed the established order of the adult world corrupted the innate virtues of the child. He wanted to see children placed in an environment where they could educate themselves, away from the malign influence of adult authority. Despite his own famous aversion to child rearing (all five of Rousseau's children were abandoned to foundling hospitals), *Émile* is today celebrated as the founding text of progressive education.

During the nineteenth century, inroads made towards progressive education occurred away from Britain. On the continent, Johann Heinrich Pestalozzi and Friedrich Fröebel pioneered new methods of learning through play and pupil self-direction, with Fröebel famously establishing the first ever Kindergarten in Bad Blankenburg. Later, the Italian Maria Montessori would devise her own Montessori Method based on similar principles. Importantly, these ideas were applied to pre-school and primary aged children to prepare them for the more formal atmosphere of high school.

At the turn of the twentieth century America, John Dewey began to apply these ideas to the whole range of a pupil's education. Dewey was already a prominent liberal philosopher before he turned his mind to education in 1894, and moved to Chicago to establish an experimental school. This led to the publication of his two most important books on education, *The School and Society* (1900) and *The Child and the Curriculum* (1902). In these, he outlined a broadly child-centred view of 'the learning process'. He claimed that a child's learning 'must be assimilated, not as items of information, but as organic parts of his present needs and aims', and opposed the didactic teacher, adding: 'In the last analysis, all the educator can do is modify stimuli.' His experimental schools aimed to teach literacy and numeracy indirectly, through engaging young pupils in activities such as cookery or carpentry. Later in life, Dewey renounced many of these earlier beliefs in *Education and Experience* (1938), and admitted that he had underestimated the need for direct teacher instruction.[8]

Dewey's ideas fell on receptive ears in his homeland, where an aversion to tradition and love of personal liberty were firmly established within American popular culture. In 1934, William Bagley, an American critic of progressive education, was driven to write:

> If you wish to be applauded at an educational convention, vociferate sentimental platitudes about the sacred rights of the child, specifying particularly his right to happiness gained though freedom. You are likely to get an extra 'hand' if you shed a few verbal tears over the cruelty of examinations and homework, while if with eloquent condemnation you deftly bring into every other sentence one of the favourite stereotypes of abuse, such as Latin, mathematics (geometry, especially), grammar, the traditional curriculum, compartmentalization, "chunks of the subject matter" to be memorised, discipline, formal discipline, and the like, you may be fairly certain of an ovation.[9]

In pre-war Britain, progressive education only existed in a handful of independent schools, with The New Education Fellowship (NEF) at the centre of the movement. Founded in 1921 by Beatrice Ensor and influenced by the ideas of Froebel and Dewey, the NEF had its own journal *New Era*, which had a heavy focus on the emerging academic discipline of child-psychology.[10] In particular, Susan Isaacs, a founding member of the NEF, popularised the new theory of 'developmentalism', stating that children pass through various stages of intellectual development and must be allowed to do so at their own pace – a theory employed by teachers to criticise whole class instruction and to promote individual learning. Isaacs became head of a short-lived progressive primary school in Cambridge called Malting House, before setting up the Department of Child Development at the London Institute of Education in 1932.[11] Isaacs's lasting legacy was to popularise the work of Swiss developmental psychologist Jean Piaget, whose theory of 'constructivism' still dominates the reading lists of trainee-teachers today.

The NEF influenced a number of progressive independent schools, including Summerhill, King Alfred School in Hampstead and Dartington Hall. Set on a 1,000-acre site in South Devon, Dartington Hall was briefly fashionable amongst Britain's liberal intellectuals, catering for the offspring of Bertrand Russell, Aldous Huxley, G. E. Moore and the grandchildren of Sigmund Freud. Another pupil was the future literary critic Miriam Gross, who later wrote of her memories of the school. Whilst admiring its open-mindedness, Gross criticised the squandering of pupil potential. She wrote that 'the absence of grades for school work, the disapproval of competition, the distaste for ambition, the disdain for structure and discipline, the unlimited freedoms' resulted in a general atmosphere that was 'sapping of our energy'. Accordingly, Gross has 'never quite forgiven' the school for allowing her youthful potential to founder on the rocks of their liberal indulgence.[12]

These early experiments have had a lasting influence on education wholly inverse to their own institutional success. Isaacs's Malting House lasted just five years, and Dartington Hall was shut down in 1987 amidst reports of drugs, theft and the death of a pupil in their nude bathing pool.[13] Summerhill continues a stunted life to this day under the command of A. S. Neill's daughter. It has become a little stricter, and the lessons have become rather more conventional, but the pupils continue to underperform. Despite charging £3,000 to £5,000 a term, their GCSE results remain 10 per cent below the national average.[14] These trailblazers in progressive education have publicly failed, but their model of child-centred learning and renouncement of adult discipline has triumphed in capturing the imagination of the education establishment.

Reading Wars Round 1

The growth of progressive education in Britain began in primary schools, before moving upwards to encompass the whole range of schooling. Progressive ideas were already evident during the inter-war period. The 1931 Hadow Report entitled *The Primary School* stated: 'We are of the opinion that the curriculum of the primary school is to be thought of in terms of activity and experience, rather than of knowledge to be acquired and facts to be stored.'[15] This message was reiterated in the 1933 Hadow Report *Infant and Nursery Schools,* to which psychologist Susan Isaacs contributed: 'The principle underlying the procedure of the infant school should be that, as far as possible, the child should be put in the position to teach himself.'[16]

However, such ideas only had a marked effect on the classroom after the war. The most important early development was in the teaching of reading, where 'look-say' methods were promoted to replace the teaching of 'phonics'. This is a crucial but rather technical debate that is still alive within education today. Phonics teaching, known colloquially as 'ABCs', was the near-universal method of teaching children how to read up until the mid-twentieth century. It involves first teaching pupils the relationship between written letters and sounds, and then teaching pupils to blend these letter-sounds into words. Only once this had been mastered would pupils move onto reading books. Phonics began to be criticised for a number of reasons. On a linguistic level, it was said to be unsuited to the English language, which is bedevilled with unconventional spelling and varied letter-sounds – think of 'thought', 'though', 'through' and 'cough'. For this reason, Samuel Taylor Coleridge complained of 'our lying alphabet' whilst teaching his own son to read.

More significantly though, phonics instruction requires a teacher-led, whole-class approach, often involving chanting and memorisation. As child-centred ideas gathered pace, such formal teaching was criticised for being boring and joyless (as it often would have been), and even for instilling in children a lasting aversion to reading. In 1975, the former headmaster of St Jude's Church of England primary school explained this development:

> Now the teaching of reading through sounds of the letters demands a great deal of teacher-direction and systematic training, and these features of learning are anathema to the child-centred theorists. There has been such emotional condemnation of didactic methods that any sign of teacher-direction and the inculcation of facts is condemned as authoritarian.[17]

In addition, developmental psychology popularised the idea that pupils will only learn to read when they are at the right stage of 'reader-readiness', so the practice of simultaneously teaching a whole class to read lost popularity.

In place of phonics, an alternative approach known as 'look-say' (later known as 'whole-word') was developed. This reversed the process of learning to read, so that instead of learning individual letter sounds and then applying them to words, pupils would recognise the meaning of words, often from picture books, and from this divine the sound created by each of the component letters at their own pace. The look-say method appealed enormously to teachers, as it suggested that autonomous pupils would be able to teach themselves to read whilst simultaneously developing a love of books, and many teachers came to defend its merits with a fervent passion.

As early as the 1950s, there is evidence to suggest that look-say overtook phonics as the preferred method of reading instruction in British primary schools. In 1954, the reading specialist Joyce Morris surveyed 60 primary schools in Kent, and found that only six gave systematic phonics instruction to all their pupils in their first year. In 48 out of the 60 schools, an 'informal approach' to reading was preferred, where teachers would spur pupil interest in reading in their first year of school through toys, images, picture books and activities. Also widely accepted in the sample schools was the concept of 'reader readiness'.[18] This idea that pupils should only learn to read once they had reached the requisite 'developmental stage', led to a worrying situation by the 1960s when a growing number of pupils were completing primary school having had little or no formal teaching in reading. In 1965, the National Child Development Survey, which tracked a group of 15,468 children born in 1958 throughout their lives, found that aged seven, 10 per cent of the children had not yet begun learning to read.[19]

The steady dominance of the look-say method can be seen in the popularity of its reading schemes, most notably *Janet and John*, which was originally published in the USA and imported to Britain in 1949. The *Janet and John* books included illustrations and repetitive text designed for pupils to learn to read without the instruction of a teacher. A survey of reading schemes in 1968 showed that *Janet and John* was used in 81 per cent of primary schools, and the old-fashioned Beacon scheme, with its emphasis on phonics, had almost disappeared.[20] In 1967, the remedial literacy teacher Keith Gardner recorded:

> In the post-war infant school it has been considered slightly old-fashioned to teach reading at all. The belief is that children will learn to read in their own way and in their own good time. Anxious parents have been fobbed off with such pious statements as 'He will learn to read when he is ready'. Inspectors have actually criticised schools that try to teach reading. In the modern craze for child-centred education, reading has become something that is acquired – not taught.[21]

The idea that reading was acquired, not taught, also led to primary school teachers being given decreasing levels of guidance during their teacher training on how to teach reading. One account from a primary school teacher who trained in 1950-52 recalled challenging her infant tutor on this matter, only to be told 'one must never "teach" reading. If one's classroom was sufficiently interesting, reading would "emerge".'[22] A survey by the Inner London Education Authority (ILEA) in 1969 found that less than one in eight junior school teachers in London had received specific training on how to teach reading.[23]

What was extraordinary about this steady disappearance of phonics teaching was the lack of evidence that the alternative methods were superior. On the contrary, there was mounting evidence by the late 1960s to suggest that phonics worked best. In the United States, where the teaching of phonics had been dethroned a generation earlier, there was a gathering campaign for its restoration by the 1950s. This was spearheaded by Rudolph Flesch's bestselling 1955 defence of phonics instruction *Why Johnny Can't Read*. In 1967 Dr Jeanne Chall, a Harvard professor, published *Learning to Read: The Great Debate*. Her work, financed by the Carnegie Corporation, was a systematic review of half a century of research that conclusively showed the teaching of phonics was superior to the look-say approach. These findings were confirmed by smaller British studies, but those unsympathetic to phonics simply dismissed them as unrepresentative.

By the start of the 1970s, there was good reason to believe that the spread of look-say teaching in primary schools was causing a decline in national literacy levels. The best study into this matter came courtesy of the National Foundation for Educational Research (NFER) and their 1972 publication *The Trend of Reading Standards*. Intermittent sampling of primary school leavers showed a steady rise in reading rates from 1948 through to 1964, aided by the very low level of literacy created by World War II. However, the survey of pupils in 1971 at the 69 sample schools showed an average fall in reading age of 4.38 months compared with 1964 – a significant drop. There was not such a large fall in the survey of 15 year olds, but the researchers explained that this was skewed in a positive direction by two setbacks rather characteristic of the 1970s. Firstly, high levels of truanting meant that many of the low-ability readers were probably excluded from the survey. Secondly, a postal strike meant that only the 50 per cent of schools that replied promptly took part, creating a positive selection bias. At the very best, the report concluded, literacy levels in British schools had stagnated.[24]

Awash with paint

Look-say was not the only child-centred reform to have become established in primary schools by this stage. Its corollary in numeracy was a movement dubbed 'new maths'. The Nuffield Maths Project 5-13, which began in 1963, moved mathematics away from the practice and rote learning of arithmetic and basic computation, and towards the early understanding of mathematics on a conceptual level. Its proponents hoped that the early formal learning of times-tables and sums could be replaced by mathematical activity and discovery, which would allow pupils to become numerate through application – a back-to-front approach to learning characteristic of progressive education. A popular argument of the new maths pioneer during the 1960s was that betting shop regulars became highly numerate with no formal instruction, proving that motivation and activity were all that was needed.

In 1967, the Nuffield Foundation published a handbook for teachers of new maths. It was dedicated to Jean Piaget and entitled *I do, and I understand,* a title taken from the Chinese proverb beloved of progressive educationists, 'I hear and I forget. I see and I remember. I do and I understand.' The General Introduction stated:

> The stress is on *how to learn,* not on what to teach. Running through all the work is the central notion that the children must be set free to make their own discoveries and think for themselves, and so achieve understanding, instead of learning off mysterious drills.[25]

The handbook further claimed that the version of mathematics that valued presentation, computation and speed, was the legacy of an outdated need to train the 'Victorian clerk' to use his ledger book. Now, 'computers' and 'simple counting machines' would be able to take care of everyday computation, and humans were free to focus on problem solving instead. The alternative contention – that arithmetic is a vital component of problem solving – was blissfully ignored. The handbook also offered two useful maps to show how the modern primary classroom should be rearranged from rows of paired desks, to islands designed for group work. The caption described: 'the same classroom rearranged to make better provision for active learning.' An article in the new maths journal *Bulletin* told teachers to abandon the old fashioned approach of teacher explains to the class, teacher demonstrates on the blackboard, teacher asks pupils to practise what they have learnt. Instead, the teacher must 'make possible the discovery of a mathematical truth' and 'endeavour not to instruct, but to guide.'[26] In primary mathematics, it was dearly hoped that discovery could replace drudgery.

More generally, primary schools during the 1960s witnessed a widespread turn away from academic content towards 'self-expression' and 'creativity'. In 1963, the *Times Educational Supplement* (*TES*) reported: 'a cynic might suppose that a primary school is judged nowadays not by how far its pupils can read but by how far the place is awash with paint'. These ideas came of age two years later in 1965, when the *TES* published a special edition entitled 'Self-expression in the primary school', with contributions from the various leading lights of the progressive movement.[27]

By the end of the 1960s, newly published textbooks for primary school trainees unanimously endorsed progressive methods. Sealey and Gibbon's popular textbook *Communication and Learning in the Primary School*, first published in 1962, pronounced against whole class teaching, lesson periods, classroom competition and marking creative writing, which was described as the 'mutilation of a page of sincere and personal expression'.[28] In addition, Piaget's theories became accepted as unquestionable fact, and in 1966 Molly Brearley and Elizabeth Hitchfield (both from the Froebel Institute) published the highly popular *A Teacher's Guide to Reading Piaget*, which was republished four times over the next six years.[29] However, nothing leant the developing orthodoxy of progressive education as much credence as the publication of the Plowden Report of 1967.

The 1967 Plowden Report

Lady Bridget Plowden was a magistrate and the wife of an eminent civil servant. The story goes that, at an official dinner in 1963, she was seated next to Conservative Education Secretary Edward Boyle who invited her to become Chair of the Central Advisory Council for Education.[30] Four years later, with the help of 25 council members, seven advisers and three civil servants, Plowden delivered her famous report. It was two volumes and over 1,000 pages in length and from its opening declaration – 'at the heart of the educational process lies the child' – the report was suffused with the presumptions of progressive education.[31] Following its publication, it was said by two educationists to contain 'the semi-official ideology of primary education'.[32] Though the Plowden Report did not introduce progressive education to Britain, it gave the movement official endorsement and ensured its continued spread.

The hero of the report's first few chapters was Jean Piaget, and his developmental theories were entirely endorsed. However, the most important part of the report came in Part V. These chapters celebrated the progressive education movement, warmly announcing 'Rousseau, Pestalozzi, Froebel, Whitehead, Dewey, Montessori and Rachel Macmillan, to mention only a few, had all written on lines that encouraged change and innovation'. The following passage was illustrative of the Plowden Report's child-centred temper:

> A school is not merely a teaching shop... The school sets out deliberately to devise the right environment for children, to allow them to be themselves and to develop in the way and at the pace appropriate to them. It tries to equalise opportunities and to compensate for handicaps. It lays special stress on individual discovery, on first-hand experience and on opportunities for creative work. It insists that knowledge does not fall into neatly separate compartments and that work and play are not opposite but complementary.

The Plowden Report expressed doubts over the benefit of repeated practice, rewards and sanctions, subject divisions, correcting pupil work, reading schemes and learning by rote; and gave support to learning through play, reader readiness, discovery learning, look-say and new maths. As the report famously concluded: ''Finding out' has proved to be better for children than 'being told'.'

In a chapter entitled 'The Child in the School Community', the report advised all primary schools to make a transition from being run along 'traditional lines' to being run along 'free lines', and stated that: 'The change is a major one which is beginning to revolutionise the primary schools of England.' The Plowden Report made frequent use of the term 'revolution', and in one particularly romantic flight of fancy, it described how a lesson in a post-revolutionary primary school may proceed:

> When a class of seven year olds notice the birds that come to the bird table outside the classroom window, they may decide, after discussion with their teacher, to make their own aviary. They will set to with a will and paint the birds in flight, make models of them in clay or papier-mâché, write stories and poems about them and look up reference books to find out more about their habits. Children are not assimilating inert ideas but are wholly involved in thinking, feeling and doing. There is no attempt to put reading and writing into separate compartments; both serve a wider purpose, and artificial barriers do not fragment the learning experience.

The Plowden Report has been caricatured as 'an anarchist's charter' by both its followers and its detractors.[34] In truth, the Report did deliver nods towards the need for whole-class teaching and school rules. However, these parts read more as attempts to forestall criticism than statements of conviction. Throughout, the rudiments of traditional education are at best tolerated, whilst progressive education is enthusiastically embraced.

According to a survey conducted by Her Majesty's Inspectorate on behalf of the Plowden Report, around 21 per cent of schools were already rated as 'good' or 'very good' at exhibiting the features recommended by the committee. A further 47 per cent were rated as 'average'.[35] These desired features were divided into five categories: 'provision for individual rates of progress'; 'opportunities for creative work'; 'readiness to reconsider the content of the curriculum'; 'awareness of the unity of knowledge'; and rather unbelievably 'permissive discipline'. So, the report came at a crucial time. It supported the nascent revolution, heaping praise on the sizeable minority of primary schools that had stormed the palace, and encouraging the rest to hurry up and abandon the *ancien régime*.

The Report received significant criticism on publication, notably from the educational philosopher R. S. Peters who published a collection of essays in 1969 entitled *Perspectives on Plowden*. Peters's own contribution was the most damning, pointing to the fact that Plowden's call for revolution was based on hardly any research evidence. He wrote: 'Talk of "development", like talk of children's "needs", is too often a way of dressing up our value judgements in semi-scientific clothes'; and observed: 'The doctrine of self-direction... is based almost entirely on teachers' hunches not on objective evidence.'[36] Unfortunately, many teachers who never read Plowden but felt an intuitive sympathy with its conclusions would assume that the Report contained incontrovertible evidence in favour of the informal primary school. In reality, it was a weighty distillation of strongly held opinion cloaked in the language of disinterested science.

Twenty years after its publication, the secretary to the Plowden Committee, Maurice Kogan, echoed this verdict. Once a precocious civil servant, Kogan later lost his idealism about progressive education – due in no small part, one assumes, to sending his children to and being a governor of the notoriously poor Islington Green Comprehensive. Writing in 1987, Kogan admitted that where evidence did not fit their liberal presumptions, the Plowden Committee had instead followed 'its instinct or professional intuitions'. He concluded that progressive methods had been badly implemented in many British schools.[37]

The Plowden Report represents a high point in British society's faith in the innate goodness of the child. With scant regard for evidence, it codified the romantic liberalism of the 1960s into a profoundly impactful document. Remarkably for a Government report, it sold 68,000 copies in its first year, and 117,000 copies after three.[38] Two years after its publication, Plowden wrote in the *TES*: 'The effect of the Report has been to accelerate the pace of change – to endorse the revolution in primary education which has been taking place since the war.'[39]

Secondary waves

Secondary schools would have to wait until the 1970s before progressive education really took hold, but the intellectual shift was discernible a decade earlier.

The impact of the 1960s on educational practice was aided by demographics. In 1951, there were 3.5 million 5-10 year olds, and by 1968 this number was 4.5 million. Consequently, many members of the 'generation of '68', who had witnessed the campus revolutions as students, joined the teaching profession. In 1952, there were 25,000 trainee teachers, but by 1968 there were 95,000 – a generation of educators that would have an enormous influence on British schools.[40]

Perhaps the first truly progressive English state secondary school was Risinghill. Located next to Pentonville Prison in Islington, the area was described at the time as 'a sordid, depressing neighbourhood' characterised by prostitution, poor housing and ethnic division.[41] This north London borough has played a unique part in the recent history of British education. Due to its mix of ethnic minorities, working-class communities, and a newly arrived bohemian middle-class, it became something of a laboratory for educational experiments during the 1960s and 1970s, and the proximity of Fleet Street ensured that these experiments never lacked media attention.

Michael Daune, a left-wing ex-army major and close friend of A. S. Neill, took over Risinghill in 1960, hoping to apply the Summerhill approach to a state comprehensive. It lasted just five years before closure.

Daune was a charismatic individual and the school was credited with an initial improvement in academic results, but this did not last. He introduced a regime of no formal discipline, humanist assemblies and a pupil-led School Council. An Inspector's Report two years into the Daune régime detailed that the school had rapidly descended towards 'an atmosphere of indiscipline which is difficult to describe'. Pupils were 'uninterested', teachers suffered from 'tiredness' and 'frustration' and the amount of wasted time was 'enormous'.[42] Parents voted with their feet, and the school roll fell from 1,323 pupils when it first opened in 1960, to 854 by the time it closed in 1965.[43] Risinghill was a decade too early – had it opened in 1970, it would have been indistinguishable from dozens of other new comprehensive schools championing the philosophy of A. S. Neill.

Proponents of progressive education appear to have gained institutional power at a remarkably early stage, such that the initial drivers for change in secondary schools tended to be government agencies and local education authorities (LEAs). Most notably Oxfordshire, Hertfordshire, Leicestershire and the West Riding led the charge against traditional teaching methods. In 1968, the role of HMI was diminished, and local authority advisers were given a much-expanded brief. The newly stated approach of these advisers was to help schools improve rather than to pass judgement. As a result, local authority advisers became the core apostles for the progressive creed, often tempting schools with generous funding for 'innovation'. By 1968, there were 1,260 of them visiting schools.[44]

In July 1969, a letter sent to *The Times* from R. Wickham Partridge complained of the advisers' meddling ways:

> Many head teachers, encouraged by schools advisers and inspectors and by education officers, all trying to be 'with it', are imposing the adoption of so-called 'progressive' (I

> call them 'digressive') methods upon unwilling members of their staffs... there is not enough actual teaching and far too much messing about in many primary schools today, and at tremendous and wasteful expense.[45]

Similarly, in 1968 the National Association of Schoolmasters complained of local authority advisers using 'hard-sell' techniques such as the promise of additional finance for schools that would adopt 'fashionable' teaching ideas.[46] Local authorities also set up training centres, often in old country houses, to spread the gospel of progressive education to teachers. In 1967 there were 270 such centres; by 1972 this had grown to 617.[47]

Much of the energy behind this progressive embrace came from an understandable rejection of traditional British education, in particular the divisive influence of the 11+. R. A. Butler's 1944 Education Act had been a watershed piece of legislation, creating a new settlement where all secondary schooling until the age of 15 was free, but pupils were divided from the age of 11 between grammar, secondary modern and the much-neglected technical schools. This was called the tripartite system. By the 1960s, a convincing body of evidence had been assembled to demonstrate that not only was 11 too young a stage at which to decide on a child's academic future, but that the exam was increasingly selecting pupils along the lines of class. A pioneering study of this pattern was conducted by Hilde Himmelweit, who in 1951 surveyed 700 13- to 14-year-old boys in four districts of Greater London and found that 52 per cent of the pupils at grammar schools were working-class (two thirds of them upper-working-class), whilst the figure at secondary moderns was 80 per cent.[48] What is more, the secondary modern gained an unenviable reputation, in Corelli Barnett's famous words, as 'a mere educational settling-tank for academic failures'.[49] Disquiet over the tripartite system came as much from the middle class as from the working class, for whom the fear of a child failing the 11+ could be unbearable. Many contemporary polls showed a widespread public support for reforming the tripartite system.[50]

Nor was everything perfect inside the classroom. Britain's peculiar attachment to the cane was opposed by growing numbers and, in addition, much unimaginative teaching is sure to have given didacticism a bad name. Twenty years after the Butler Act, Britain's schools were ready for imaginative reform. Sadly, they got wholesale revolution.

Comprehensivisation

Having been appointed Education Secretary in 1965, Anthony Crosland confided in his wife: 'If it's the last thing I do, I'm going to destroy every fucking grammar school in England. And Wales. And Northern Ireland.'[51] Such opposition to the grammar school system was not uncommon amongst public-school educated socialists of the time. However, the comprehensivisation of Britain's school system need not have been the disaster it is generally regarded as today. When Crosland issued Circular 10/65, requesting that LEAs begin the process of amalgamating all secondary schools into a comprehensive system, it was assumed that such a measure would spread virtues of the grammar school. During the 1964 election, Labour party leader Harold Wilson campaigned with the slogan 'grammar schools for all', and circular 10/65 declared the reform would 'preserve all that is valuable in grammar school education for the children who now receive it and make it available for more children'.[52] If comprehensivisation had remained true to this ideal, it could have been successful. Unfortunately, the increasing influence of progressive education ensured that it was not.

The founding text of the comprehensive movement was Robin Pedley's hugely popular *The Comprehensive*

School. First published in 1963, it went through five reprints or new editions by 1969, and seven more thereafter. Pedley was a conscientious objector during the Second World War and taught history at a Quaker school in Yorkshire before joining the education department at Leicester University. According to one historian: 'Robin Pedley probably had more influence in winning popular support for comprehensive education than any other single individual.'[53]

However, 'grammar schools for all' was not the comprehensive ideal that Pedley envisaged. His book contained many of the prejudices of a mid-1960s progressive educator. He derided his own grammar school education, mocking the 'elaborate apparatus devised to get boys to do what the staff wanted' and disparaging the use of essays and tests, quotas of marks, colours, house points, prizes and lines. Having been copied from the 'Public School Olympians', he seemed to believe that these 'formal rituals' had no place in a comprehensive school. Pedley criticised grammar school lessons for having 'much chalk and talk, a good deal of note-dictating' and 'frequent tests', concluding 'such teaching is bad for all children'. Instead, he called for mixed-ability classes, permissive discipline and classrooms where one sees 'the people who matter – the children – busily concentrating on their particular jobs' with the teacher 'moving around unobtrusively'. In the 1967 edition, he praised the trailblazing progressive schools Summerhill and Dartington Hall, and wrote supportively of the 'minority of state schools' choosing to follow in their wake. Pedley also paid tribute to A. S. Neill:

> Neill, more than anyone else, has swung teachers' opinion in this country from its old reliance on authority and the cane to hesitant recognition that a child's first need is love... The magic of the inspired reformer is there in Neill's books, in his talks to teachers, who still flock

> to hear him, above all in the absolute sincerity which marks his own school community.[54]

Such sentiments also filled the leading journals of comprehensivisation during the late 1960s. The two most important were *Comprehensive Education*, edited by Caroline Benn, the American wife of the Labour MP Tony Benn; and *Forum*, edited by Brian Simon, a professor at Leicester University and education spokesman for the Communist Party. In 1970, Benn and Simon joined forces to write *Half Way There: Report on British Comprehensive Schools*. Their book, a guide to comprehensivisation, was strongly in favour of mixed-ability teaching. This was a new idea, as the approach taken by early comprehensives to deal with a wide ability range was, in the words of the Education Officer of the London County Council, 'to put them all together and stream like mad'.[55] Many parents had their fears of comprehensive education appeased with the promise that their child, if they worked hard, would be placed in the 'grammar stream'.

This approach was soon overturned by the doctrinaire egalitarianism of progressive educationists. Addressing a headmasters' conference in 1965, one secondary-school head teacher claimed: 'If comprehensive schools were the educational battle-cry of the last election, non-streaming may be that of the next.'[56] Benn and Simon believed that it was against the founding ideal of comprehensive schools to group pupils according to ability, writing that the conjunction of streaming and comprehensive schooling was a 'contradiction in terms'.[57] These egalitarian arguments were nicely fused with child-centred teaching: it was reasoned that if pupils were of differing abilities, then whole-class instruction could be minimised and individual or group learning promoted. Channelling the language of economic struggle, Benn and Simon wrote that mixed-ability classes would end 'the more rigid structures of the past – in particular the system of subject teaching to "homogeneous" classes supported, usually, by hierarchical forms of government and control.'[58]

Elsewhere, Benn and Simon promoted the non-hierarchical role of the teacher, writing that the 'expositor and conveyor of knowledge' should now give way to the 'mediator of learning resources'. Pedley also endorsed this change, writing the teacher's prime task was to assemble resources from which individual pupils could devise their own lessons: 'work sheets varying in content and level to meet the needs of everyone in the class; schemes of programmed learning, pictures, radio and TV tapes; film strips; newspapers and magazine cuttings.'[59] On top of this dethroning of the teacher, the comprehensive literature was often opposed to traditional subject divisions and content. A contribution to *Forum* from 1966 on this topic bears a striking resemblance to the anti-knowledge arguments put forward today, as Peter Mauger, a headteacher from Nightingale County Secondary School in Redbridge, wrote:

> Children cannot be expected – in any type of school – to see school work as relevant to their needs while their curriculum is fragmented into uncoordinated subjects... Moreover, the subject-based curriculum is clearly inadequate in view of the knowledge explosion... The idea that our schools should remain content with equipping children with a body of knowledge is absurd and frightening. Tomorrow's adults will be faced with problems about the nature of which we can today have no conception. They will have to cope with the jobs not yet invented. They need a curriculum that will teach them to ask questions, to explore, to enquire, to recognise the nature of problems and how to solve them: a curriculum that they can see as an organic whole, related to their present and their future needs.[60]

Due to an absence of contemporary surveys into teaching practice, it is difficult to assess accurately the extent to which such views were disseminated to and implemented in schools. However, Benn and Simon did conduct a survey of 673 comprehensive schools in 1968, which found that 22 per cent of schools taught with predominantly mixed-ability classes. In 1971 they conducted a smaller follow-up sample survey of 44 comprehensives, and found the proportion had by then risen to 34.5 per cent. Rigid streaming across subjects in comprehensive schools had fallen from an incidence of 19.5 per cent to just 4.5 per cent.[61]

The same pattern can be seen in the use of traditional house systems. The house system was first developed by public schools, widely copied by grammars, and then dismissed by proponents of progressive education. In 1965, the NFER surveyed 331 comprehensive schools and found that 90 per cent used a house system. However, by the time of their next survey of 59 schools in 1970, only 36 per cent did so, a figure corroborated by Benn and Simon's survey.

This was a precipitous drop in just five years, illustrating the changing fashions within comprehensive education. During the 1960s, progressive heads rejected the collective identity and competition that house systems sought to create on the principled grounds that they were tribal and elitist. In 1969 Margaret Miles, the head teacher at the Mayfield Comprehensive School, articulated this position in her own book *Comprehensive Schooling: Problems and Perspectives*:

> In the house system, there is a tendency to encourage the sense of belonging by making all the pupils want to make their house the 'best' house; house competitions, whether for games or drama or for a system of house points for school work, encourages this rather artificial idea of 'our house' being the 'best house', an idea that

> has always struck me as being immature and unfruitful of real educational and social development.[62]

Not all schools followed suit. One comprehensive that clung defiantly to its house system was Highbury Grove School in Islington, which swam against the tide due its pugnacious headmaster Dr Rhodes Boyson. Educated at a grammar school, Boyson was a northern Methodist with a thick Lancashire accent and distinctive mutton-chop side-burns. He would go on to become a cabinet minister for Margaret Thatcher, and his steadfast defence of corporal punishment made him a hate figure for the British left. However, at this stage the 'Wackford Squeers of modern Britain' was a one-time socialist, former Labour Councillor and a founding member of the Comprehensive Schools Committee. A believer in the original comprehensive ideal, he established single-sex Highbury Grove School in 1967 with the aim of 'giving many more boys the opportunity of academic achievements.' It amalgamated three local schools, but tellingly retained the smart blazers, badges and ties of Highbury Grammar – a symbolic endorsement of Wilson's original ideal. The school had a house system, strict discipline, lots of sport, academic streaming and a curriculum stretching from Latin to motor engineering.[63]

Highbury Grove achieved excellent examination results, and it was continually oversubscribed. Having left as head in 1974, Boyson wrote that one of his 'saddest thoughts' was:

> ...the remembrance of the deep disappointment of the working-class parents whose sons do not obtain admission to the school and are directed to a school whose academic record and disciplinary framework are very different from ours. Such parents – dockers, prison warders, policemen, shopkeepers – in their letters and interviews communicate to us their anguish that their sons have to go elsewhere.

Boyson became a Member of Parliament in 1974, but for the next decade Highbury Grove hung on to its traditionalist ethos. In 1978 pupils at the school achieved 220 O-level passes and 40 A-level passes, compared to just 22 O-level passes and 2 A-level passes at the nearby Islington Green School.[64] The left-wing Inner London Education Authority (ILEA) loathed this school that sang Jerusalem and the National Anthem on prize day and, embarrassed by its strong academic record, made repeated attempts in later decades to kill off its distinctive ethos.

Boyson was precisely the sort of head that comprehensive campaigners such as Benn and Simon wanted to see excluded from their brave new schools. The most ominous aspect of their advice manual *Half Way There* was their aversion to school discipline and ethos. During the liberated 1960s, when personal fulfilment and liberal individualism were sacred, the belief that pupils should be conditioned by the ethos of a school was often ridiculed. Similarly, any authoritarian interpretation of a head's role was seen as oppressive – gaining lazy allusions to the Third Reich that continue to this day. Benn and Simon recommended a new concept of leadership, which involved 'necessarily abandoning the strict authoritarian interpretation of the role of head and incorporating more of the managerial and organizational skills required in running complex educational and social units.'[65] With two leading lights of the comprehensive movement promoting such a change in philosophy, it is not hard to see the out-of-control, ill-disciplined 'comp' of the 1970s lurking just around the corner.

Black Papers

In July 1968, two English Literature professors went for a walk on Hampstead Heath. Brian Cox was down from Manchester University to visit his friend Tony Dyson and discuss how they could boost sales for their influential poetry journal *Critical Quarterly*. They decided to publish a special edition on education that would criticise the student and academic radicalism engulfing universities that summer. Jokingly, Tony recommended they call it a 'Black Paper', in contrast to a Government White Paper. The idea stuck.

Black Paper: The Fight for Education was published in March 1969. Robert Conquest, Kingsley Amis and a number of prominent academics contributed their thoughts on the recent campus turmoil and, almost as an afterthought, Cox commissioned two articles on primary schooling. Cox had briefly taught at a secondary modern, and was deeply unimpressed by the education received by his own child at an open-plan, progressive primary school in Cottingham in Yorkshire. One of the pieces entitled 'Freedom in Junior Schools' was written by C. M. Johnson, the head of Prendergast Grammar School, and caused uproar. Later Cox recalled, 'we had no idea how Miss Johnson's simple reflections would offend the progressive establishment.'[66]

Johnson's article was mainly concerned with the decline in reading standards that she had witnessed amongst pupils moving from primary to secondary schools. She laid the blame for this decline with the following changes in educational fashion:

> According to some present day psychologists, all teaching of young children must be child-centred: the teaching must grow from the child's interests and not be limited by any time-table divisions. Freedom of expression is all-important and the method of conveying it is relatively unimportant... Some of my friends in junior schools tell me that marking and correcting is a thing of the past as it may bring a sense of failure to a child. So one sees mistakes becoming firmly implanted in the child's mind.

Johnson ended her article by arguing that a permissive atmosphere places a strain on young children, who are in reality crying out for adult direction and leadership. She concluded: 'This feeling was expressed in a delightfully naïve manner by a little 11-year-old, beginning life in an ordered secondary school, who said she liked her new school because discipline was allowed.'[67]

Much of the press reaction to the *Black Paper* was positive. John Raymond in *The Sunday Times* wrote that they contained 'blistering home truths' and were 'incisive and stimulating',[68] whilst Julius Gould in the *Observer* called it 'a brilliant critique of the modern ethos'.[69] However, Cox and Dyson did themselves few favours by giving their pamphlet a dystopic title, an alarming cover design, and a strongly worded introduction warning that 'anarchy is becoming fashionable'. The backlash was fierce. *Black Paper* contributors were described as 'a decrepit bunch of educational Powellites' in the *New Statesman*, 'elderly reactionaries' in the *Evening Standard*, and 'fascist' by Michael Duane, the former head of Risinghill School. In his address to the National Union of Teachers, the Labour Education Secretary Edward Short described the *Black Paper*'s publication as 'one of the blackest days for education in the past 100 years', before lumping its message with calls for the return of capital punishment, the removal of immigrants and the end of the welfare state.[70] For the next two decades Cox and Dyson were treated as pariahs by the education establishment; the 'Enoch Powells of education'.

Such an emotional condemnation as right wing ideologues took these two liberal English professors by surprise. Dyson lived with his partner, a Labour Party councillor, in Hampstead and was the founder of the Homosexual Law Reform Society. Cox was a working-class grammar school boy from Lancashire, raised on Methodism, Milton, and a scholarship to Cambridge University. He was a member of the Labour Party until 1964 and spent his holidays as a tutor in the Workers' Education Association. Both were active members of the Campaign for Nuclear Disarmament. The vitriolic reception of their *Black Paper* shows how polarised the topic of education had become by end of the 1960s. The radicalism of progressive education had shifted the debate to such extremes that any defence of traditional education could be depicted in the mainstream press as something akin to fascism.

Black Paper 2: Crisis in Education was published later that year, on the back of the enormous response garnered by its predecessor. Kingsley Amis and Robert Conquest enjoyed parodying the hysterical reception of the first pamphlet with an article entitled, 'The Anti-Sex, Croquet-Playing, Statistic-Snubbing, Boyle-Baiting, Black Fascist Paper'. *Black Paper 2* had a sharper focus on schools, with five articles about primary schools, and nine articles about secondary schools, including Rhodes Boyson's advice on how to set up a comprehensive. In addition, some of the letters of support from teachers and parents that Cox and Dyson received were published. G. W. J. Crawford, the Head of Hobbs Hill Wood Junior School, contributed an article that testified to the strength of progressive education's developing orthodoxy. He wrote: 'Most "old-fashioned" parents and teachers, assailed with moral obloquy for not echoing progressive parrot cries, feel rather unsure of themselves nowadays.'[71] Cox and Dyson would publish three more Black Papers, all warning against the false gods of progressive education.

During the 1960s, progressive education made some radical promises. The misery of hard work, repetitive practice, memorisation, competition and strict discipline would be done away with, and replaced by creativity, inspiration, play, co-operation and friendly relationships – and not only would children be more happy, their learning would be enhanced. It was an enticing prospect, and many were seduced. Quoting H. G. Wells, Robin Pedley wrote in 1963 that this new dawn would deliver to Britain 'a yield beyond comparison greater than any yield of able and brilliant men that the world has known hithero'.[72] By the end of the 1970s, even the most sympathetic observer would have concluded that Pedley's optimism had been misplaced.

2

Riot: 1969-1979

An uncertain adventure

In 1975, the sixty-one year old Head of Commerce at Creighton Comprehensive School in Muswell Hill, north London handed in her resignation. Miss Stevens filled in the staff survey immaculately, before scrawling across the page in biro, 'I am sick and tired of pupil abuse, swearing, discourtesy, inattention, indifference to work – i.e. I am completely disenchanted with State education. It has in my opinion been completely ruined. Great pity!'

Miss Stevens had been teaching for 20 years, first at William Grimshaw Secondary Modern, before it was subsumed by the newly formed Creighton Comprehensive. She intended to continue teaching until retirement, so her sudden departure took colleagues by surprise. With her grey cardigan, dark skirt and spectacles hanging from a cord, she was a stickler for discipline and had earned the nickname 'Steve'. She was respected as a teacher, instructing generations of local girls in typing and secretarial work, and a line of cacti lined up on her window attested to their gratitude. However, the progressive ideas of the new comprehensive proved too much for Miss Stevens to bear. Hunter Davies, the journalist who recorded her discontent, concluded: 'Whatever one might think of Miss Stevens' own beliefs, it was a very sad message.'

Hunter Davies's book *The Creighton Report* was published in 1976, and is a remarkable portrait of a comprehensive school during the mid-1970s. Davies, a journalist at *The Sunday Times* and biographer of the Beatles, had written a series of education features about Creighton before deciding to stay and teach for a whole year, recording what he saw. Davies had chosen Creighton not for its radical excesses, but because it was a representative example of the modern comprehensive. The school was situated in Muswell Hill and the head was forty-three year old Molly Hattersley, wife of the rising star of the Labour Party Roy Hattersley. It had a varied intake, populated by middle-class pupils from the surrounding suburbs, working-class pupils from a nearby estate, and a number of Indian and Cypriot immigrants. The school was formed in 1967 from the merger of a secondary modern and a grammar, but retained few of the features of the latter. It abandoned prize-giving, achievement badges, the house system, prefects, pupil duties and school uniform – Mrs Hattersley did draw the line at pupils turning up in bare feet though. 'That's unhealthy', she remarked. The spirit of egalitarianism ran deep at the school. 'We're trying to avoid children saying, "I'm better than you and I've just proved it",' Mrs Hattersley stated. 'While children are at school, we want to minimise the competition.' The school rules were just one page long, mainly concerning hours and attendance. There were no punishments at the school, aside from suspension for 'serious crimes'. Wherever possible, mixed-ability teaching was implemented. Mrs Hattersley hoped to make this universal but was aware it would lead to difficulties recruiting staff.

Creighton had a 'democratic' school council, which proved a constant source of strain for Mrs Hattersley, particularly when they questioned her decision to ban a visiting speaker who intended to show the pupils slides illustrating the difference between pornography and eroticism. Mr Bamford, the young R.E. teacher who invited the speaker, complained: 'It was only going to be soft porn, not hard porn. It would have helped the students to make rational judgements.'

Davies's descriptions of the Creighton staff attest to the

enormous culture change that had taken place by 1976. On the one hand, there were members of staff such as Londoner Mr Macdonald. He was a geography teacher, head of third year, and 'one of the few young teachers in the school who believes in the old virtues, especially discipline.' The son of a policeman, he had short hair, and wore a neat blazer, clean shirt and tie. He kept excellent order in his classroom, and complained of his colleagues who 'think they're progressive' but came running to him for help once the children started to misbehave. Although he was fond of the pupils at Creighton, he did not see himself lasting long, and even considered leaving for a job in Lockerbie. He had heard that Scottish secondary schools had more successfully held out against 'the new wave of freedom and permissiveness'.

In stark contrast was David Matthews, a gentle grammar school boy from Swansea. Pupils complained that his maths lessons were too noisy, but he had no intention of clamping down. He believed that forcing pupils to work was exactly what was wrong with schools, claiming it turns them into 'prisons'. As he explained:

> I didn't become a teacher to act as a policeman. The old-timers make them sit down and shut up and write out what they're told to write out, but do they learn any more? You hear all this crap about education fitting kids for life. All it does is fit them into the system.

At the end of the year Matthews left the school to live on a farming commune in Wales, explaining that all school did was prepare 'kids' for a capitalist, materialist society.

Throughout his book, Davies retained a stance of studied neutrality on the question of progressive education. However, the pupils at Creighton were clearly underachieving. Tracey, from the local council estate, complained of the difficulty she had working in disorderly classrooms, and by the end of her first year her mother was resigned to the fact that Tracey would not learn anything at school. The bright, middle-class Jonty from Highgate was similarly held back. His father, who went to Clifton College before becoming a socialist and joining the BBC, sent his son to the school on principle but was aware of its limitations. 'It's an uncertain adventure,' he stated, worrying that at his son's age he had been learning Greek iambics. About the best that could be attributed to Creighton, on the basis of Davies's account, was contented mediocrity: it was certainly a far cry from Harold Wilson's promise a decade earlier of 'Grammar Schools for all'.

Comprehensive values

Creighton demonstrated the great misfortune that comprehensivisation suffered by coinciding with progressive education. Davies himself explained that the early comprehensive schools retained all the features of secondary school life recognisable 'since Dr Arnold's day'. This did not endure though the 1970s, however:

> After ten years the progressive comprehensive school, such as Creighton, has very few if any of these features. The typical comprehensive, if there can be such a thing, is unrecognisable, as we shall see, to anyone who left school in the fifties.[1]

As the radicalism of the sixties settled into a new set of social norms, so too did the core assumptions of progressive education become received wisdom within British schools. One such philosophy was spelt out in *Comprehensive Values* (1975), written by P. E. Daunt, the well-known headmaster of a progressive comprehensive in Crawley. Daunt believed, according to what he termed the 'equal-value principle', that no school had a right to prioritise their expectations of pupil behaviour over the behavioural choices made by the pupil, irrespective of any perceived 'moral and social faults'. Daunt praised the 'relativism' that has been popularised by psychology and anthropology, and declared that a comprehensive school should allow pupils' characters to flower in a non-judgemental atmosphere of freedom.[2] If such a philosophy defined 'Comprehensive Values', there is little wonder that vandalism, graffiti and violence were so often the result.

During the 1970s, the behaviour crisis in primary and comprehensive schools was a continual concern of national newspapers. 'Stop these trendies before they ruin ALL our children,' wrote the *Daily Mail* in October, 1973.[3] 'Order and discipline have been abandoned,' confirmed the *Sunday Express* the following July. But it was not just the conservative press who were worried. The feminist Jill Tweedie wrote a critical exposé of a progressive Islington primary school in 1975 for the *Guardian*, in which she spoke to a Yorkshire born fireman who complained that his children were not being taught 'stability, discipline and the three Rs'. Tweedie concluded that it was desperately patronising for liberal, middle-class teachers in favour of 'free expression' to tell such parents: 'You do not know what is best.'[4] That same year in the *Observer*, Alan Watkins, a left-wing political journalist born in the Welsh mining village of Tycroes, raged: 'The administration, the teachers, the sociologists, the psychologists, the education correspondents have, over the past decades, betrayed the ideals of working-class education.'[5]

Apologists dismissed such opinions as scaremongering, but poor behaviour in schools was no illusion. In the space of ten years, the number of school fires rose from 18 in 1963 to 89 in 1973, costing £6 million in damage. The ILEA ordered a special enquiry in 1973 into damage and vandalism in London schools, and discovered that one school alone was spending £1,000 a month repairing broken windows. In 1977, £15 million of damage was done to British schools and Glasgow education officials estimated that the money spent on repairing vandalism that year could have allowed them to build two new primary schools.[6] Pupil theft within such schools became endemic, and visitors to comprehensive schools commonly observed that pupils would carry their jackets and oversized bags around school, knowing that the cloakroom would not be safe.

It is important to note how the abnegation of adult authority, which took place on an intellectual level in the 1960s, so quickly translated into classroom disorder during the 1970s. This rapid deterioration left teachers shell-shocked and the general public appalled. Whilst a number of factors were blamed for this onslaught of disorder – popular culture, school architecture, the worsening economy – it took a wilful level of naivety to suppose that the spread of 'progressive' ideas about pupil behaviour played no part.

The most powerful public exposé of behaviour in comprehensive schools came courtesy of a BBC fly on the wall documentary presented by David Dimbleby for *Panorama*, entitled 'The Best Days?'. Filmed at Faraday Comprehensive in 1976, and airing the following year, it showed an 'ordinary comprehensive school in outer London', where pupils in lessons openly swore, ate sweets, wandered out of their seats, shouted at teachers and refused to work. The pupils did not wear school uniform and most of the teachers' time was occupied with simply achieving quiet. As one despairing PE teacher shouted at a class before their lesson: 'Talk, talk, talk. No wonder we have so many rubbish lessons!'

The documentary featured a young American teacher who tried to set a whole class detention for 20 minutes (the time it took the class to settle down) only for one female pupil to shout: 'Oh miss, come off it'. A housemaster dealing with a boy who had sworn at the school matron uttered the well-worn phrase of disapproving tolerance:

'Now you can see I'm not getting at you or anything. I'm just disappointed'. Even the headmaster had trouble clearing out the girls' toilets and corridors during break time. In the 'Sanctuary', a room for pupils excluded from mainstream lessons, pupils were shown sitting on sofas, playing ping-pong, listening to music and chatting to staff about their boyfriends. The documentary closed with two cleaning ladies sweeping litter from the floor at the end of the school day. One said to the other: 'Gets worse every day doesn't it? I don't know where all this dirt comes from.'[7]

In July 1974, the political commentator Ronald Butt wrote an insightful article for *The Times* entitled 'A sorry tale of two conflicting cultures in the country's classrooms'. It argued that parents were fleeing comprehensive schools not because they were elitists, but because they were repelled by the values espoused by such institutions. Butt observed that 'a basic culture conflict' had developed between many pupils' homes and their schools. He wrote: 'Until a decade or so ago, it used to be taken for granted that the values of the school reinforced the values of the home. This is no longer necessarily the case.'[8] As if to drive home his point, Butt's article was rebuked by a letter to *The Times* from a teacher the following week describing himself as 'a young, long-haired tramp who occasionally uses four-letter words in the staff-room', who believed 'there is as much, probably more good Christianity in this egalitarian, atheistic, progressive, trendy, hard-swearing, free-loving comprehensive than any religious, excellent, patriotic, single-sex, single-cast, establishment.'[9]

The professional prestige of teachers took a serious blow during the 1970s. The extreme disorder in Britain's classrooms gave the unfair impression that teachers were incompetent, and still worse it made the job of teaching seem newly unpleasant. For the first time, 'bravery' came to be a quality required by the prospective teacher. Teaching in the capital had traditionally been seen as a prestigious job, but by now the opposite was the case. Many schools in London could not fill their rolls and depended on teachers in their probationary year or from overseas, particularly Australia. The Department for Education and Science conducted a survey in 1972/3 into staff attrition, and found that teacher turnover was 18 per cent in primary schools, and 15 per cent in secondary schools. In the capital the figures were 33 per cent and 26 per cent respectively, with London schools having to recruit around 5,000 new members of staff a year.[10] In January 1974, a letter was sent to the *TES* stating:

> It is high time somebody made a tally of the casualties in our comprehensive schools – the shell-shocked, the battle-weary, the walking wounded... the physical effect is what bothers most of us. The nervous and bodily exhaustion, the enervation at the end of each week, the dog-tiredness at the end of each term, the relentless accumulation of stress.[11]

The William Tyndale affair

Awareness of progressive education peaked with the William Tyndale affair – a case that came to symbolise the movement's potential for creating havoc. From the summer of 1975 to the spring of 1976, the national press closely followed events at this small Islington primary. The school had been taken over in 1973 by a radically progressive head named Terry Ellis, although he preferred the non-hierarchical title of 'convener'. His second-in-command was Brian Haddow, later described by a colleague as 'a hard person, a trouble-maker and an ideologue'.[12] Together, Ellis and Haddow presided over two years of extraordinary irresponsibility before the school was closed down by the ILEA. Believing that traditional teaching was merely 'social control', they abolished formal lessons and gave pupils complete choice over what they learnt. Not even writing lessons were compulsory, as this was thought to be obsolete in the age of the typewriter, and no effort was made to enforce discipline. When parents complained about their children being allowed to truant and run onto the streets, the head answered: 'What do you expect me to do? Make the school into a concentration camp to keep your children in?'[13] Stories were reported of pupils 'bullying infants; laughing and swearing at teachers; and abusing the dinner ladies and playground supervisors', as well as throwing stones and spitting at pupils in a nearby infant school. In perhaps the worst story, one boy climbed on top of the roof of the toilets and began hurling glass milk bottles at the infant school pupils below. The head's solution was to have milk delivered in cardboard cartons instead.

Desperate parents removed their children from the school, and the roll fell from 230 in September 1973, to 144 one year later. After a campaign from parents and teachers, the ILEA entered into a protracted battle to get the school shut down, closely followed by the press. 'Parents boycott "School of Shame"', wrote the *Telegraph*; 'The Tragedy of William Tyndale' wrote the *Observer*. The school was finally closed in the summer of 1975 with just 63 pupils remaining.[14] There was a public outcry that Ellis and Haddow had been allowed to indulge in their ideological fantasies at the expense of the pupils, and a government report was commissioned to find out why. The Auld Inquiry called 107 witnesses, spent £55,000, and totalled 250,000 words, but it did not reach a clear answer. Dolly Walker, the remedial teacher at the school who first galvanised opposition to Ellis and Hadlow, attacked the report in the fifth *Black Paper* for not facing up to the controversial issue of educational philosophy. Walker argued the school was implementing in a doctrinaire fashion some very common ideas about primary education. She refuted the 'attempts to dismiss this as a regrettable but entirely exceptional case', and concluded, 'I venture to say that the debasement of education which it exemplifies is a reflection of the very widespread *malaise* within education in the country today'.[15]

Located so close to central London, the William Tyndale affair invited media coverage. Admittedly, very few primary school teachers were like Ellis and Haddow, but the story resonated with the general public for good reason. It was emblematic of the disorder that progressive ideas were creating throughout the country.

Comprehensive curriculum

Less commented upon but no less damaging was the continued spread of child-centred teaching methods throughout the 1970s, particularly in secondary schools. At the centre of this movement was the Schools Council. In the post-war period, nearly all British politicians observed the unspoken rule that intervening in school curriculums was 'not done' – such autocratic meddling was viewed as the preserve of foreign dictatorships. So curriculum decisions were made firmly at the level of local authorities, schools and individual teachers. In 1960, the Conservative Minister of Education David Eccles tentatively suggested that the government should be allowed access to what he dubbed 'the secret garden of the curriculum'. To this end, he formed his own Curriculum Study Group, which proved deeply unpopular amongst teachers, so Eccles's successor Edward Boyle replaced it with the teacher-led Schools Council in 1965. This organisation would play a crucial role in recasting traditional subjects in child-centred moulds over the next 20 years.[16]

The Schools Council received an annual budget of around £2 million and eventually set up over 180 projects.[17] In most cases, the Council's projects attempted to move subjects away from a curriculum defined by knowledge towards developing skills and allowing pupils to learn independent of teacher instruction. One key concern was the need to eliminate 'arbitrary' subject boundaries and teach a 'whole curriculum', particularly in the humanities. To this end, the educationist Lawrence Stenhouse led their Integrated Humanities Project, which replaced clearly defined subjects (geography, history, religious education) with 'themes' relevant to pupils. Stenhouse wrote in the introduction to his project:

> We need to establish a new climate of relationships with adolescents which takes account of their responsibility and is not authoritarian. Education must be founded on this co-operation, not on coercion. We must find a way of expressing our common humanity with our pupils, and we must be sensitive to the need to justify the decisions of authority to those affected by them. [18]

In science, an emphasis was placed on discovery learning through practical experimentation; in maths, a grounding in arithmetic was replaced by a grounding in conceptual understanding; and in languages the need to learn grammar and vocabulary was replaced by 'communicative' teaching in the target language. These projects undoubtedly led to some exciting teaching, but their orthodox aversion to subject content and teacher instruction did much to dumb down teaching in British schools.

Long characterised the archetypical old-fashioned school discipline ('kings and queens', 'Rule Britannia', 'rote learning dates'), history received the most thorough re-conceptualisation at the hands of the Council. The Schools Council History Project (later the SHP) founded by David Sylvester in association with Leeds University in 1972, moved history teaching away from understanding the past and towards developing 'historical skills' and 'concepts' such as 'source analysis' and 'understanding causation'. In this recasting of the subject, the process of building one's own historical narrative from primary sources was paramount.[19] As an early member of the SHP who is now an influential history educationist recently recalled, 'in about 1970 I would have said history's about skills and the content is neither here nor there.'[20] Indeed, when it did come to choosing historical content, relevance was the desired quality. Accordingly, the SHP developed a course covering the history of the American West, designed to appeal to the contemporary vogue for cowboy films.

Robert Thornbury, an employee with the ILEA, broke ranks in 1978 and published a lively critique of modern education. He mocked the millennial aspirations of 'the curriculum church', which claimed that the bad behaviour could be eliminated by teaching in a more child-centred fashion. Thornbury wrote:

> The curriculum development movement, indeed, resembled nothing so much as a mad tea party of neo-scholastics. Educational sociologists, project directors and researchers, deschoolers and a host of Marxists all squabbled for funding and influence... The official dogma of the curriculum papacy, the Schools Council, was that the curriculum, not social control, would carry the urban schools through difficult times to redemption and salvation.

Thornbury recorded that Stenhouse's Humanities Curriculum Pack engaged young teachers in a 'hopeless cargo-cult', adding 'Stenhouse himself admitted that this work imposed great difficulties and personal strain on the teachers, and that there had been many failures.'[21]

It was during this period that university education departments became temples to the progressive cause, particularly after 1973 when teaching qualifications became compulsory for all state school teachers. Child-centred education became the in-house orthodoxy for teacher training, and the education philosopher R. S.

Peters complained that: 'The prevailing pattern of teacher training has been to supplement a basic training in subjects and the handing on of skills by an attempt to bring about commitment to some sort of ideology.'[22] So dogmatic was this attachment to discovery learning in teacher training colleges that the tutors themselves insisted on teaching, or even facilitating, trainee teachers in this fashion. This would often result in teacher trainees feeling they had not been taught at all. A trainee from Rickmansworth called Wendy Hawkin captured the irony:

> Practising what they preach, tutors will accompany seminars prepared by students and discussed by students with gentle nods and grunts but never point out that anything said is wrong, rubbish or completely off the point. This leaves the student completely lacking in direction... In retrospect, one was expected to know already how to teach.[23]

One London grammar-school boy who trained during this period later wrote that passing out of teacher training: 'I wanted them to work independently and to be able to engage easily in group discussion. The idea that they should sit gazing at me, hanging on to my every word, soaking up the wisdom I, and only I, could impart, was abhorrent.'[24] That teacher was Chris Woodhead, and he would experience a dramatic conversion from this early instruction.

Trainee teachers from this period also witnessed an effusion of radical books on education which found their way onto university reading lists, many published as cheap paperbacks by Penguin Education Specials. These books tended to combine the anti-authority, individualistic ethos of progressive education with revolutionary politics. A. S. Neill continued to sell well, and was joined by John Holt's *How Children Fail* (1964), Carl Rogers's *Freedom to Learn* (1969), Pablo Friere's *Pedagogy of the Oppressed*

(1970), Ivan Illich's *Deschooling Society* (1971), Postman and Weingartner's *Teaching as a Subversive Activity* (1971) and Everett Reimer's *School is Dead* (1971).

An entirely new thoughtworld was being created, and the coexistence of old-fashioned schoolmasters still using the cane, and progressive teachers who flinched at the very thought of a school bell, shows just how enormous was the chasm that had emerged by the 1970s. The centre ground, where most teachers would have felt comfortable, was not an easy place to inhabit. G. Kenneth Green, a well-known head who spent 20 years setting up comprehensive schools, wrote an article in the fourth *Black Paper* in 1975 entitled 'Why Comprehensives Fail'. By now, the *Black Paper* pamphlets were arguing for a return to selection, but its authors remained concerned with the doctrines of progressive education. Green wrote of 'a persistent, vociferous, anti-intellectual faction most evident in comprehensive schools', for whom:

> 'academic', 'intellectual', have become almost pejorative terms; 'formal', 'traditional', words of abuse; 'progressive', 'forward-looking', words of divine revelation. Teachers as a group have been brainwashed into thinking that there must be something wrong with them if they are interested in the needs of the able, preserving standards of learning and attainment, of believing that things were not always done badly thirty years ago.[25]

In the third *Black Paper* in 1970, the writer Marjorie Bremner recorded the religious fervour with which progressive education was now being promoted by teachers aiming at nothing less than the salvation of mankind through education:

> The dispute becomes moral, religious, separatist, polarised. All 'the Light' is on one side; all the powers of Darkness on the other. And so it is that the passionate

denunciations of the *Black Papers* are couched in a fervent, violent, chiliastic vein.[26]

All schools experimented with aspects of the progressive revolution, from non-uniform to project work, but some embraced it to the letter. The most famous secondary school of this type was Countesthorpe College, formed in 1970 by the forward-looking local authority of Leicestershire and described by Benn and Simon in *Half Way There* as 'a prototype of the school of the future'.[27] The three school leaders all came from the Nuffield Resources for Learning team, a group associated with the Schools Council, and the building was designed to accommodate their child-centred philosophy. Instead of 'the usual rows of box-like classrooms', the school was designed around a large circular hall, with interdisciplinary areas for group work and team teaching spanning from the centre. The 'warden', not 'head', was Tim McMullen. There was the now familiar abandonment of lesson periods, rewards and sanctions, examinations and traditional subject distinctions. Instead, pupils at Countesthorpe studied 'the individual and his group' (known as IG); 'creative and expressive work in words, music and movement' (CW); and 'creative and expressive work in two and three dimensions' (2D-3D).[28] Brian Simon, the comprehensivisation guru, was a school governor. He announced that what Thomas Arnold's Rugby was to the Victorian public school system, Countesthorpe would be to the twentieth century comprehensive.[29]

Tim McMullen left after just two years due to ill health, and later declared his time there to have been a failure.[30] One year later, disaffected parents were demanding that the local council inspect the school, due to their concerns about poor behaviour and lack of pupil progress. An inspector arrived in November 1973 and his confidential report was leaked to the press. It offered stories of vandalism, defective architecture, misbehaviour and the theft of school property.[31] Under the new head John Watts, the school reined in some of the wilder reaches of its philosophy, but struggled under threat of closure for the rest of the 1970s.

The demands placed on teachers by schools such as Countesthorpe caused frequent reports of teacher exhaustion, and 'innovation fatigue' was a common complaint. Even the most ardent proponents of child-centred teaching admitted that its complexity posed a considerable challenge. According to the new principle of 'personalisation', teachers found themselves expected to create three or four different lessons within a lesson, and the dreaded term 'resources' entered the professional lexicon. The era of the 'pupil worksheet', which could be completed at a pupil's own pace according to their varied ability, had arrived. In *The Comprehensive School,* Robin Pedley wrote that a successful teacher must have reserves of energy, 'comparable, let us say, to those required by successful Prime Ministers'.[32] An NUT pamphlet from 1978 entitled *Teachers Talking* even used the demands of new teaching methods to argue for a rise in teacher pay. The Deputy Head of a Gloucestershire Junior School with 40 years of experience wrote:

> The complexity of modern education means greater and greater strains being put upon individual teachers and partly accounts of the substantial wastage which is a significant feature of this present time.[33]

Progressive decline

To what extent this new style of teaching led to a direct decline in standards was then, and remains now, a subject of considerable debate. Examination results were not monitored and nationally administered primary school tests were still two decades away. As was often commented upon at the time, there was a severe lack of quality educational research, considering the level of experimentation and increases in expenditure taking place. This paucity of official figures meant that debates over standards were mired in speculation, informed mostly by small-scale studies that could be easily dismissed.

Neville Bennett, a Professor of Educational Research at the University of Lancaster, conducted the most discussed research of the 1970s. He studied 37 primary school teachers from Lancashire and Cumbria, classifying them according to teaching method. Between those teachers classified as 'formal' and those classified as 'informal', there was a clear difference. In the formal classes, pupils were not allowed to move around freely, whilst they were allowed to do so in 51 per cent of the informal classes. In the formal classes, 100 per cent of the teachers requested quiet during classwork, compared with 31 per cent in the informal. Of the formal teachers, 97 per cent regularly awarded marks to the pupils, compared with three per cent of the informal teachers.[34]

The classes were tested in mathematics, English and reading in September 1973, and retested in June 1974 to measure their progress. Bennett's conclusions, published in 1976, shocked the education establishment:

> The results form a coherent pattern. The effect of teaching style is statistically and educationally significant in all attainment areas tested. In reading, pupils of formal and mixed teachers progress more than those of informal teachers, the difference being equivalent to some three to five months' difference in performance. In mathematics formal pupils are superior to both mixed and informal pupils, the difference in progress being some four to five months. In English formal pupils again out-perform both mixed and informal pupils, the discrepancy in progress between formal and informal being approximately three to five months.[35]

Bennett added that spelling and punctuation were better in the formal classrooms, and that the informal classroom was particularly detrimental for the 'anxious' or 'insecure' child. Even on measures of creativity, a sacred pillar of the informal classroom, there was no evidence that informal classes outperformed formal classes. The Bennett Report had far reaching effects, warranting a leader in *The Times* entitled 'Progressive is not progressive'.[36] It even led the American psychologist Jerome Bruner to revise his opinions in favour of formal teaching. He wrote in *New Society* in April 1976:

> We are just at the end of an era in the human sciences in which concepts of self-direction, self-realisation and self-reward lived unchallenged in a world where self-determination was the ideal... Common sense and technical enquiry are finally catching up with romantic excess.[37]

Many hoped this research would put to bed the utopian schemes of progressive education, but debates in education rarely progress along rational, evidence-based lines. Reason has always been a slave of the passions and, in education, passions remained in favour of the liberated child. In a letter to *The Times*, the psychologist Professor Eysenck observed that the Plowden Report was wildly influential despite a paucity of evidence, so the likelihood of Bennett's Report spurring a counter-reformation was low:

> It would be nice to think that we had learned our lesson, but it is difficult to be optimistic. Ideological thinking is not easily swayed by factual evidence; it is only too easy to change one's claims when disproof stares one in the face, and demand new and more extensive contrary evidence, *ad infinitum*, while refusing to back up one's own claims with equally good evidence.[38]

On an anecdotal level, the sheer weight of complaints emerging from parents and employers, particularly with respect to the elementary teaching of the 'three Rs', was notable. In 1976, the CBI submitted the following memorandum to the Select Committee at the House of Lords:

> Employers are becoming increasingly concerned that many school-leavers, particularly those leaving at the statutory age, have not acquired a minimum acceptable standard in the fundamental skills involved in reading, writing, arithmetic and communication. This shows up in the results of nearly every educational enquiry made among the CBI membership, and is backed up by continuing evidence from training officers in industry and further education lecturers that young people at 16+ cannot pass simple tests in mathematics...[39]

Similar concerns were voiced in public by Sir Arthur Bryant, the director of Wedgwood pottery, and the managing director of the GEC who wrote an article in the *TES* in January 1976 entitled 'I blame the teachers'.[40] In the *Financial Times,* the managing director of an engineering company wrote that his firm was unable to find a single school leaver over the summer who could answer the following question : 'Express ¼ as a decimal'.[41]

In real terms, expenditure on education rose by more than four times from 1953 to 1976, and at its peak consisted of 13.3 per cent of public expenditure.[42] New buildings, curriculum 'innovations' and a significant reduction in the pupil/teacher ratio were all achieved, but at best the standards in schools stagnated. Maurice Kogan, the reforming civil servant who had been Secretary to the Plowden Committee, admitted in 1978: 'Education is a gigantic case study of how increased social and individual activity and commitment – more expenditure, more building, more people, and more public support – does not necessarily lead to satisfaction and success.'[43]

Hey! Teachers! Leave them kids alone!

In 1979, Pink Floyd were recording their album 'The Wall', and decided that one of the tracks required the backing vocals of schoolchildren. They sent their sound recordist to Islington Green Comprehensive where the maverick music teacher Alun Renshaw, who was well known for swearing, smoking in lessons, and encouraging pupils to make music by banging on the classroom walls, leapt at the idea. Renshaw's pupils duly recorded the chorus to what is perhaps the most well-known rock song about education, 'Another Brick in the Wall Part 2'. Gerald Scarfe provided his famous cartoon of a demonic gown-wearing teacher feeding children through a meat mincer, whilst the pupils sang: 'We don't need no education. We don't need no thought control. No dark sarcasm in the classroom... Hey! Teachers! Leave them kids alone.'[44]

In a remarkable case of intellectual dissemination, Pink Floyd and the pupils of Islington Green were articulating an idea developed by sociologists earlier in the decade, which subsequently swept through teacher training colleges. In his 1971 collection of essays *Knowledge and Social Control*, Michael Young developed the 'new sociology of education'. He argued that the dominant forms of curriculum knowledge, decided upon by industrial elites, allowed schools to play a key role in the reproduction of a class-based society. According to this thesis, working-class pupils failed at comprehensive schools because they were being taught a syllabus that was designed to favour middle-class pupils and perpetuate social inequality. Young* described the traditional school curriculum as 'constructed realities realised in particular institutional contexts'.[45] A similar conclusion was reached by the educationist Vic Kelly, who in 1977 wrote *The Curriculum: Theory and Practice*, which ran to six editions and became a staple of teacher training reading lists. It stated: 'one must see the imposition of any one version of knowledge

---

* Michael Young, who is now Emeritus Professor at the University of Education, has since experienced a conversion. In 2009 he described *Knowledge and Control* as 'deeply flawed'.

as a form of social control and as a threat to all of the major freedoms identified as essential constituents of a free and democratic society'.[46] The number of teachers who actually read and understood Young's collection of essays was probably small. However, it gave a new intellectual authority to criticisms of teaching based on the transmission of knowledge. The knowledgeable teacher hoping to pass on to pupils the best that had been thought and said, could now be dismissed as a middle-class agent of industrial capitalism who was suppressing the working class.

In the third *Black Paper*, Robert Conquest and Kingsley Amis mocked the new sociology of education with their 'Short Education Dictionary'. 'Teach' was defined as 'Impose irrelevant facts and bourgeois indoctrination upon', 'spelling' was 'a bourgeois pseudo-accomplishment designed to inhibit creativity, self-expression, etc.' whilst 'discipline' invited the reader to 'see fascism'.[47] Reality can quickly followed satire, as a letter from the head of English at Crofton High School, Wakefield, sent to the *TES* in 1976 illustrated. It wrote that enforcing spelling standards was 'wasteful and irrelevant, and they are used to put people down and make them feel inadequate... So am I advocating a lowering of standards?' the head of English asked. 'Yes' was his answer.[48] The ramifications of Young's ideas were keenly felt. In June 1974, a headmaster wrote to the *TES* complaining of the ideas held by newly recruited members of staff. He wrote such teachers were:

> ...imbued with newer notions about repressive middle-class culture. These come out of college with *Knowledge and Control* in the bloodstream. They assume that to get on with working-class children you must pretend to be working-class. But children do not want you to play a patronising role.[49]

Young's ideas gave momentum to a new philistinism which derided the very idea of an 'academic' education for the majority of the population. In an argument that would persist for decades, educationists attacked their own calling, and everything from reading novels to upholding correct spelling became seen as a middle-class imposition.

These ideas fused with the popular cultural relativism of the period, mocked by Richard Hoggart as 'the "the Beatles are in their own way as good as Beethoven" nonsense'.[50] In 1973, Brian Jackson wrote an article for *New Society* entitled 'How the poorest live: education'. He suggested that pupils were bored and restless at school because of the misguided attempts to teach them an academic curriculum, and recommended instead that state education be fitted to their existing interests. Jackson suggested teachers take their pupils outside of the classroom to chalk on walls, build cars out of junk, make dresses and perform street theatre.[51]

Amongst public figures of both the right and the left, there was due outrage. In the *Observer* Alan Watkins, whose parents had been teachers in the Welsh mining village of Tycroes, railed that an academic education was not elitist but the entitlement of all. He recognised that the new sociology of education contained a 'terrifying inverted snobbery', which sought to deprive the working class of their cultural inheritance. Watkins wrote of the miner with whom he used to discuss Hegel, and demanded to know: 'Was Aneurin Bevan elitist when he spent hours in the Tredegar public library?' Watkins concluded his furious article with a broadside against 'the sociologists, the education correspondents and some of the teachers, many of whom are little better than criminals against the working classes of this country.'[52] Another figure of the left appalled by the new sociology of education was the novelist Iris Murdoch, who opened the fourth *Black Paper* with an essay in favour of academic selection and streaming. She ended her essay by writing of the 'danger' that 'learning itself may come to be regarded as a "middle-class value", repugnant to those who hold "proletarian values"... It would be hard to exaggerate the brutalizing effect of such a development.'[53]

There was another aspect to the new sociology of education, which in the long run would prove even more destructive. This was the belief, popularised by the sociologist Basil Bernstein, that socio-economic circumstances had an overpowering effect on educational attainment. Bernstein was Michael Young's mentor at the Institute of Education and specialised in the study of 'speech codes'. He claimed that whilst middle class children are raised to speak in an 'elaborated code', working-class children are raised to speak in a 'restricted code'. An academic education, he argued, was only ever going to exacerbate, and not bridge, that divide, so the dice of school were always loaded against the working class. As with Young, Bernstein's arguments were complex and nuanced, but it was the simplified message that 'deprivation is destiny' that filtered through to the teaching profession. The title of Bernstein's celebrated essay from 1970, 'Education cannot compensate for society', became something of an adage within state education.[54] Schools, it came to be believed, were powerless in overcoming a child's socially predetermined chance of success.

This 'sociological view' gave birth to a damaging excuses culture, whereby the underperformance of schools could reliably be pinned on the inequalities and injustices of society. David Hargreaves, one of the legions of educators who fell under the spell of Bernstein's sociological view, would later rise to public prominence during the New Labour years. In 1982, Hargreaves argued that the poor behaviour in British schools could be explained as a revolt of the working class, who felt a loss of dignity due to their industrial livelihood being destroyed.[55] The possibility that this poor behaviour, from working and middle-class pupils alike, was due to the leniency promoted by progressive education was thereby avoided.

For this reason, the 'sociological view' made a convenient alliance with progressive education. Just as the consequences of the mistaken creed were becoming clear to the general public, educationists found the perfect escape clause: it was social inequality, not the defects of their pedagogy, causing all of the problems. As such, progressive educationists took away the discipline and formality that held a school community together, and blamed the ensuing chaos on socio-economic deprivation. One former headmaster wrote in the fourth *Black Paper*:

> It is interesting for observers of the educational scene to note that as methods in British schools have become increasingly informal and a noticeable decline in standards of reading and writing has become associated with this trend, apologists for the new progressive modes of teaching seem to have become more and more concerned with such apparently irrelevant matters as the social background of the pupils in the school. [56]

Aside from all else, the 'sociological view' was deeply insulting to working-class culture. In his magisterial history, *The Intellectual Life of the British Working Classes*, the historian Jonathan Rose documents the memoirs of Edwardian working-class autodidacts who lived long enough to see the arrival of progressive education. He quotes from the autobiography of James Williams, who grew up in rural Wales reading Dickens, Scott, Trollope and even Prescott's *The Conquest of Peru*. Writing in 1971, Williams lamented the spread of 'pappy' children's books, writing of the 'deplorable tendency in the last 30 years to keep the child away from difficulties'.[57] Dolly Walker, the remedial teacher during the William Tyndale affair, recounted that staff were told not to criticise pupils for obscene language as it was deemed 'unfair discrimination' against working-class culture. Walker protested that it was the working-class duty staff, and not the middle-class teachers, who were most appalled by children's use of four letter words.[58]

In addition, the poor behaviour at urban schools such as William Tyndale was often pinned on ethnic diversity. However, many recent immigrants were used to traditional schooling and were amongst those most shocked by progressive education in Britain. Mike Phillips recalls leaping to his feet when the teacher walked in on his first day at school in London, just as he would have done at school in Guyana, only to find his fellow pupils 'laughing and swearing at me'. He later recalled: 'All the mistakes I made in the first week or two were to do with being polite, with treating the school work as if it was a good thing to do'.[59]

The editor of the *Black Papers* Brian Cox, himself from a working-class background in Grimsby, was keenly aware of the troubling development of a 'sociological view' during the 1970s. He wrote:

> The teacher who uses poor social conditions as an excuse for poor teaching is the cause of greater deprivation than the home background itself. At a time of rising living standards since World War II the teacher, by becoming a second-grade social worker, has become a third-grade teacher. It is far easier to blame the lack of an internal water closet for the failure of a pupil to read than to slog at teaching that pupil to read.[60]

Enter the politicians

One figure for whom the sociological view did not wash was Labour Prime Minister James Callaghan. Born in Portsmouth, the son of a Chief Petty Officer, Callaghan did well at school but resented the fact that his family could not afford to send him to university. Nevertheless, he rose to become Prime Minister and retained an abiding faith in the value of hard work and personal discipline. Having been brought up a Baptist and serving his beloved Royal Navy, Callaghan's Labour politics were always wedded to a strong social conservatism. As Home Secretary, his approach to law and order earned him the nickname PC Jim, and he was sceptical of the permissive excesses espoused by the left during the 1960s. As such, he was inclined to confront the wilder extremes of progressive education.

By 1976 public discontent over state education was much enflamed by the Bennett Report and the William Tyndale affair, obliging the Prime Minister to address the issue. He was keen to do so, but knew he was venturing into unknown territory. Previously, politicians steered clear of the 'secret garden', observed to be the preserve of teachers, schools and local authorities. However, by 1976, this accord was breaking down. Society's broad consensus over how schools should operate had been broken by progressive education and there was an increasing sense that intervention from central government was necessary. The *Black Paper* pamphlets, and their associated pressure group the National Council for Educational Standards, were already calling for reforms such as primary school testing, league tables and a national curriculum by the mid-1970s.

Much of the impetus behind Callaghan's foray into educational came from the head of his Policy Unit, Bernard Donoughue. Donoughue was born into a poor family in Northampton and his abusive father split from his mother when he was 11. However, his grammar school propelled him to Oxford University and a career in journalism and politics. He cared deeply about education, and knew the contemporary debate well. His wife was a teacher and soon to be a schools inspector, and he was critical of the poor education his four children had received at London state schools. Like many former grammar school pupils,

Donoughue retained a deep conviction in the values of a traditional education.[61] As he later recalled:

> There was clear evidence that working-class parents and children wanted education and what they wanted was not the same as the middle-class Labour people from Islington, the trendy lecturers from higher education who wanted education at the expense of working-class kids. Jim and I talked about this. Whenever I heard those people talk I got very angry... Their thinking was based on *Guardian* style ideologies and prejudices.

Callaghan later recalled that he hoped to distance his party from 'every idiotic teacher who was sympathetic to the Labour Party'.[62] Spurred on by Donoughue, he decided to enter the secret garden with a speech at Ruskin College, Oxford, where he had been invited to lay the foundation stone for a new accommodation block. Where better, he thought, to air his misgivings about modern education than at a college formed for working-class scholars, and named after the Victorian art critic who wrote about the elevating effect of study? It was a cause dear to Callaghan's heart; five members of his government were former Ruskin Scholars.[63]

To test the water, a confidential briefing paper was authored with the DES and leaked to the press. It was called the *Yellow Book*, and covered areas such as the primary curriculum, vocational education, and the gap between schools and industry. However, the most controversial area was the questioning of modern teaching methods. The *Yellow Book* criticised 'these newer and freer methods', suggesting that the 'uncritical application of informal methods' had allowed some primary school pupils' performance to suffer. On the topic of secondary education, the *Yellow Book* recognised the public's concern 'that schools have become too easygoing', and hinted at the introduction of a national curriculum.[64]

The press reaction was not positive, and over the weekend Callaghan softened his criticism of progressive teaching methods.[65] By the time he made his speech at Ruskin College on 18 October, all he did was suggest that parents felt 'unease' about 'new informal methods' in the hands of poor teachers, but thanks to the *Yellow Book* a strong message was still heard. Subsequent press reaction was mixed, but generally positive. A letter to *The Times* on 22 October from a state school teacher, who had revealingly just moved to the independent sector, read: 'May one offer an admiring welcome to the courageous concern shown by the Government for the *quality* of education... It is indeed a refreshing change for a leading politician thus to express anxiety for the health and content of the curriculum.'[66] However, the teaching profession was not impressed. A *TES* editorial wrote that Callaghan had 'gathered his Black Paper cloak around him' and accused him of appealing to public sentiment in order to divert attention from the faltering economy. Callaghan was incensed by what he called the 'appalling educational snobbery' of the education establishment, as he was accused of being an 'amateur educationalist' in *The Times*, and of engaging in 'political demagoguery' in the *TES*.[67]

After Callaghan's speech, the Education Secretary Shirley Williams took over, organising what was optimistically entitled 'The Great Debate' in early 1977. This consisted of a series of eight regional one-day conferences, each attended by a government minister and prominent figures from industry, education and politics. Williams also introduced a Green Paper in 1977 called *Education in Schools*, which warned against the uncritical application of child-centred teaching methods which had descended 'into lack of order and application' in the classroom.[68] It also suggested the establishment of a national curriculum. Williams was opposed by the teaching unions, who resented the potential loss of professional autonomy and interpreted this desire to raise standards as 'teacher bashing'. The well-known headmaster of Westminster School, John Rae, remarked on the 'hysterical' comparisons made between Labour's interest in a national curriculum and Nazi control of education.[69] However, with inflation, trade union negotiations and unrest in Northern Ireland all pushing Britain to breaking point, the state of schools seemed like a peripheral concern, and Labour were unable to capitalise on the public support for school reform.

Callaghan's 'Ruskin Speech' remains a significant turning point in the history of British education. Up until this point, the education establishment held the keys to the secret garden. However, the destructive idealism of the 1960s and '70s left public trust in the profession irrevocably damaged, and the education establishment forfeited its exclusive access to the secret garden. Had progressive teachers not taken leave of their senses, politicians may never have felt the need to exert central control over British schools. Those who today complain of Ofsted, league tables and the national curriculum have the educators of the 1970s to blame.

However, those who hoped for an educational counter-revolution following the Ruskin Speech were disappointed. The scandals at William Tyndale, Countesthorpe and Faraday schools were not aberrations consigned to the 1970s. As the 1980s began, the disorderly classroom of the 1970s became the norm.

3

Reform: 1979-1986

Educashun isn't working

Margaret Thatcher came to victory in 1979 following Saatchi and Saatchi's famous campaign poster 'Educashun isn't Working', and promised to restore some sense to Britain's battered educational landscape. However, once in power her government put little energy into solving the crisis. Figures in the Labour party such as Callaghan, Donoughue and Williams had gained a working understanding of the problems created by progressive education, but the Conservative government lacked both insight and concern. A succession of ministries pursued an education policy that combined indifference with hair-brained market ideology, greatly retarding any recovery of the comprehensive ideal.

Thatcher's first Education Secretary was a wet named Mark Carlisle. Educated at Radley, Carlisle was a willowy barrister able to deliver a convincing brief with little conviction. He spent just over two years in the role and never got to grips with undercurrents that swirled beneath the surface of education policy. He also lacked government support. The unimportance of the Education Department was symbolised by its relocation to an ugly concrete office block beside Waterloo Station called Elizabeth House, and even Carlisle's own department joked that he spoke 24th in a Cabinet of 23. Carlisle cut spending in schools, but he did not cut fast enough, and was replaced by Keith Joseph in September 1981.[1]

The two most significant reforms passed by Carlisle seemed to confirm that the Conservatives were most concerned with the life-chances of the few. In July 1979, Carlisle's first Education Act ended comprehensivisation, after it had been made mandatory in 1975. Those redoubtable LEAs such as Kent, Buckinghamshire and Birmingham, that had held out for three years, often in protracted court battles, were now allowed to keep their grammar schools. As a result, there are still 164 grammar schools across the country, historical anomalies from the political battles of the 1970s. The following year, another Education Act introduced the Assisted Places scheme, intended to restore the opportunities for non-wealthy pupils formerly provided by Direct Grant Schools. At an eventual cost of £70 million a year, between 12,000 and 15,000 academically gifted pupils from modest backgrounds would have their fees paid for them by the government at independent schools. The *TES* condemned the reform as elitist, writing: 'It offers to snatch a few brands from the burning fire while doing nothing for those same city comprehensives.' The *Guardian* called it a 'miserable measure'.

The one Conservative politician who did have the knowledge and experience to fight the culture war in British comprehensives was Rhodes Boyson, the former headmaster of Highbury Grove Comprehensive and *Black Paper* co-editor. By this stage Boyson had become an MP, and was dying to get his hands on schools, but was given the derisory position of Under-secretary for Higher Education instead. He rightly assumed he was being marginalised as his knowledge and opinions of schools would have threatened the Secretary of State. The party confined him to Higher Education, using him as a populist able to shore up the Tory party's working-class support with pro-capital punishment, anti-homosexuality speeches. The so-called 'Minister for Flogging' rapidly became the wrong person to restore public faith in the traditionalist position on education debates.

If Boyson had the experience to combat the spread

of progressive education, the new Education Secretary Keith Joseph could not have been more different. The chief intellectual architect of Thatcherism, Joseph was a fiercely intelligent barrister and policy expert who had previously set up the monetarist Centre for Policy Studies in 1974. Rarely had a minister been more unsuited to his brief. By this point a discernible divide had developed amongst the Conservatives in approaches to education reform. The 'One Nation' Tories believed in introducing stronger government control through inspections and a national curriculum to drive up standards, something also promoted by Her Majesty's Inspectorate and the Education Department. The Thatcherite wing of the party did not like the sound of such interventionist policies. Instead, they wanted to see the principles of the free market applied to school reform, trusting that parental demand and competition between schools would drive up standards.[2] This was to be achieved through a neo-liberal proposal, long promoted by free-market reformers, known as 'vouchers'. A vouchers system would fully privatise all state schools, and the government would grant parents a 'voucher' to spend on the education of their child wherever they saw fit. Joseph was a leading exponent of this position and shut himself away in Elizabeth House to work out how it could be implemented, surrounded by advisers and academics including a bright young upstart named Oliver Letwin. Joseph held interminable discussions exploring the vouchers idea in the tone of a university seminar, infuriating Boyson who passed the time reading detective novels. Joseph treated school reform as an intellectual exercise, not a practical matter, and in June 1983, after nearly two years of deliberation, he announced that vouchers were, in fact, unworkable.[3]

All the while, Britain's state schools showed little sign of improvement. The morale and prestige of the teaching profession was dealt a severe blow by Joseph, whose position as the figurehead of monetarist retrenchment meant he refused to raise school spending and teachers' salaries in line with inflation. As his own biographer wrote, 'there was a point when Keith Joseph perhaps needed to be saved from his own financial conscience'.[4] Even the Treasury was amazed that the Minister of a major spending department never once requested more resources, and Joseph earned the enduring hatred of the teaching profession. This came to a head in 1985, with the largest teachers' strikes Britain has ever seen. The NUT wanted a 12.4 per cent pay rise but the government offered only four per cent. The NUT began a 'withdrawal of goodwill' action, with teachers refusing to complete extra duties or events such as parents' evenings. Between 1985 and 1987, a total of 910,000 working days were lost as a result of industrial action in schools.[5] British schools were on the verge of meltdown: teachers took early retirement, heads were unable to fill vacancies; pupils played truant *en masse*; and modernist comprehensive buildings became increasingly dilapidated with no capital funds for their repair. On 11 October 1985, the former head of Banbury School wrote in the *TES* that: 'the morale and confidence of the education service is now at a desperately low point... [the present mood] is without precedent'.[6] The consequences of strike action in schools were serious and the teaching profession entrenched its unenviable reputation for being both militant and poorly paid.

Having realised that his vouchers system was a busted flush, Joseph belatedly turned his mind towards school standards. However, his desire to see state education fit with Britain's overall project for economic recovery led him down an anti-academic path not wholly dissimilar to that of the progressive theorists. Joseph was greatly influenced by Correlli Barnett's book *The Audit of War* which attributed Britain's economic decline in part to its favouring of a classical education over a more vocational or scientific path. Joseph believed that an academic education was only suited to a minority of pupils, and worked on a Technical and Vocational Educational Initiative (TVEI) and the Lower Achieving Pupil Project (LAPP) as potential alternatives for the majority. However, drained of energy by industrial action and the failure of his prized vouchers scheme, Joseph could not achieve much. In May 1986 after a botched attempt to remove university grants for wealthy students that alienated Conservative core support, he resigned. Just prior to his resignation, Joseph was asked in an interview with a teachers' magazine whether he would see his time in office as a success. 'No', was his reply.[7]

Progressive continuity

Comprehensive schools by now educated around 80 per cent of British children. With Boyson sidelined and Joseph busy building castles in the air with his coterie of free-market ideologues, progressive education was able to continue unchallenged.

In 1982, a prospective Parliamentary candidate for the Conservative party named Elizabeth Cottrell wrote an essay for the Centre for Policy Studies entitled 'The Two Nations in Education'. As a teacher, Cottrell had worked in a large comprehensive, followed by an independent all-girls school ten miles away, and concluded that the two schools belonged to entirely different worlds. Like most, the independent school had been immune to the winds of educational change, largely preserving a traditional ideal of what education should be. However, Cottrell lambasted the comprehensive school for having low academic expectations, an unwillingness to enforce a common standard of behaviour, a uniform policy that was passively resisted, and a habit of excuse making on behalf of pupil background. Interestingly, Cottrell claimed that the secondary modern where she began her career was far more like the independent school in its ethos and ideals than the new comprehensive. However, she saved the worst of her ire for her own Conservative party. 'In its approach to education during the last 20 years, the Conservative party has exhibited some of its worst features', she wrote. These were lack of will and ignorance.[8]

Many in education, at the time and since, would have challenged Cottrell's depiction of comprehensive schools by the 1980s as dominated by the ideas of progressive education. There was even the occasional reference to a 'conservative counter-revolution' in education after Callaghan's Ruskin Speech. However, there is little evidence for such a view. Only a small minority of comprehensive schools were fulfilling Harold Wilson's original vision of 'grammar schools for all'. There were schools and teachers who rejected the ideas of progressive education but it was always a stance that placed them outside of the new educational orthodoxy. The HMI surveys from the late 1970s were often cited as evidence that talk of a 'progressive revolution' in schools was unfounded, and they offer a picture of continuity and good sense in most English schools. For example, the 1978 HMI report into Primary Education stated that whilst three quarters of teachers employed a 'mainly didactic' approach, only one in twenty relied exclusively on 'exploratory methods'.[9] However, such results conceal more than they reveal. The bias in favour of progressive methods within the inspectorate, which was already well developed, means that the definition of 'mainly didactic' is ambiguous. In addition, the style of the report shows an unwillingness to confront key issues. Phonics and new maths are not mentioned once in the entire report, nor are issues such as uniform and behaviour about which so many parents were concerned.

A similar academic study, which sought to show the lack of 'progressivism' (or 'Plowdenism') in British primary schools took place at Leicester University in 1980 and was known as ORACLE (Observational and Classroom Learning Evaluation). It was pioneered by

Maurice Galton, Brian Simon and Paul Croll. Strangely for a one time educational progressive such as Simon, the researchers concluded that progressive education in primary schools was neither widespread, nor effective. Their research showed that British primary schools still emphasised English and maths, still had lessons directed by the teacher, and only gave a small amount of time to creative arts. According to their analysis: 'one thing that does seem clear is that "progressive" teaching, if by this is meant teaching having the characteristics defined by the Plowden Report, hardly exists in practice.'

However, by defining 'progressive education' as the extreme end of Plowdenism and by classifying schools according to categories which overlapped with both progressive and traditional approaches, the ORACLE research did not pick up on the more subtle way in which Plowden's ideas had percolated through primary schools. Pupils may have been doing maths and English, but they were likely to be pursuing the progressive innovations of look-say and new maths. Lessons may have been at times teacher-led, but they probably did not contain clear discipline, silent study, homework or testing.

On that last point, it is a distinctive feature of progressive education that its effect was felt more strongly in what was abandoned than what was embraced. Whilst few schools during the 1980s persisted with the far-reaching child-centred experimentation of Countesthorpe College, many would have exhibited the generalised rejection of traditionalist methods evident at Creighton Comprehensive. The sociologist Bernice Martin in her 1981 book *A Sociology of Contemporary Cultural Change*, characterised this process as part of society's more general rejection of authority in favour of personal expression and individual liberty:

> In schools, too, this progressive movement involved a sharp attack on boundaries, categories, roles, rules

> and ritual and was characterized by a fundamental mistrust of institutions as such... Those rituals which traditionally embodied and expressed collective identity (communitas), group symbols such as uniform, speech day, school assembly, school sports and the house system, all fell out of favour as constricting individual liberty. Hierarchy, authority, and honourable, achieved leadership roles (prefect, house captain and so on) were also frowned on as anti-egalitarian. So instead of formal rituals of overall communitas, many schools came to be dominated by the symbolic vocabulary of anti-structure and new, informal rituals of peer group conformity.[10]

Once the features of traditional schooling were abandoned, pupils found themselves in primary and comprehensive schools with educational ideals as featureless as the modernist glass and concrete structures in which they were housed.

High priests of dumbing down

A central reason behind the failure of the reforming agenda of the 1980s was that it left the gatekeepers of progressive education firmly ensconced in their LEAs, university departments and government agencies, and their political and intellectual hegemony over state education unchallenged. In 1985, the ever astute commentator on England's schools, Ronald Butt, wrote a piece in *The Times* after attending an event populated by the education establishment. Butt observed that these figures were sanguine about their continued influence, and it was against them that the battle in education now needed to be fought. He concluded: 'Education is too important now to be left to the educationists.'[11] Unfortunately, Butt's call for a new battle went unheeded. By this time, the psychological and sociological theories developed to defend progressive education had become firmly established as academic disciplines, codified in the new jargon of 'eduspeak', and dispensed to trainee teachers in 'professional studies' courses across the country. Whenever the right of educationists to do so was challenged, the high priests of education would close ranks and defend teacher 'professionalism' – a misleadingly neutral term for what was in reality instruction in the progressive orthodoxy.

The DES provided university education departments with an estimated £440 million a year to train teachers, but their requests to know what the training consisted of went unheeded. However, the education campaigners Caroline Cox and John Marks did glean some information. Cox and Marks met whilst working as academics at the Polytechnic of North London (PNL) during the 1970s. At the time, both saw themselves as members of the left, and Marks was a member of the Labour Party, but the violent derailing of the PNL at the hands of left-wing political radicalism distressed them. In 1975 they published their account of these disturbances, entitled *The Rape of Reason*. During the following decade, they turned their attention to state education. In 1989 they wrote a report into teacher training, which concluded that courses, particularly in psychology and sociology, were 'at best an irrelevance and at worst a positive hindrance to good teaching'.[12]

The Durham University PGCE course was broken down into 'subject studies' and 'professional studies'. In 1990, their stipulated reading for a course on 'Learning and Intelligence' included *How Children Fail* by the American John Holt, which was published in 1964 and republished in 1982. Holt's book consisted of a series of meandering diary entries which charged the very institution of school, due to its promotion of examinations and fear, with created educational failure. The Durham course also required trainees to read David Hargreaves's *The Challenge for the Comprehensive School* (1982), perhaps the most read text by trainee teachers during the 1980s. His book argued that pupils misbehave due to the injustices of capitalism, schools are designed to foster 'social control', and that all examinations should be abolished. It also proposed that the secondary school curriculum should consist of only two subjects: 'community studies' and 'expressive arts, crafts and sport'. Hargreaves's book did not prepare trainees to teach in British schools, but to subvert them.[13]

Teacher training courses also promulgated the 'sociological view', encouraging schools and teachers to use socio-economic background as an excuse for failure. Typical of this was Warwick University's PGCE course, which included a 'professional studies' course that 'considers the powerful influence of social factors such as home and community background, gender, race and culture on the work of children and schools'.[14] Instead of resolving to look beyond social divisions, teachers were taught to obsess over them. There was also significant infiltration of the 'New Left' ideas about race and gender into teacher training courses, with some even encouraging trainees to use their jobs to fight established power relations. Trainee teachers at Goldsmiths College attended a compulsory course delivered by a Marxist-Leninist called Madan Sarup based on his book *The Politics of Multicultural Education*. Sarup's work outlined the struggle between the British state and the black community, suggesting: 'teachers should intensify the struggle on a large number of sites', and his book described black Britons who sought assimilation to mainstream society as: 'a class of collaborators who justify the ways of a capitalist state to the blacks and are engaged in domestic neo-colonialism'. The BEd course at Brighton Polytechnic involved a second year course that posed questions such as: 'To what extent do schools reinforce racist stereotypes?' Their reading list included the Marxist *Schooling in Capitalist America* (1976), the anarchist *Deschooling Society* (1971), and the progressive education bible *The Comprehensive School* (1964).[15]

An HMI report from 1982 entitled *The New Teacher in School* criticised the paucity of training in crucial areas of the teacher's craft, with reading tuition, assessing pupils and managing classroom behaviour amongst the areas where many new teachers felt underprepared. Where craft was covered, a progressive education bias was almost inevitable, with one teacher noting: 'the teaching from the education studies department tended to concentrate on the integrated day, open-plan schools and informal teaching'.[16] Almost half of the trainees believed too much time had been given to 'Education Studies', and complained the overly theoretical sessions had little relevance to their ensuing career. The most neglected aspect of training was subject content, as educationists who disdained 'mere knowledge' always favoured instructing trainees on pedagogy. The author of a 1990 report, Sheila Lawlor, wrote:

> Despite the time given to subject studies, this does not mean a concentration on the subject itself. Rather, the aim is to encourage trainees to see the teaching of their subject in terms, almost exclusively, of recent educational theory... That there are no subject studies, but something much worse, is one of the most disturbing features of the PGCE.[17]

A survey conducted between 1972 and 1980 by John Wilson, a member of the Oxford Department of Educational Studies, demonstrated quite how radically the worldview of the average educationist differed from that of normal British people. The study interviewed around 1,000 parents, pupils, teachers and educationists on two unfashionable topics – 'Discipline' and 'Moral Education' – and recorded their views. Whilst 99 per cent of parents and 91 per cent of pupils believed rules should be backed up by sanctions, only 34 per cent of educationists agreed. On the opinion that discipline is not adequately enforced in schools, 90 per cent of pupils and 99 per cent of parents concurred, but only 41 per cent of educationists. In response to the idea that discipline means obedience to authority, 73 per cent of pupils and 81 per cent of parents agreed, but only 24 per cent of educationists. Interestingly, on each question teachers hovered somewhere between educationists and parents. Many teachers would have chosen to disregard what they were told during their training, but the ability of such courses to enforce the gospel of progressive education should not be underestimated.[18]

Attempts were made during the 1980s to encourage a more sensible approach to preparing teachers for the classroom, such as the creation of the Council for the Accreditation of Teacher Education (CATE) in 1984. However, any attempt to alter teacher training radically – such as proposals for teachers to train in schools on 'apprenticeship schemes' – were overturned by university departments which successfully defended their right to ensure 'teacher professionalism'. By the close of the 1980s, it remained business as usual in teacher training. This was revealed by Ed Pilkington in 1990, when he wrote an exposé for the *Guardian* of the 'dangerously' one sided BEd course at the Roehampton Institute:

> ... already, only five weeks into the course, (students) have begun to absorb the message that will be hammered home with monotonous regularity throughout their four years at Roehampton: children should not be told what to do, but encouraged to learn for themselves. Their tutor, Graham Welch, assistant dean of education, tells the class that the key to learning is play: 'You have to realise that everybody including big kids like us, learn through play.'

Pilkington's article gave some idea of how the hegemony of the progressive thoughtworld operated on a BEd course:

> All the fourth-year students I talked to, without exception, were passionately in favour of child-centred learning. Part of the reason for this unanimity is that dissenters are likely to drop out or transfer to other subjects, and thus never become teachers. Others have their doubts ironed out through the sheer weight of argument... It is as if Roehampton were a desert island, with eulogies on child-centred learning its only discs.[19]

LEA confidential

The other institutional strongholds of progressive education during the 1980s were the local education authority. One particular authority gained more national attention than perhaps all of the others combined, before it was shut down in 1988. Combining wild spending with dire results, the Inner London Education Authority (ILEA) rates as perhaps the most extravagant educational failure in British history.

As could be seen in the previous chapter, from the 1960s onwards London was at the forefront of the progressive revolution in British education. As the nation's capital, it was the first to feel the ebb and flow of educational fashions, and it could depend on a steady supply of idealistic young teachers willing to implement them. The ILEA gave institutional support to this culture, and stories abounded of their 'loony' policies, from non-competitive sports days to removing funding from the London Scouts brigades due to their being 'para-military organisations'. In May 1983, their insistence that schools spend extra-curricular time on anti-racism, anti-sexism and 'political education' lessons even led to a union strike.[20] Within the ILEA was the more radical Inner London Teachers' Association (ILTA), which published its magazine *Teaching London Kids* from Monsoon Primary School in New Cross, blending child-centred teaching ideas with a Marxist critique of society.

The ILEA would bully into conformity any school that

did not subscribe to its ideology. In 1986, Brian Dugan was the head of St Jude's Primary School in Southwark. An old-fashioned teacher from Australia, Dugan encouraged competition and strong discipline at his primary school, and appeared the archetypal schoolmaster of old in his tie, jacket, side parting and neatly trimmed moustache. He took over the school in 1980, when it had only 100 pupils on roll and a clear attachment to progressive education. After six years under Dugan's more traditional guidance, St Jude's was full to capacity with 208 pupils. It was popular amongst local parents with two applicants for every place and the pupils achieved highly – nine had won scholarships to public schools. Unfortunately, the ILEA took exception Dugan's old-fashioned approach, and local authority inspectors gave his school a damning report. They wrote: 'St Jude's has become a cause for concern. It is an extremely formal school with a highly competitive ethos and, as such, stands well outside the established tradition of primary education in this authority.' As the journalist Lynda Lee-Potter observed: 'one scarcely need criticise the ILEA when it damns itself so efficiently.'

In June 1968, Dugan was suspended from his headship on full pay and placed in front of a disciplinary tribunal that recommended his dismissal. After a sustained campaign from parents against two ILEA nominated school governors, the ILEA judgement was finally overruled and Dugan was reinstated as head.[21] His only crime had been a refusal to toe the progressive line. The ILEA combined their fondness for progressive education with a militant pursuit of gender and race politics in the classroom. They caused a national scandal when at a primary school in Lewisham, boys of seven were made to dress in petticoats and carry handbags, whilst cooking, doing embroidery and playing with dolls. Girls, meanwhile, were encouraged to play with engineering sets and toy cars. This ILEA sponsored scheme to 'combat sexism and stereotyping' amongst small children was judged 'psychologically damaging' by Professor David Smith.

The 1980 Education Act made it compulsory for schools and local authorities to publish their examination results, and a light was finally shone on the ILEA's much suspected academic underachievement over the following years. In 1986, the ILEA was the highest spending of all 96 Local Academies, with £2,085 spent on each pupil, and it had the most favourable pupil/teacher ratio in the country. However, in terms of examination results, it ranked 86th out of 96 with only 16.2 per cent of pupils achieving what was then called 'defined results' (five or more good O-levels or CSEs). Unsurprisingly, the ILEA tended to blame their woeful attainment on the socio-economic background of London pupils, but Inner London only ranked 56th out of 96 authorities for deprivation. Equally, their frequently made argument that a large number of racial minorities in London gave ILEA schools a unique challenge could not be upheld: some of their worst performing pupils were of British origin, whilst Pakistani and Indian pupils in London did significantly better.

Such a damning evidence of the failure of the ILEA approach led their last Chairman Neil Fletcher to address the Socialist Education Association in 1987 with some significant soul searching. He asked: 'Does our system let down these children? For too many of them, if we are honest, the answer is yes.'[22] Later that year in an interview with *The Sunday Times* Fletcher admitted: 'mixed ability and progressive teaching methods have failed to equip children with basic skills of literacy and numeracy' and added that parents were right to be concerned about basics such as spelling, handwriting and homework.[23] It is little wonder that independent schools in London thrived during this period. Education campaigners Cox and Marks, who both sent their children to comprehensive schools, caustically wrote of the London liberals who supported progressive education during the 1970s before 'going private' with their own children: 'The system which they engineered for other people's children looks less appealing for their own.'[24] After a decade of trying, the ILEA was finally abolished by the 1988 Education Reform Act and two years later the administration of inner London schools passed to the individual boroughs. This grand educational folly, which combined unparalleled financial resources with dreadful results, was not much lamented.

Another example of LEA sponsored decline occurred in Leeds between 1985 and 1991. Britain's third largest city, Leeds, had one of the worst primary records in the country. So, in 1984, Leeds Council successfully applied for an Education Support Grant to implement a detailed proposal named 'Primary Needs Programme' (PNP). The PNP contained many of the usual euphemisms for progressive education: they aimed to teach a 'broadly based' curriculum in 'a stimulating and challenging working environment' with 'flexible teaching strategies' and work that met 'the identified needs of individual pupils'.[25] Money was spent on extra staff, training and refurbishment of schools – which involved knocking down walls to create open plan 'learning environments'. There was team teaching of multiple curriculum areas in single lessons and a large emphasis on pupil discussion and discovery learning. All in all, nearly £14 million was spent over the six years on the Leeds Primary Needs Programme. The result? Reading scores at 7+ and 9+ initially stayed the same, then declined. The decline was steepest in the inner city, where PNP resources were most concentrated.

In a report published in 1991, Professor Robin Alexander laid bare the disaster in Leeds. He condemned the widespread implementation 'of post-Plowden progressivism', which had been before it was embraced by Leeds Council. Speaking to the press, he was scathing: '...many of the most widely endorsed practices simply don't work. As a result, millions of children have had a raw deal – they've wasted such a hell of a lot of time.'[26] At the time the new national curriculum was being devised and Alexander recommended that those designing it be wary of the ideas used in Leeds 'reappearing in another guise'.[27] Such prescient advice went unheeded.

Poor behaviour

The chaotic comprehensive of the 1970s shocked the British public but, by the 1980s, poor behaviour in comprehensive schools was simply tolerated as a feature of national life. However, as the decade drew to a close there was an upsurge in public concern about school discipline, as a series of damning teacher surveys turned the spotlight back on the issue. In 1985, a survey conducted by the union NASWUT concluded that 80 per cent of teachers believed violence and disruption had become more commonplace in schools over the last ten years, whilst four per cent reported being attacked in the preceding six-month period. This was followed by a similar report from the union PAT, which in 1987 surveyed its members and found that 94 per cent believed indiscipline to be on the increase and 32 per cent had been attacked at some point during their career. Lastly, a survey by the NUT in 1988 confirmed that 91 per cent of their members thought discipline in schools was worse than it was ten years previously.[28]

Whilst concern during the 1970s tended to focus on vandalism and disruptive classroom behaviour, during the 1980s this shifted to violence towards staff and bullying. A DES report from 1988 showed that 68 per cent of pupils believed bullying to be a problem in schools.[29] The national press covered a series of tragic stories concerning pupils committing suicide, or accidently dying, at the hands of playground bullies.

In 1987, a former Labour MP who had stood down from his Merseyside constituency the previous year took up the cause of bullying and school discipline in his new BBC chat show *Kilroy!* In an opinion piece for *The Times*, Robert Kilroy-Silk noted that over the past year in Liverpool alone there had been 87 cases of teacher assaults, and concluded: 'It is only a matter of time before a teacher is killed.'[30] In one of his shows, Kilroy-Silk featured the story of Mark Perry, who rode his bicycle under a van after being taunted by bullies for being mixed race. After a crescendo in public dismay, the Professional Association of Teachers wrote to Margaret Thatcher in December 1987 asking for a 'commission of inquiry into discipline in school throughout the United Kingdom'. In response, Kenneth Baker commissioned the Elton Report.

As with so many of its type, the Elton Report published in January 1989 had a surplus of recommendations but lacked an accurate diagnosis of the problem. It may not have helped that Lord Elton, who led the committee, was an elderly life peer educated at Eton and Oxford. His report endorsed many of the permissive, non-hierarchical behaviour policies that had got schools into such trouble in the first place, and wasted time on irrelevancies such as suggesting broadcasters show fewer violent television shows. The Report also surveyed 3,500 teachers, with revealing results. The most popular strategy for dealing with misbehaviour was the progressive staple of 'reasoning with a pupil or pupils in the classroom setting' with 55 per cent using such a strategy 'often or quite often'. In comparison, only 17 per cent of teachers 'often or quite often' used sanctions such as detention, suggesting non-punitive approaches were widely preferred. The lack of hierarchical enforcement of behaviour policies was reflected in the fact that just two per cent of teachers reported that they 'often or quite often' sent poorly behaved pupils directly to senior members of staff. Overall,

52 per cent of teachers surveyed said their school needed 'tougher sanctions for certain forms of indiscipline'. Surveys of adult opinion concurred. The British Social Attitudes survey, which began in 1983, asked members of the public which one factor would most improve schools. In each of the years 1983, 1985, 1987 and 1989, 'stricter discipline' was chosen as the second most popular choice behind 'training for jobs' – with around one in five adults choosing it as the most important factor.[31]

When the views of children were sought, the results were quite unexpected. In 1977, Capital Radio interviewed 1,000 London teenagers, and found that two thirds of them would have liked to see more discipline in their schools.[32] Similarly, in 1986 a three part survey into the attitudes and opinions of young people conducted by *Times*/MORI found that education was the second biggest concern amongst 16-24 year-olds, after unemployment. Discussion groups held in Bath, Nottingham and Leeds revealed:

> Thatcher's children want more discipline in schools, not less. This may come as a surprise to educationalists; it certainly will to those who grew up in the 1960s, when the tide of school liberalisation was in full flood. Over and over again, these young people spoke with contempt of the slack school regimes of which, they readily admitted, they had taken advantage.

One of the interviewees was Michael Hufton, an 18-year-old apprentice printer from Nottingham, who stated: 'I wanted discipline, I could have done with it earlier. I wanted somebody to guide me. I wanted somebody to say, that's wrong, don't do that. [At school] you could go up and smack somebody and get away with it, they (the teachers) don't bother.'[33] The institutional values of most comprehensive schools were clearly out of kilter with children, parents and even teachers.

With such an image of unruly schools implanted in

the public imagination, it is unsurprising that very few people during the 1980s wanted to become teachers, and the breakdown in discipline had a direct effect in depressing the quality of future generations of teachers. In January 1988, despite unemployment for the previous year standing at 10.5 per cent, there were 2,000 vacancies in secondary schools, amounting to around one per cent of the teaching force in England and Wales. Primary vacancies were even higher, at around 1.5 per cent.[34] In addition, many head teachers were taking early retirement and in 1988, in Sheffield alone, 70 heads had applied for early retirement. Only four were successful.[35] Poor pay, disruptive schools, and little prospect of sensible reform: the 1980s was not a good decade to be a teacher.

Reading Wars: Round 2

After the watershed of 1976, there may have been a slight return to teaching reading through phonics. Joyce Morris, whose work for the NFER during the 1950s and '60s made her sceptical of the benefits of 'look-say' methods, had her alternative phonics based reading scheme *Language in Action* published by MacMillan during the late 1970s. However, by the 1980s the winds of fashion had once again changed, and 'look-say', or whole-word (as they were increasingly called due to pupils initially learning the 'whole word' before individual letter sounds) methods were given a significant new lease of life. Morris' reading schemes went out of print in 1983.[36]

The 1980s saw a revival in the reading wars. Debate was so intense that in 1991 the Education Secretary Kenneth Clarke commissioned a report from the NFER entitled *What Teachers in Training are Taught about Reading*. It revealed quite how biased teacher training courses had become towards 'look-say' methods during the 1980s.[37] All 92 institutions of initial teacher training in Britain were asked to submit their core reading lists, and the NFER team chose half of the lists at random to analyse, and ranked the thirty most popular titles. Every one of the thirty texts had a preference for 'look-say' methods of instruction while there was not a single text on the systematic instruction of phonics. Additionally, not one text presented an objective review of the experimental research into initial reading instruction – although many had been published. In response to the survey's results, the reading specialist Bonnie Macmillan concluded: 'A careful examination of these materials exposes the staggering bias in current teacher training, a bias that amounts to nothing short of indoctrination on a very wide scale.'[38]

The fourth most popular book, according to the NFER reserach, included on 52 per cent of initial teacher training reading lists, was *Reading* by the Canada based psycholinguist Frank Smith. With no teaching experience and a background in philosophy and linguistics, Smith managed to attain 'guru' status within teacher training colleges. He reinvigorated the child-centred, look-say approach with a method known as 'real books' – the idea being that pupils could begin their journey of word recognition by reading and memorising the content of 'real books' as opposed to the 'boring' reading schemes. Smith was emphatically anti-teaching, proclaiming in *Reading* that: '*Children cannot be taught to read.* A teacher's responsibility is not to teach children to read but to make it possible for them to learn to read.'[39] A more counterproductive message for trainee teachers is hard to imagine. However, he was a very charismatic individual. As one critic later wrote:

> I have seen him at conferences and it is like a Billy Graham meeting. He talks of [teachers] as keepers of the imagination and flatters them about their important role in society. He has made (phonics) a political and ideological thing and created a perception of phonics as a right-wing affair.[40]

In third place on the NFER's survey was *Learning to Read,* a 1982 book by the Institute of Education's 'whole-word' specialist Margaret Meek. Meek, who also occupied seventh place on the list, was greatly influenced by Smith. Her work reiterated his belief in the non-importance of phonetic understanding for early readers, claiming: 'The child who plays at reading by imitating what readers seem to do is in a better position to begin to read than those whose first step is instruction in the alphabet.'[41] Like nearly all advocates of 'look-say' methods, Meek advanced her ideas with a startling lack of scientific evidence, preferring to call upon philosophical speculation, non-quantative research and stories. As she admitted in 1988: 'Any significant research I have done rests on my having treated anecdotes as evidence.'[42]

Occupying first place on the survey was *Read With Me* by Liz Waterland. Appearing on 68 per cent of teacher training reading lists, Waterland's offering was perhaps the least credible of all the new wave of 'look-say' advocates. *Read With Me* was not an academic text, but more of a professional memoir of one Peterborough primary school teacher. The book recounted how she grew bored with the reading schemes used in her classes, and was referred to the work of Frank Smith and Margaret Meek by a colleague at the local Educational Development Centre. She wrote about how these ideas revolutionised her conception of reading, and made her realise that reading 'cannot be taught'. Instead, Waterland concluded that reading is caught 'like a cough'.[43] Her particular brand of look-say teaching was dubbed the 'apprenticeship' method, and proposed that adults or classmates should repeatedly read and reread the same text with an 'apprentice', until they begin to recognise the words and read along at the same time. Throughout the book, Waterland assembled a series of erroneous claims: 'In many ways the acquisition of written language is comparable with that of spoken language'; 'reading cannot be taught in a formal sequenced way any more than speech can be'. Justification for such claims was almost always rooted in anecdote. Two senior lecturers at Leeds and Sussex Universities were so shocked that they wrote a conclusive rebuke of Waterland's 'apprenticeship' method. It concluded: 'The teaching of reading has, for too long, been monopolised by fads, fashions and the viewpoints of a few persuasive and charismatic advocates.'[44]

Smith, Meek and Waterland were not a niche interest. They provided three of the four most popular texts on reading for trainee teachers on university courses during the 1980s, each appearing on over half of the university reading lists submitted to the NFER. These books were distinguished by their lack of scientific evidence, in place of which the authors incestuously footnoted each other (along with Ken Goodman from the University of Arizona), building an academic Ponzi scheme of unsubstantiated 'expert' opinion. In her critique, Bonnie Macmillan observed that the 'look-say' revival was predicated almost entirely on 'non-experimental' research, tending to be descriptive, naturalistic, ethnographic, qualitative or just plain anecdotal. At the same time, there was a large array of experimental research from America that was scientific, controlled and quantative that regularly demonstrated the importance of phonics. However, it was ignored by British universities.[45] As the educational psychologist Martin Turner wrote: 'Writers and lecturers genuinely seem never to have considered scientific evidence and, given a choice, always to prefer sentimental excitement.'[46] In an abnegation of their original ideal, education departments in British universities gave up on the responsibility towards the disinterested pursuit of truth in favour of reinforcing their existing child-centred prejudices.

The superiority of phonics as a method of instruction was established as far back as 1967 by Harvard professor

Jeanne Chall in *Learning to Read*. During the intervening years, the case for phonics had only grown stronger. In 1990, the US Department of Education commissioned the cognitive psychologist Marilyn Jager Adams to provide a synthesis of all available evidence in order to bring an end to the reading wars. Her resulting book *Beginning to Read* was damning of the likes of Smith, and conclusive on the importance of phonics in learning to read. Such a conclusion was not confined to America. In England, Jane Oakhill and Alan Garnham introduced their 1988 work *Becoming a Skilled Reader* by writing: 'the evidence in favour of phonics-based approach is, if anything, stronger than it was'.[47] Even the HMI, who by this time tended to beat the drum for the progressive cause, wrote in 1990 that there was 'a clear link between higher standards and systematic phonics teaching' in primary schools.[48]

Despite this, phonics instruction during teacher training remained extremely rare. A questionnaire of teacher training graduates across 13 different institutions, conducted by the NFER, concluded that 52 per cent of new teachers had been taught 'little or nothing' about phonics. Amongst those that did, it is probable that 'teaching' on phonics often consisted of a brief dismissal of such methods as 'old-fashioned' and 'boring'. In most cases, the report concluded that a philosophy of 'mixed methods' was favoured, as one graduate observed, 'eclecticism rules'.[49] Such a pluralistic view on reading instruction, which is still common, gains support for appearing reasonable and even-handed, but often involves a watered down and devalued version of phonics. According to an HMI report in 1990, 85 per cent of primary school teachers taught through 'mixed methods', whilst only three per cent of primary school teachers were teaching their pupils mainly through phonics.[50]

This small minority of phonics adherents, who held out against the opprobrium of their colleagues, achieved outstanding results. During the early 1990s, Kevin Cassidy was the headmaster of the Catholic St Clare's Primary School in Handsworth, inner-city Birmingham. Writing under the pseudonym 'Peter Benedict' in the *Guardian*, he confessed to his use of traditional phonics instruction. Despite the sort of intake which many sociologists claimed made school failure inevitable (90 per cent from ethnic minorities, 60 per cent from single-parent families), Cassidy ensured every pupil read fluently by the age of seven. He blamed the inability of other schools to emulate such successes on the malign influence of 'advisers, teacher trainers and other experts', and recalled travelling to London to share his success with a room full of fellow heads:

> ...half of them walked out, disturbed at the challenge to their current beliefs... One experienced head teacher has told me that all reading schemes and phonetic approaches should be thrown in the dustbin. Perplexed by this methodology, I asked how any tangible assessment of children's individual progress could be made, in such an unstructured environment. The answer offered in all seriousness was that it would be obvious from the look of excitement on their faces.[51]

Cassidy devised his own resources from which to teach phonics and implemented annual tests to keep a track of pupil progress. By 1992, St Clare's Primary was oversubscribed and recognised for its great achievements with a £100,000 Jerwood Award for education.[52] A similar story was seen at Raglan School in Bromley, where a parents' revolt in 1987 against 'real books' teaching methods led to a change in leadership and the introduction of phonics. Raglan went from having one-third of year six pupils at least two years behind in reading age in 1987, to having 96 per cent of the seven-year-olds reading either at or above their chronological age by 1990. The head who had introduced phonics told *The*

Sunday Times: 'This method has made all the difference, even though it sounds old-fashioned and boring.' Quoted in the same article was Liz Waterland, author of *Read With Me*, who protested: 'I passionately dislike reading schemes. They offer a poverty-stricken experience of literature.'[53] Sadly, primary schools such as Raglan and St Clare's remained exceptional cases.

By the early 1990s, there was a growing consensus that the mania for the 'real book' method during the 1980s had led to further falls in literacy levels. An educational psychologist called Martin Turner, who from 1984 was employed by the Croydon Educational Authority, noticed a polarisation between the local authority advisers who were evangelical about look-say methods, and educational psychologists who were employed to help those pupils with 'learning difficulties' who were struggling to read. He became the informal coordinator of a group of dissenting educational psychologists, and in 1990 he published *Sponsored Reading Failure*, arguing that reading failure was caused by methods actively endorsed by the education establishment. He assembled the results of ten anonymous local authorities (representing around six per cent of Britain's primary population) and showed that in eight of them a significant decline in reading ability had taken place.[54]

Turner was ostracised by the education establishment and dismissed as 'ideological' in teacher training literature. He was accused of fabricating evidence and lost his job in Croydon, moving to become head of psychology at Dyslexia Action.[55] However, only a year later, the NFER vindicated Turner's findings. On the request of Education Secretary John MacGregor, the NFER asked for reports on reading levels from each of Britain's 116 local authorities. Of all the authorities, only 26 had carried out authority-wide tests that would allow the NFER to make year-on-year comparisons. Of these 26 authorities that submitted data, 19 reported a decline in literacy levels, with the reading age of pupils declining on average by four months between 1981 and 1990. The research also revealed that many schools that claimed to teach phonics as part of a programme of 'mixed methods' were using phonics as a supplement to a look-say course, and not teaching it in the systematic fashion needed for success.[56] Although Turner's results were widely dismissed by the education establishment as flawed, similar results were recorded by the NFER the following year. In a survey of two sample groups totalling 2,170 pupils, the NFER saw reading scores fall (in the *Reading Ability Series, Test A*) between 1987 and 1991 from 100 to 97.5 in one sample, and from 101.3 to 98.7 in the other.[57]

In 1994, a MORI poll found that 90 per cent of British parents were concerned with the teaching of reading at British primary schools, and many stated a desire for a return to more traditional methods.[58] However, despite parental pressure, the overwhelming weight of objective evidence from America, and the success of exemplar primary schools, phonics instruction was not given special emphasis in the newly developed national curriculum. The sentimental attachment to the child-centred alternatives prevailed, and it would take until 2006 before the education establishment finally capitulated to the fruits of research and allowed the government to recommend phonics in all British primary schools.

The birth of the GCSE

In 1986, British 14-year-olds started studying for a new examination, the General Certificate of Secondary Education (GCSE). It had been introduced to replace the two-tier system of GCE O-level, originally intended as the 'grammar school exam', and CSE, which was introduced in 1965 as a qualification for less able pupils. The DES and HMI had been pushing for it for years, arguing that it was inconvenient and divisive to have pupils taking two different types of examinations within the same school.

The hope was that a new 'universal' exam would cater for all ability groups, according to the newly fashionable concept of 'differentiation'. The GCSE was in a sense the last step in the comprehensivisation of the British school system.

The GCSE was introduced during Keith Joseph's time in office and there is little more convincing evidence of his blind spot when it came to school standards. Examinations are the most powerful lever a government has in dictating what schools teach, and how subjects are taught. For this reason, the rigorous O-levels had up until 1988 been a gatekeeper for traditional academic standards, although too few pupils were entered for them. Had its principles been writ large across the GCSE, Harold Wilson's vision of 'grammar schools for all' could have been reinvigorated and a clear stand in defence of academic rigour could have been made. Unfortunately, the opposite occurred.

Joseph liked to stand aloof from the pedagogical arguments within the classroom, and paid scant attention to the detail of the new examination. Despite being passed under a Conservative administration, the GCSE was generated almost entirely by the education establishment, embedding many aspects of progressive education. Joseph may have been oblivious to this, and may even have sympathised with some aspects of progressive education when they were dressed up in the language of modernisation and economic renewal. Consequently, the GCSE was probably the greatest missed opportunity in educational policy during the Thatcher years.

The organisation entrusted with designing the new examination was the Secondary Examinations Council (SEC), made up of heads of the exam boards and other figures from the education establishment. The SEC developed the 'National Criteria' for GCSEs which all examination boards had to follow. Published in 1985, the National Criteria's stated aim was to overturn the 'grammar school curriculum' of the O-level and enshrine the ideas developed in comprehensive schools over the preceding three decades. It was explicitly against the disinterested pursuit of knowledge and prized 'relevance' of subject material instead, stating: 'all syllabuses should be designed to help candidates to understand the subject's relationship to other areas of study and its relevance to the candidates' own life.' There was a general trend away from 'negative' marking, which deducts marks for mistakes, to 'positive marking' which seeks to reward pupils for what they *do* know – a principle that can allow repeated mistakes to go unheeded.[59] The National Criteria warned that no syllabus content should be 'excessive in its demands', and stipulated each subject should have a large component of coursework so that project work and activities could become part of the candidate's grade.[60]

A handbook entitled *All About GCSE* was published in 1986 by four educationists who were involved in its creation. It explained to schools and teachers how far the new GCSE aimed to move away from those of the old, 'academic' type of examination:

> The aim of the GCSE is to introduce courses where all pupils can perceive the content as being relevant, where learning is active and pupil-centred, with the stimulus of varied activities, and where a wide range of skills is valued. In addition, the coursework component will give importance to day-to-day classroom activities.

One section even suggested that the new skills-based GCSEs would necessitate a pedagogical change for many British teachers:

> Skills cannot be taught in the traditional didactic manner. A teacher may demonstrate or describe a skill, but a pupil can learn or acquire it only through practice and experience – that is by *doing*. Therefore, some teachers

> may need to change their teaching methods so that they may become facilitators rather than givers of knowledge.

These messages filtered through to the individual subject criteria. The SEC booklet on GCSE mathematics declared a departure from how maths was 'traditionally' taught, which involved 'knowing the rules to deal with numbers, percentages, areas, equations, and so on'. Instead, it was stated that 'GCSE should lead pupils to see that mathematics can be used to solve practical problems in everyday situations'. Similarly, the booklet on English declared that because the GCSE is aimed at the whole ability range, it should have less of a focus on 'traditional discursive essay questions', deemed unsuitable for 'students lower down the ability range.' A number of other measures were taken to make the English GCSE less demanding, including open-book exams, an oral component, and a high degree of coursework. The history GCSE took a significant departure from the history O-level, which tended to ask for five essays to be written in the space of two-and-a-half hours. The new GCSE enshrined many of the child-centred ideas developed by the Schools History Project, such as downgrading the importance of historical content, replacing chronological overviews with a topic-based approach, and emphasising 'historical concepts' and skills such as source-evaluation. The Schools History Project even developed its own GCSE curriculum, which included an in-depth study of the American West, and the entirely 'skills-based' Paper 2, containing a series of short questions on historical sources for which, they stated, 'no prior knowledge of the subject matter or the source material will be required'.[61]

From 1988, it was illegal to take the O-level in Britain, but the exam continued to be written in England and taken around the world, particularly in Commonwealth countries such as Singapore. For British teachers who respected the academic ambition of the O-level, forcibly converting to GCSE was distressing. In 1987 the history department in Lewes Priory School, a comprehensive in East Sussex, decided to take a stand. Their head of department, Chris McGovern, chose to offer the academically rigorous Scottish O-grade (similar to the O-level) to his pupils. This led to furious rows with the school headmaster, and McGovern, his deputy head of department, and a third history teacher all lost their jobs. McGovern was blacklisted by the East Sussex Education Authority and was unable to find another job. He retrained as a primary school teacher and went on to teach in a preparatory school in the independent sector. In order to demonstrate the basis for his opposition to the 'skills-based' syllabus of the history GCSE, he offered a group of primary school pupils (10 or 11 years old) a GCSE history paper from the 1989 examination, and they all scored respectable GCSE grades. In May 1990 he wrote up the results in the *Guardian* education supplement and concluded that such an exam required little knowledge, and the 'skills' they assessed were simple common sense. A *Guardian* columnist named Melanie Phillips, who was rapidly becoming a *bête noire* amongst British teachers for her trenchant opposition to progressive teaching, took up McGovern's cause. She concluded in her column: 'the result of the affair is undoubtedly that other teachers who share these dissident views are too frightened to speak out. We have an education system in which teachers have to pay for their job security by intellectual conformity.'[62]

Allowing for the GCSE to be introduced in this form was a spectacular own goal for a Conservative government nominally dedicated to higher standards within state education. The education campaigners Cox and Marks recognised the paradox, that a government committed to raising educational standards had allowed a watershed reform which did the exact opposite to slip by unnoticed. They wrote: 'little trust can be placed on the GCSE examination – devised as it was by the very education establishment against which the Government has now been compelled to take legislative measures.' This paradox was a harbinger of things to come.

Must do better

The Conservative reforms of the early 1980s did have some positive impact. The stipulation of the 1980 Education Act that schools and LEAs must publish their results allowed for greatly improved levels of school accountability. Three years later, in June 1983, Cox and Marks published *Standards in English Schools,* which crunched the numbers of the 1981 school examination results and found that striking variations existed between schools in similar areas that could not be explained by socio-economic background. More worryingly, they found that comprehensives underperformed compared to grammar schools and secondary moderns with equivalent intakes. Worried by the implications of such conclusions, the supposedly impartial DES leaked an attack on Cox and Marks's research methods, leading to it being lambasted as 'crude', 'amateurish' and 'seriously flawed' in the national and trade press. Such allegations were unfounded, and two months later the DES and Keith Joseph agreed to a statement, announced in the House of Commons, which vindicated Cox and Marks' research. *The Times* covered the affair in a leader in December 1983, drawing attention to worrying 'prejudice' within the DES that had led them to discredit important and valuable research.[63]

In addition, some efforts were made by Joseph to shut down underperforming organisations, most notably the ILEA and the Schools Council. He commissioned a report on the Schools Council, the organ of child-centred subject innovation, by an Oxford academic named Nancy Trenaman. She found it to be overfunded, ineffective and full of infighting. Significantly, Trenaman discerned an 'anti-academic flavour' within the organisation, noting that the term 'academic' was never used save in a pejorative sense.[64] The Council was closed in 1985. There were also the reforms to school funding in the 1984 Education Grants and Rewards Act, which limited the spending power of LEAs, placing more power in the hands of the DES.

Important though these reforms were, tinkering with the structures of British state schooling was never going to combat the problem of standards. Whilst explaining his philosophy of reform, Keith Joseph said: 'One is always as a Minister looking for a single lever that would transform attitudes... One looked for the same sort of lever in Education.' This was not the correct approach for fighting an entrenched orthodoxy. The pulling of levers in Whitehall was never going to overturn the cultural revolution that had taken control of Britain's classrooms.[65]

All the while, schools continued to underperform. A series of international comparisons during the early 1990s shocked the British public. According to a 1991 report by the National Institute of Economic and Social Research, the proportion of 16-year-olds gaining the equivalent of three GCSE grades above a C in maths, the national language, and one science, was 62 per cent in Germany, 66 per cent in France, 50 per cent in Japan, and 27 per cent in England.[66] A senior research fellow at the National Institute of Economic and Social Research, Professor Sig Prais, spent much of the decade conducting international comparisons of mathematical ability. In 1988, he asked a comparable group of 14 year olds the same set of maths questions in Japan and Britain. Whilst 89 per cent of Japanese children could calculate two-thirds plus three-eighths, only 42 per cent of British children could do so. Amongst Japanese children, 48 per cent could solve a simple algebraic equation, which only 22 per cent of British children could solve. Prais laid the blame on the 'new maths' revolution of the 1960s, but caustically observed that educationists in Britain would probably reply to such criticism: 'We're glad we are not wasting our children's minds with these questions.'[67]

This fall in standards did filter through to the British public. The British Social Attitudes Survey found that, in 1983, only 39 per cent of British people thought that standards had improved in schools since they were young, dropping to 37 per cent the following year. By the 1980s, education in Britain had become a national embarrassment.[68]

4

Reform: 1986-1997

Baker's monster

In 1986, the incoming minister Kenneth Baker injected a boisterous new energy into the Education Department. Baker was a traditional Tory with none of the neo-liberal dogmatism of his predecessor. He took the job as Education Secretary on Margaret Thatcher's assurance that he would not have to introduce vouchers; instead he wanted to centralise power with the DES to drive up school standards. At the heart of this new direction would be the national curriculum. This reform had been waiting in the wings of Whitehall since Jim Callaghan first mooted the idea in 1976; ten years later the DES and HMI were keenly in favour, and there was a high degree of support amongst the public. Baker shared none of his Thatcherite colleagues' fears of centralised bureaucracy, and had the knack for showmanship and political ambition to force the reform through.

Perhaps naively, Baker assumed that his national curriculum would be able to impose factual content and regular assessment upon the nation's classrooms, providing the sort of traditional education from which he had benefited at St Paul's Boys School during the 1940s. In October 1988, he said:

> When I talk about traditional values in teaching, I mean that children should learn their tables, and learn their tables by heart. And when it comes to English I'm quite unashamed in wanting children to read and to write and speak fluently and to be taught grammar, spelling

> and punctuation... And when it comes to history I want children to know about the main events.[1]

Not surprisingly, the education establishment had very different ideas. They saw the national curriculum as an opportunity to enshrine the last forty years of progressive education with statutory authority. The ensuing conflict between the rival philosophies shocked Baker and his successors, and brought the education culture war from British classrooms to the corridors of Whitehall. Many key battles would be won by the education establishment.

Baker took two years to pass the 1988 Education Reform Act – a considerable achievement. It laid the groundwork for a national curriculum that consisted of three 'core' subjects of maths, English and science, a further six 'foundation' subjects (history, geography, technology, music, art and physical education), and a modern language and an RE course devised at a local level. It further divided schooling into four 'key stages', with nationally overseen tests in each subject at the end of each stage. Thatcher was perturbed by the enormity of Baker's project, teasing him for his 'socialist interventionism' and complained, 'all I wanted was the three Rs!'[2] However, passing the Baker Act would prove to be the easy part. Once done, the battles over establishing curriculum content, attainment targets and testing began.

Baker appreciated that the teaching profession would have to support the new curriculum, so he established 'working groups' staffed by educationists to devise the content for each subject. Though admirably consensual, this was a major mistake. Such a decision left the door wide open for university academics, local authority employees, subject associations and inspectors to commandeer the national curriculum. As Baker's special adviser Tony Kerpel recalled: 'I asked Kenneth Baker why are we turning to these people who are the very ones responsible for the failures we have been trying to put right?'[3] Baker should have been more cautious. He had been shocked on assuming office by the GCSE content smuggled past his predecessor, and the HMI had already shown its progressive colours by publishing its own curriculum proposals in 1985 that recommended replacing traditional subjects with a 'whole curriculum' structured around 'areas of learning and experience' such as 'aesthetic and creative', 'human and social' and 'linguistic and literary'.[4] Baker later declared himself 'astonished' by the doctrinal wrangling that the working groups threw up. As he recalled in his memoirs, *The Turbulent Years*:

> Of all the Whitehall Departments, the DES was among those with the strongest in-house ideology. There was a clear 1960s ethos and a very clear agenda which permeated virtually all the civil servants. It was rooted in 'progressive' orthodoxies, in egalitarianism and the comprehensive school system... Not only was the Department in league with the teacher unions, university departments of education, teacher-training theories, and local authorities, it also acted as their protector against any threats which ministers might pose. If the civil servants were the guardians of this culture, then Her Majesty's Inspectors of Education were its priesthood.

Baker wrote enviously of his more dictatorial equivalent M. Chevènement. During the same period, the French Minister of National Education took a Napoleonic approach, personally putting together a French national curriculum in happy isolation from subject association and unions.[5]

The individual subject working groups each experienced protracted battles between government-appointed traditionalists and civil service-appointed progressives. In the mathematics working group, Sig Prais from the National Institute of Economic and Social Research wasted no time in announcing he had been chosen by Margaret Thatcher to bring to the proceedings a commitment to mathematical rigour. At the other end of the spectrum, two educationists from Nottingham and Cambridge Universities stated their principled opposition to testing young children and declared that long division and the learning of times tables was no longer necessary in the age of the calculator. Sig Prais eventually submitted a note of dissent and left the working group, complaining that 'so many of you believe that "having fun" is one of the prime objectives of mathematical teaching'.[6] Representing such divergent opinions, the maths working group's reports became impossibly inflated – one interim report included 354 attainment targets. Baker labelled the group 'disgraceful' and later wrote that they provided him with a steep learning curve:

> By then, I had become suspicious of certain phrases widely used in education which had a meretricious ring about them. One was 'problem solving' and the other was 'child-centred'. These were euphemisms for a much softer and less demanding approach to teaching.[7]

As ever, history proved to be controversial. Baker appointed an old Etonian retired naval captain named Michael Saunders Watson as the chair of the history working group after meeting him at a party. Aside from taking visiting pupils around his family seat at Rockingham Castle, Saunders Watson had little knowledge of school history. He had even less knowledge of its raging pedagogical debates, and was no match for the educationists on the group, many of whom were keen supporters of the Schools History Project. The actual curriculum specified a reasonable level of historical content, but the attainment targets were designed exclusively in terms of skills with no mention of historical knowledge. Baker was passionate about history (that year he had edited *The Faber Book Of English History In Verse*) and was infuriated by the group's interim report. In June 1989, he sent it back demanding significant alterations.

The working group played for time and in March the following year the final report was submitted unchanged to a new education secretary, the hapless John MacGregor. He was not prepared for a full-scale fight with the history-teaching establishment and capitulated to their vision of the subject. This prompted a last minute intervention from a furious Margaret Thatcher, who tried unsuccessfully to amend the final draft. Her anger at MacGregor's handling of the history affair was, according to many, a key reason behind his dismissal the following autumn.[8]

If there was one working group where Baker must have felt he appointed well, it was English. The chair was Brian Cox, the infamous *Black Paper* pamphleteer who lambasted the excesses of progressive education during the 1960s and '70s. English was the subject that Baker was most concerned they 'got right', but Cox would prove to be a great disappointment. Having been decried as a 'fascist' and an 'educational Powellite' during the 1960s, he took the opportunity of the working group to re-establish his reputation as a sensible centrist. In his own words, he wanted 'to ensure that a true balance was achieved between traditional and progressive modes of teaching.'[9] Unfortunately, this meant reneging on some of the government's and the general public's key areas of concern. The teaching of grammar (euphemistically referred to as 'linguistic terminology') was underemphasised, the fashionable view that 'Standard English' is just one dialect amongst many was endorsed, and phonics was not given preference in the early teaching of literacy.[10] Public anger was most animated when Enid Blyton was left off the list of recommended children's books, on grounds of racism. The first working group meeting was graced by Roald Dahl, whom Baker had also met at a party, but Dahl only lasted one meeting before declaring himself unsuited to such deliberations. Baker did achieve one small coup though. As a lover of poetry, he ensured that the English curriculum stipulated pupils memorise poetry, and gained a ringing endorsement from the poet laureate Ted Hughes as a reward.[11]

Working groups in the seven other subjects were similarly dominated by progressive educationists. In modern languages, the explicit teaching of grammar was discouraged, suggesting that it should be 'practised rather than the subject of theoretical exposition'. The correcting of mistakes in spoken language was also discouraged as inhibiting progress. Teaching in the target language (known as the 'Berlitz Method') was offered as a way of avoiding any boring, grammatical drudgery and achieving it instead through 'osmosis'.[12] Science also caused trouble for Baker, as the working group promoted investigations and projects over scientific knowledge.[13]

Overseeing the tortured progress of these working groups were two new government agencies established by the 1988 Baker Act. The National Curriculum Council (NCC) was charged with developing the curriculum detail, and the School Examinations and Assessment Council (SEAC) with assessment. Again, Baker naively agreed to the recommendation of the DES to appoint chairmen from within the education establishment. The man placed in charge of the NCC was Duncan Graham, a former teacher, council education officer and a moderate, consensus-seeking figure. In 1993, he published his own account of the creation of the national curriculum, in which he wrote that ideas such as 'child-centred education' and 'learning by doing' on which the education establishment were 'hooked', were 'perfectly respectable philosophies'. It was his contention that these ideas had simply been taken too far by 'a small number of their more extreme colleagues', and as a result public opinion was unduly negative towards them.[14]

However, Graham's views were moderate by comparison with those appointed to accompany him. Tony

Edwards, the head of education at Newcastle University, joined the NCC review team having previously written of the national curriculum in the *TES* that there was 'ample scope for creative subversion... there is almost everything still to play for'.[15] The Director of Education in Newcastle, Martin Davis, wrote in 1987 that he disagreed with the 'subject-based' curriculum and favoured schools 'planning their curriculum in a more progressive way'. Two years later he was made director of the National Curriculum Council. Such appointments were extraordinarily counter-productive for Baker, as these individuals could purposefully stall the curriculum's development.[16]

It was a similar story with assessment at the SEAC. They were charged with introducing end of key stage assessments, a difficult task as much of the education establishment since the 1960s had been firmly against testing. As Baker recalled:

> Many teachers, various experts in the assessment of children and virtually everyone in University Education Departments were passionately opposed to the whole idea of testing and assessment... trying to introduce such a system became one of the most emotive aspects of my reforms.[17]

The solution of the educationists appointed to the SEAC was to design a testing regime so byzantine in its complexity that it hardly resembled 'testing' in the commonly understood sense of the word. The government had envisaged what they dubbed 'pencil and paper tests'– short, easy to mark, and a reliable indication of pupil ability. Such a style of testing was anathema to the educationists, as was revealed by the Task Group on Assessment and Testing (TGAT) placed under the control of Paul Black of Kings College, London. Black, it transpired, believed that traditional tests were harmful to young pupils and put too much pressure on teachers. He later wrote that he was content to dismiss 'a return to traditional didactic teaching, a return to traditional testing, a return to the O-level'.[18] As one critic later observed, placing Black in charge of an assessment regime was 'like asking a goat to look after the cabbages'.[19]

In 1988, Black's TGAT report was delivered. It opposed the 'summative' nature of 'pencil and paper' tests, which Black thought were designed to make pupils fail. Instead, he wanted 'formative' assessments, which would allow pupils to show what they *do* know, and not penalise them for what they *do not* know. To allow for such 'positive' testing, he suggested that each subject be assessed according to ten 'levels' covering all four key stages, each offering a painstaking taxonomy of what attainment involved at every stage of development.[20] In attempting to devise tests that were not really tests, the progressive educationists at the SEAC created a maddening regime of levels and procedures, which would almost derail the national curriculum. Once again, appointments to the SEAC included figures intent on sabotaging its very purpose, such as the well-known progressive English teacher, formerly of Holland Park Comprehensive in London, Terry Furlong. At an education conference in 1991, Furlong declared that educationists had to 'man the barricades – to get inside groups and turn the [national curriculum] around'.[21] The same year, he told the *Guardian* that reading Shakespeare plays line by line was 'arse-achingly boring'.[22]

In 1991, seven-year-old pupils sat Key Stage 1 Standard Assessment Tests (SATs) for the first time. The original hope for a 'pencil and paper test' was a distant memory. Not an examination hall, ticking clock, nor invigilator, were in sight. Instead, the tests were informal, co-operative and collaborative, taking great care to ensure the pupils did not feel as if they were being tested. Over the course of half a term, pupils were grouped in fours according to ability and asked to complete their SATs in a naturalistic manner. For example, in place of a straightforward spelling test, pupils were invited to do creative writing, so that the spelling level of the prose could be assessed. Aside from the great difficulty of marking such assessments reliably, their conduct was maddeningly complex. In all, the cost of administration the tests was reckoned to be £60 million, and all primary schools were sent four glossy booklets of SATs instructions totalling 224 pages, which alone cost £6 million to develop.[23] The signatories of a letter to the *TES* declared themselves to be 'astonished that anybody could really believe that this neat, new system of ticking boxes, compartmentalising and dehumanising education would actually work... The National Curriculum is too weighty, wordy and jargonistic.'[24] All the while, the cost of the national curriculum project spiralled towards many billions of pounds, with its launch predicted to have cost £2.8 billion alone.[25]

At the receiving end of this monstrous concoction, brewed in a cauldron of committee infighting and contradictory interests, were the teachers. Rival organisations, the DES, the NCC, the SEAC and HMI, subjected schools to a barrage of warring documents over how to implement the curriculum. Teachers were dismayed by the sheer weight of paperwork, with one head calling it 'death by a thousand ring binders'.[26] Simplicity is rarely achieved by committee, in particular committees of progressive educationists, and their aversion to the founding principle of the national curriculum led them to develop needlessly complex guidance and practices. Many laid responsibility at Baker's door, accusing him of negligence when it came to supervising the follow up detail of his grand 1988 'Baker Act'. His Deputy Education Secretary Angela Rumbold stated that after the 1988 Act was passed, 'Ken went out to lunch'.

In the summer of 1989, Baker finished his stint at the DES and became Conservative Party Chairman, leaving an awkward inheritance.

Taming the beast

John MacGregor was the first Education Secretary charged with bringing Baker's beast under control, and he was not ready for the fight. A consensus-seeking politician, his political profile was so low that he was depicted on the television show *Spitting Image* with a bag over his head. He did not take well to the factional world of education, complaining that 'you constantly move in a maelstrom of argument'. His political adviser, Eleanor Laing, declared MacGregor's task to be 'the worst job in government'. In April 1990, he made the decision to cut SATs tests for all subjects aside from English, Maths and Science, angering Baker in the process. MacGregor made repeated concessions to the education establishment winning the enmity of his own party, and lasted just over a year – the shortest serving Education Secretary since 1968.[27] He was replaced by another ambitious Tory maverick named Kenneth.

Famed for his beer drinking, jazz loving, cigar smoking ways, Ken Clarke was ordered as Education Secretary to 'get tough'. He prided himself on being a straightforward, common sense politician with a dislike of the ideological wrangling from both right and left. Unsurprisingly, Clarke quickly developed a disdain for progressive education. He recalled:

> Ken Baker's reforms were the best thing he ever did, but Ken is not a details man… He had set up all these bloody specialist committees to guide the curriculum, he'd set up quango staff who as far as I could see had come out of the [notoriously progressive] Inner London Education Authority, the lot of them. There wasn't anybody there who agreed with the government's approach to education at all.[28]

In only a year and a half, Clarke did his best to clear out what he perceived to be the worst offenders, removing the chairmen of the NCC and the SEAC and two top-ranking civil servants. The DES made a lasting impression on Clarke, who later claimed they were 'more trouble' than any other department in which he had worked. A particular challenge was trying to simplify the assessment regime developed by Black, 'those wretched SATs' and 'elaborate nonsense' in Clarke's words. In an interview with *The Times* he expressed his exasperation with those educationists who refused to even entertain the notion of 'a short written examination'. His adviser, Tessa Keswick, claimed: 'Working in education was like walking in treacle. The civil servants were terrible, very cynical and deliberately obstructive.'[29]

The last Conservative education secretary to approach the job with any real designs of taking on the education establishment was John Patten. He began his time in office with a swashbuckling last charge on the progressive orthodoxies in the national curriculum, which turned into a brutal defeat. The new Prime Minister, John Major, had a deeply felt concern for state education and backed Patten to once again 'get tough' with schools. Like Jim Callaghan, Major was largely self-educated and never went to university. As he wrote in his memoirs: 'Not having had much education myself, I was keen on it.'[30] Soon after becoming Prime Minister, he made a strongly worded speech about what he saw to be the dreadful legacy of progressive education:

> This was a mania that condemned children to fall short of their potential… A mania that undermined common-sense values in schools, rejected proven teaching methods, debased standards – or disposed of them altogether. A canker in our education system which spread from the 1960s on, and deprived great cohorts of our children of the opportunities they deserved. I, for one, cannot find it easy to forgive the Left for that.[31]

So, Patten did get tough. Clarke had already appointed

the businessman and former policy adviser David Pascall as chairman of the NCC, and Thatcher's former head of policy Brian Griffiths as chairman of the SEAC. Patten further sought to 'pack' these committees with figures sympathetic to the government's reforms, including the Cambridge don John Marenbon, the education campaigner John Marks, and the Warwick Professor Lord Skidelsky. The teaching profession characterised such figures as belonging to the 'radical right' but their opinions were probably closer to the sympathies of the general public. Their opinions only appeared radical when compared to the education establishment's progressivism. In any case, to associate pedagogical beliefs with political positions is always crude: Lord Skidelsky, who had co-founded the traditionalist History Curriculum Association, was also a founding member of the Social Democratic Party.

Nevertheless, the profession was unimpressed with the strident line Patten was taking, with the *TES* complaining: 'Every week we see the appointment of another bogeyman to a key committee.' To demonstrate their disapproval, the teaching unions campaigned to boycott the SATs tests in the summer. In January 1993, the NUT balloted their members and received a 90 per cent approval for the boycott. This was a potential disaster for the government, and they took out full-page advertisements in the newspapers to persuade the teachers to change their minds, but to no avail. In June 1993, after years of preparation, a mere 150 schools administered the SATs and returned them to the SEAC. The fiasco of the SATs boycott was a profound demonstration of the inability of the government to force through a programme of reform that did not have the approval of the profession. Patten found the protracted struggle intolerable, and in the summer of 1993 his health broke down and duties passed to his deputy Baroness Blatch whilst he recovered. Reforming zeal had squared up to the entrenched culture in state schools, and lost.

After the boycott, Patten stayed in education for one more year but had to change his entire approach, staging a number of humiliating climbdowns. Pascall and Griffiths were bid farewell from the NCC and SEAC, and Ron Dearing was placed in charge of a new amalgamated agency called the School Curriculum and Assessment Authority (SCAA). Dearing, a career civil servant who had formerly been head of the Post Office, was an apolitical and conciliatory figure whose appointment clearly signified that the fight for academic rigour in the national curriculum was over. Many of the government placemen on the committees resigned and December 1993 saw the publication of the Dearing Review. It necessarily streamlined the bloated curriculum, but also made a number of key concessions. Prescribed subject knowledge was narrowed, less time would be spent on testing, and geography and history became optional at Key Stage 4. Patten's deputy Baroness Blatch, a strident campaigner for traditional standards in schools, was not happy: 'The appointment of Dearing was unforgivable. John Patten was weak… he had been bullied by [his permanent secretary] Geoffrey Holland. I came as close to resigning as I ever did.'[32]

In 1994 Gillian Shepherd replaced Patten, and she saw out the last three years of the Conservative government. As a former teacher and inspector for Norfolk County Council, Shepherd was an education insider explicitly chosen to appease the profession. She had no intention of continuing the battles of bruisers Baker, Patten and Clarke, and chose instead to see her time in office as one of consolidation and stability. For the sake of the profession, this was a sensible decision. However, it did signal the end of any hopes for fundamental change. The animating spirit behind the battles waged from 1986 to 1994 was a conflict between the traditionalist intentions of elected politicians against the progressive stance of the education establishment. Baker underestimated them, MacGregor capitulated to them, Clarke disdained them, and Patten was destroyed by them. Once established, the national curriculum was decried for being both an endorsement of progressive nonsense and a reactionary throwback to the Secondary Regulations of 1904: a testament to the ongoing culture war in education still being waged by the mid-1990s. However, in many regards, the former interpretation was apt.

Although the national curriculum was legislated by a Conservative government, its implementation was wrested from them. Ultimately, the government got a national curriculum, but it was a long way from the traditional curriculum that Baker envisaged in 1988. It was not a complete disaster: in many areas, a structured overview of subject content was established, and schools previously wandering towards the false dawn of a 'whole curriculum' were checked. However, it did endorse many progressive dogmas, reinvigorating them with the authority of law. Worse still, central government control over the curriculum in British schools was now an established fact. In less wary hands, the curriculum could be further reformed to enshrine the very ideas it was established to defeat.

The paradox of education reform

At the heart of the national curriculum story is a distressing paradox, which has continued to hamper educational reform over the past 20 years: educational reform has to be implemented by the education establishment, even when it is the ideas of the education establishment that these reforms aim to overturn. Thus, measures initiated by the government can be captured by the education establishment, and promptly subverted. Early on, *The Times* recognised this problem:

> The Government originally sold the idea of a National Curriculum to parents as a conservative reform, a switch

> in emphasis towards traditional teaching techniques, which would squeeze out the wilder notions to which teachers – left-wing ones of course – were said to be tempted. Nobody in government appears to have asked what would happen if the curriculum itself moved that way, and caused teachers, many of them staunch traditionalists already, to abandon their well-tried methods for imposed educational novelties.[33]

Members of the education establishment made no secret of their intention to subvert the national curriculum, and regularly declared as much at education conferences. *The Sunday Telegraph* wrote a story in 1993 uncovering the secretive meeting of senior figures in the education establishment every four months in Oxford. Dubbed 'the All Souls Group', it included education officers from local councils, *TES* journalists, civil servants, and heads of teaching associations, all united in opposition to the government reforms.[34] Senior members of the education establishment even circulated a 'green paper' to reassure members of the profession that the reform posed little threat, brazenly stating: 'We have people in place at every level of education to subvert the National Curriculum.'[35]

This organised subversion continued to bedevil all other areas of educational reform, from examinations to teacher training, inspections to accountability measures. On stepping down as Chief Inspector of Schools, Chris Woodhead wrote that 'politicians need professionals to work through the detail and implement their reforms, but most senior figures in the world of education, however cleverly they hide the fact at interview, are enthusiastic supporters of the status quo that the Government wants to change.' For this reason, he took to calling the education establishment 'the Blob', after a 1958 science-fiction film about a giant amoeba-like alien that terrorises a small American town.[36] The Blob seeps into every corner of the community, subsumed all attempts to destroy it, and becoming more powerful with every attack. It would prove to be a fitting metaphor for the education establishment.

Classroom realities

For all the effort from central government during the early 1990s to steer British schools in a traditionalist direction, little effect was felt on the ground. Reforms were watered down and most schools were not prepared to steer away from the firmly established progressive mould. In the autumn of 1996, a reporter from the *Guardian* travelled to Birmingham's very first comprehensive school to see how it was getting on. The conclusion was not positive. Shenley Court in Northfield was a large school, with a mixture of pupils from the nearby council estate and the city's smart southern suburbs. Built in 1963, the report concluded: 'The idealism that lay behind the comprehensive system has worn as badly as the buildings.'

Just like reports from the 1970s, lessons were stymied by continual low level disruption, lesson changeovers were 'frightening', pupils carried their possessions in oversized bags for fear of theft, and any sense of academic life was absent: 'I never saw a child read so much as a comic'. As usual, the influence of progressive education was more powerful in what it led schools to abandon, than what it led them to embrace:

> There is no school ethos, not really; no school song, colours or motto... The front of the staff handbook is graced by the quote 'Empowerment through working towards a total learning school community', which is not as catchy as *Floreat Etona*.

Pupils paid so little attention to the head that the reporter compared his school tour to a walkabout with John Major. National curriculum reforms had been felt in the classroom, but with no accompanying revolution in the school's attitude. The reporter concluded: 'It is not immediately obvious what more Shenley could do for its pupils, given the system, the finances, the raw material and the fact that most teachers are not geniuses but human and stressed.' Cynical resignation reigned.[37]

Unfortunately, the absence of widespread surveys makes it difficult to build up a statistical picture of comprehensive school practices during this period. One exception is *Thirty Years On*, published in 1996 by Caroline Benn as a sequel to her 1972 offering *Half Way There*. Benn and her co-author Clyde Chitty sent out a survey to all British comprehensive schools in 1993-94. They gained a response rate of 35 per cent (compared with 81 per cent in 1972), but the numbers remain instructive. The number of schools using a house system as the main form of pastoral organisation had dropped even further from its low rate in 1972, to just eight per cent. Schools using year groups as the main form of pastoral organisation had increased to 46 per cent. The proportion of comprehensive schools requiring their pupils to wear a full school uniform was 42.5 per cent, but one can assume few of these were particularly formal. Around six per cent of schools had no uniform whatsoever. Streaming and setting were still relatively unpopular, especially in the lower years. Just over 50 per cent of the schools used entirely mixed ability classes in year 7 and, by year 9, 25 per cent of schools still used mixed ability teaching in all or almost all of their lessons. Harold Wilson's promise of 'grammar schools for all' remained unfulfilled.

The persistence of progressive prejudices was even stronger in British primary schools, becoming the subject of a controversial government discussion paper in 1992. Authored by Chris Woodhead and two primary specialists, Robin Alexander and Jim Rose, it became known as 'The Three Wise Men Report'. The report attacked the 'highly questionable dogmas' hampering Britain's primary schools, criticising the ubiquity of topic work, complex teaching methods, sociological explanations of pupil failure, Jean Piaget's developmental psychology and the Plowden Report. Counterpoised to this, they diagnosed a notable lack of subject-specific teaching, whole-class teaching, explanation and questioning, and curriculum content within the primary school. Most insightfully, the report concluded that whilst progressive education was rarely embraced to the letter, it was frequently used as a convenient excuse for poor practice – 'rhetoric' used to support practices that 'might look attractive and busy' but resulted in precious little being learned.[38]

The effect of the national curriculum was felt in the primary sector. Research from London University in 1996 found that some schools were abandoning 'child-centred approaches' and focusing more on the three Rs, with around half of the teachers surveyed claiming to be doing a more 'didactic' form of teaching. One of the researchers, Professor Gipps, was positive about these changes, telling *The Times*: 'From the children, one overriding comment was that what they really liked about the tests was everyone was quiet and they could think.'[39] However, national tests alone were not going to spur a professional counter-reformation. The Three Wise Men Report recognised this, stating that government reform will never have the authority or power to change how teachers teach, without a simultaneous 'radical rethinking' within the profession.[40]

In 1994, one of the three wise men, Chris Woodhead, was appointed Chief Inspector of Schools and placed in charge of the newly reformed schools inspectorate, named Ofsted. Due to his trenchant opposition to progressive orthodoxies and the occasional unguarded pronouncement (he claimed there were 15,000 incompetent teachers in Britain), Woodhead became the most controversial figure in British education.

Ofsted was created by Ken Clarke's Education Schools Act in March 1992 as a centralised inspection body to replace a system administered by local authorities. Such a system was subject to inconsistencies and some inspectors were suspected of having strongly held progressive prejudices that led them to penalise more traditional schools. Inspection reports were not made public so verifying such a suspicion was difficult, but some reports did spill out. A well-publicised case was the 1989 inspection of a highly regarded grammar school in Stratford-Upon-Avon, King Edward VI School. Despite acknowledging that the pupils were 'well motivated, well behaved and receptive', and achieved excellent examination results, overall the report was critical. It claimed that the school had a 'narrow range of teaching styles', a 'reliance on 'traditional' methods', and classroom furniture that 'limits the range of teaching'.[41] Two years previously Ken Baker had voiced similar concerns to the public over the HMI Report on Longdean, which had fallen into his hands. Longdean was a successful comprehensive in Hemel Hempsted, but was criticised by inspectors for having 'passive' pupils and mathematics lessons 'often unrelated to real-life problems'.[42] The 1992 Act stipulated that Ofsted inspections would follow a National Framework, occur every four years, be made available to the public, and involve at least one 'lay inspector' from outside the educational world. It was hoped that such measures would prevent any progressive prejudices from harming schools.

Woodhead did not have an easy job. He experienced repeated battles to get his inspectors to follow the National Criteria, and was forced into making public pronouncements that inspectors should not penalise schools according to their own pedagogical preferences. However, he still received complaints from heads about inspectors with a progressive bias.[43] Having stepped down as Chief Inspector in 2001, Woodhead wrote that this problem was widespread and added that he never could have admitted to its extent whilst still in charge:

> [Inspectors] drag the baggage of their beliefs about the nature of education, how teachers should teach and schools be managed, what it is reasonable to expect inner-city kids to achieve, into the classrooms they inspect... If their baggage was the flotsam and jetsam of progressive education, then, in my judgement as Chief Inspector, we had a problem.[44]

Once again, the paradox of educational reform was painfully clear. A beefed up inspectorate was legislated by a Conservative government to push for higher standards in schools, but many of the individuals charged with carrying out these inspections were not prepared to follow the National Criteria. In the face of a professional culture so impervious to reform, it seemed there was little that the government, or Chris Woodhead, could do.

Other reforms did attempt to break the hold of the education establishment. The 1988 Baker Act offered schools the opportunity to 'opt out' of local authority control and become grant maintained schools, directly funded by central government. The ultimate aim was that all schools would eventually opt out and the power of local authorities would be broken, but the results were disappointing. Opting out was a protracted process and there was hostile obstruction from local authorities. By 1997, only 1,000 schools had taken up the offer. All schools did gain increased autonomy from local authorities through the Baker Act's 'Local Management of Schools' section, but such reforms were only ever going to deliver incremental change.

A more encouraging development was the City Technology Colleges (CTCs), also established by the Baker Act. These new schools were developed to combat Britain's poor record on vocational and technological education. One-fifth of their costs was met by private business sponsors and they were encouraged to form close links with business and industry. Only 15 were ever established, but their academic record and innovation provided the basis for Labour's City Academies a decade later. The CTCs were free from local authority control and able to innovate in a way that the one-size-fits-all comprehensive could not. For example, Emmanuel CTC in Gateshead was sponsored by the car showroom entrepreneur Sir Peter Vardy and developed a strong emphasis on discipline and academic rigour. Perhaps most famously, the BRIT school in Croydon was established by George Martin, Richard Branson and the British Record Industry Trust with an emphasis on the performing arts, becoming known as the 'Fame Academy'. It achieved a good academic record and became a source of future stars: in part we have Kenneth Baker to thank for the careers of Adele, Amy Winehouse, Jessie J, The Kooks and Leona Lewis.

Despite the positive reception of CTCs, vocational education remained a significant problem. The National Council for Vocational Qualifications was established in 1986 in the hope of overcoming this historic black spot, but its progress was lambasted in a 1994 report entitled *All Our Futures: Britain's Education Revolution*. Its author, Professor Alan Smithers of Manchester University, wrote that vocational education was a 'disaster of epic proportions'. He judged the newly developed NVQ qualifications to be 'utterly lightweight, ridden with ideology and weak on general education'. Vocational education had for too long been treated as an easy 'non-academic' alternative but, as Smithers emphasised, the skills needed by many such jobs still depended upon a certain level of rigour and knowledge. This was borne out by international comparisons, which showed that the level of mathematics required for equivalent vocational qualifications in France, Germany and Holland was far higher than in the UK. Smithers wrote of the situation in Britain:

> All rigour has been sacrificed to flexibility. The students are not stretched. Remarkably, even the basic skills of

> literacy and numeracy, principal concerns of employers and, one might have thought, of vital importance to electricians and plumbers, are neither taught nor assessed. They are simply 'inferred' from project work.[45]

Far too late into their period in power, the Conservatives came to realise that university education departments, the guardians of state education's thoughtworld, were at the root of many of these problems. John Patten claimed in 1994 that overhauling teacher training should have been the Conservatives first priority when they got into power 15 years previously. The 1994 Education Act established the Teacher Training Agency (TTA) to try to exert some central control over how teachers were trained, stipulating that the majority of the training should take place outside the lecture hall and on school placements. It even tried to establish school-based teacher training.[46] However, this reform was too little too late and the TTA did not do much to combat the ingrained notions in teacher training. A trainee teacher recorded her experiences on an English course in 1995, one year after the Education Act was passed:

> The course wasn't incredibly rigorous... We never got down to the nitty gritty. For example, we were told the government wanted us to teach grammar. I've never done grammar myself but I could learn it. The tutors told us they didn't approve of this and they refused to teach it to us.[47]

A far-reaching shift?

The trainee English teacher's experiences were recorded in an influential book entitled *All Must Have Prizes,* written by the *Guardian* and *Observer* columnist Melanie Phillips in 1996. Phillips' defined progressive education as a combination of liberal individualism and cultural relativism, and she poured scorn on the Conservative government for failing to take its reform seriously. The book gained much attention, and was generally seen as a timely intervention. Future Blair adviser Michael Barber wrote that the education establishment, of which he counted himself a member, should resist dismissing the book as 'deranged rantings from the far right' but instead pay it close attention.[48] The philosopher John Gray stated: 'It should be clear to everyone that a far-reaching shift of educational theory and practice is underway in Britain.'[49] In a rare moment of optimism, even Chris Woodhead wrote: 'I think we are standing on the threshold of a new era in which there is a real possibility that the old ideological restraints are loosened.'[50]

Due in some part to Phillips's persuasive attacks, there was by the mid-1990s a growing political consensus that combating progressive education was a necessary step for improving Britain's schools. Contemporary teaching methods were even mocked on the BBC radio comedy series *People Like Us*, in which a television reporter interviews a teacher at a local school. The teacher explains what is happening in the classroom: 'the pupils actually own the ownership of their own knowledge. What happens is, they sit in groups and interview each other, and then they go on to cut out things from magazines, draw graphs, so that they can establish for themselves that they don't know what the questions are.' When the interviewer asks what the teacher does in all this, the teacher responds: 'Well, he hands out the glue.'[51]

This critique of progressive education spread across party lines. The opposition leader Tony Blair and his education spokesman David Blunkett were remarkably critical of the functioning of British state schools. In a 1995 speech, Blair stated:

> Those people who suffer for lack of pressure are not the well-off and the articulate; it's traditional Labour voters who lose out when the teaching is poor, discipline

> non-existent and low standards excused on grounds of background.[52]

David Blunkett, who had trained as a teacher and held a PGCE, was equally scornful of what he deemed 'trendy teaching'. In 1995, he wrote in his autobiography *On A Clear Day*: 'Yes, I am a fundamentalist when it comes to education: I believe in discipline, solid mental arithmetic, learning to read and write accurately, plenty of homework, increasing expectations and developing potential – all things which are anathema to many modern children.'[53] When he was being touted as shadow education secretary, Blunkett's two young sons even drafted a letter to the party leader asking him to reconsider, arguing their strict father would make schoolchildren's lives a misery.[54] Once appointed, the fears of Blunkett's sons were confirmed as he vowed to go 'back to basics' on education – he even declared his admiration for Chris Woodhead.[55] The Conservatives meanwhile entered the 1997 election with 17 years of bitter experience leading them to believe that the comprehensive school was beyond salvation. John Major rather desperately promised a return to selection, declaring that he would like to see 'a grammar school in every town'.[56]

However, reports telling of the death of progressive education were exaggerated. In 1996, *The Sunday Times* paid a visit to Islington to find out why many resident members of the Labour Party (such as Margaret Hodge, Frances Morell and Tony Blair himself) did not send their children to the local schools. It concluded that 'the progressive ideologies of the 1960s... are still very much alive in [Tony Blair's] backyard'. Chris Pryce, the Liberal Democrat leader of the opposition at Islington Council, told the reporter:

> The people running Islington schools believe that personal achievement, especially in exams, is 'middle-class' and

> therefore suspect, and that failure of individual children should not be recognised because it is 'discriminatory'.

Pryce had conducted his own research and estimated that as few as ten per cent of homeowners in the by-then affluent borough of Islington sent their children to a local state school. Instead, they chose to go private or find faith schools such as the London Oratory in Fulham, the grant maintained school where Tony Blair sent his sons – a source of political embarrassment, since Blair's Labour Party remained opposed to grant maintained schools.

Blair could have sent his sons to the local Highbury Grove School, the traditionalist and high-achieving Islington comprehensive founded by Rhodes Boyson. However, since 1987 Highbury Grove had been led away from its founding ideals when Boyson's successor Lawrie Norcross retired, and the school was taken over by Peter Searl. A progressive head, Searl banned assemblies, introduced mixed-ability teaching, emphasised the 'struggle for social justice' in the school curriculum, and encouraged the pupils to call him 'Pete'. By 1992, only 18.4 per cent of pupils gained five good GCSEs and visiting inspectors commented on bad behaviour, poor punctuality and unsatisfactory lessons. Highbury Grove's unique approach had been dismantled.[57]

The period of educational reform from the 1988 Baker Act to the election of New Labour in 1997 was overwhelmingly one of centralisation. During the 1960s, Harold Wilson would joke to Bernard Donoughue that the Department of Education was 'little more than a post-box between the teachers' unions and their local authority employees.'[58] By 1997, the same could not have been said. The government now had unprecedented power to intervene in schools, dictating how and what was taught. The Conservatives had hoped to use this power to drive up standards and counter progressive education, but this power was mediated through the education establishment who had some very different ideas. This was a dangerous inheritance to pass on to New Labour. Once Blunkett and Blair's resolve to confront 'trendy teaching' had dwindled, the newly centralised education system in Britain was turned around to give progressive education a powerful new lease of life.

5

Reform: 1997-2010

A sure start

In May 1997, teachers turned out in droves to help New Labour toward their historic election victory. According to a March poll from ICM, 59 per cent of teachers planned to vote Labour, 21 per cent Liberal Democrats, and only 15 per cent Conservatives.[1] However, those who hoped a return to Labour would mark a break with Conservative policies were mistaken. Once elected, Blunkett retained league tables, SATs tests, the national curriculum and even Chris Woodhead. His first white paper *Excellence in Schools* struck a disarmingly traditionalist tone, daring to criticise the original implementation of comprehensivisation, stating that: 'The pursuit of excellence was too often equated with elitism.'[2] The paper promoted setting in core subjects, national guidance on amounts of homework, and introduced the National Strategies for literacy and numeracy. *The Sunday Times* hailed 'plans to eliminate fashionable teaching methods from Britain's classrooms', and the *Daily Express* happily reported a 'School Blitz as Blunkett Goes Back to Basics'.[3]

The National Strategies, though far from perfect, would prove to be the one generally acknowledged success of Labour's drive on standards. These strategies developed clear classroom guidance and resources for teaching basic literacy and numeracy in primary schools – an idea inherited from the last year of Conservative government, and eagerly promoted by Chris Woodhead. Starting in 1998, the National Literacy Strategy (NLS) prescribed a daily 'literacy hour' for all primary schools. This hour was to be a structured, formal, teacher-led lesson, beginning with a 'starter activity', moving on to the main task, and ending with a plenary session – giving birth to the now ubiquitous 'three part lesson'. It was backed up by the ambitious target of 80 per cent of primary school pupils reaching the expected standard of literacy (Level 4) in their Key Stage 2 SATs by 2002, rising to 95 per cent by 2007.

The education establishment was generally unsupportive. Stephen Ball from London's Institute of Education claimed that it would dominate teaching time at the expense of 'cross-curricular, open-ended, real world problem-solving tasks to encourage group work, creativity, initiative and the application and transfer of learning'. Some traditionalists were also critical because, although it did specify a certain level of phonics, the NLS promoted a fundamentally whole-word approach. Nevertheless, the strategy did lead to a steady improvement, and between 1997 and 2001 the proportion of pupils reaching the expected standard of literacy by the end of Key Stage 2 rose from 62.5 per cent to 75 per cent. In 1999, the National Numeracy Strategy was introduced, heralding a more modest rise in standards.[4]

Many noted the wider implications of this return to whole-class teaching. The schoolteacher Alan Kerr wrote to *TES* in October 2000, heralding this final defeat of the 'Plowden ideology':

> Many of us who argue against the progressive ideology legitimised by the Plowden Report broadly, if not unreservedly, welcome the more structured approach to learning which young people experience today. Plowden was a huge mistake and recovering from it has been a long and painful process.[5]

The malady of agitation

Unfortunately, Blunkett's success with primary standards

contrasted with a surfeit of less well thought-through reforms. Blair wanted quick returns on his pledge to transform Britain's schools, so a blizzard of initiatives and directives issued forth from the Education Department* and its newly formed Policy and Innovation Division, in the hope that at least some would hit their intended target.

'Education Action Zones' (EAZs) were introduced to give new freedoms to schools in disadvantaged areas, and potentially place local authorities in the hands of private companies. By 2001, this was costing £60 million a year, but Ofsted reported two years later that there was little change in pupil attainment.[6] EAZs were quickly overtaken by the 'Excellence in Cities' programme, which offered an increased provision of resources for pupils in urban schools. By 2005, the programme, which was administered by local authorities, had an annual budget of £386 million but yielded only negligible improvements.[7] The Fresh Start scheme, which gave a number of failing schools £1.5 million to re-open with new staff, new management and a new name, was a disaster. Perhaps the most amusing example of hopeful profligacy was an attempt to introduce Performance Related Pay through a bonus scheme, which saw almost every teacher who applied for the bonus receive it, leading to meaningless salary increase and leaving the Education Department with a bill for £737 million. This cascade of legislation and initiatives was accompanied by an unprecedented level of centralised direction. In 1998 alone, Blunkett sent out 322 directives to schools and LEAs, more than one per working day. Little wonder that many in the profession began to complain of 'initiativitus'.[8]

---

* I shall refer to the 'Education Department' throughout the chapter, to cover its different incarnations over the period: Department for Education and Employment, Department for Education and Skills, and Department for Children, Schools and Families.

In order to implement these successive waves of government policy, agencies were formed or remodelled and a vast education quangocracy developed. The acres of parchment this new bureaucracy produced were wasteful enough, but worse still was the unprecedented bonanza created for those members of the education establishment who came to hold many of the top jobs. After two decades sequestered in university education departments and local authorities around the country, the door was opened for progressive educationists to choose from a bevy of influential positions. Such figures gained an increased level of influence and their progressive ideas enjoyed a powerful new lease of life. This was felt most keenly in the area of teaching methods and curriculum design, where the child-centred ideas of the 1960s and 1970s witnessed a significant rejuvenation.

Often, this revived progressivism masqueraded under new terms and developed new conceptual justifications, meaning that their true nature was not always clear to ministers. Child-centred learning became 'personalisation' or 'independent learning', and knowledge-lite curriculums were said to promote '21st century skills'. By the turn of the millennium, the direction of educational fashion was in stark contrast to Blunkett's original vision of going 'back to basics'. This only worsened after Blunkett moved to the Home Office in 2001 and the Education Secretary's office enjoyed a revolving door with four ministers, Estelle Morris, Charles Clarke, Ruth Kelly and Alan Johnson, entering and leaving in the space of six years. With so little time to build up experience, the real direction of reform was decided by the growing education quangocracy. Blunkett had initially kept on a number of important appointees inherited from the Conservatives, such as Chris Woodhead at Ofsted, Nicholas Tate at the QCA and Anthea Millett at the TTA, who generally kept the progressive wolf from the door of central government. However, by 2000 they had all drifted away and little caution was exercised in appointing their successors.

Duck! Here comes the pendulum

There is little that testifies more to the resurgence of progressive education around the year 2000 than the uncontrollable outbreak of the word 'learner'. Its semantic implications are subtle but profound. Whilst schools are traditionally seen as institutions defined by teaching, the new emphasis on 'learners' implied a preference for children to educate themselves with minimal adult direction.

Tony Blair's principle education adviser Michael Barber wrote *The Learning Game* in 1996, and the year 2000 witnessed the passing of the Learning and Skills Act, followed in 2004 by the Five Year Strategy for Children and Learners. Amongst the numerous fads that filtered down to schools, there was Deep Learning, Personalised Learning, Lifelong Learning, Leading Learning and Learning to Learn (L2L). The latter was a concept promoted by the government-funded charity Campaign For Learning, which in 2000 published a collection of essays entitled *Schools in the Learning Age*. With a foreword from David Blunkett, and essays from Michael Barber, Guy Claxton and Ken Robinson, it was the progenitor of a bold new concept called 'learnacy'. The aforementioned Guy Claxton, Professor of Learning Sciences and the co-director of the Centre of Real-World Learning, developed the 'Building Learning Power' programme that became highly popular in schools. In addition, ideas once deemed too unpleasant for progressive educators re-entered the teaching lexicon once qualified with the affix 'for learning': see 'behaviour for learning', 'assessment for learning', and 'leadership for learning'. The government enquiry into behaviour in schools was entitled *Learning Behaviour*, and Blunkett's report on Further Education was entitled *The Learning Age*. In this sustained assault on the English language, schools were encouraged to exchange the word 'pupils' with 'learners', and even dub teachers 'co-learners'.

These concepts and fads often originated with the new education quangocracy. One of the most powerful was the Qualifications and Curriculum Authority (QCA), which emerged from the SCAA (an organisation created by the Conservatives to oversee the national curriculum). During the nine years from 1999 to 2008, the QCA's budget tripled to £157 million.[9] In 2000, it was given a new chief executive, the well-known educationist David Hargreaves. Even by the standard of educationists, Hargreaves is a man of radical views, as was established by his well known 1982 book *The Challenge for the Comprehensive School* (see Chapter 3). The series of publications he wrote for the think tank Demos over the following two decades gave little indication that his views had altered. In one 1994 offering, *The Mosaic of Learning*, Hargreaves endorsed the ideas of the educational-anarchist Ivan Illich and wrote: 'Schools are still modelled on a curious mix of the factory, the asylum and the prison.'[10] For a government still nominally dedicated to 'driving up standards', this was akin to placing the Paris Peace Conference in the hands of the Kaiser.

Hargreaves only lasted a year before resigning in 2001 after the botched introduction of the AS level. However, the QCA continued in much the same vein under new leadership, and in 2007 published a revised national curriculum – a document that is perhaps the crowning glory of dumbing down during the New Labour years. Hargreaves, meanwhile, moved to be associate director of another powerful government agency: the Specialist Schools and Academies Trust (SSAT). This organisation was formed by Cyril Taylor in 1987 to support the formation of Ken Baker's new City Technology Colleges and by the early 2000s had responsibility for guiding the newly emerging City Academies. In his 2006 pamphlet for the SSAT, *A New Shape for Schooling*, Hargreaves explained the concepts of 'personalisation' and 'co-construction', and lapsed into anti-teaching rhetoric indistinguishable from the first wave of 1960s progressive thinkers:

> The learner is neither an empty vessel into which teachers can pour the curriculum, nor the tabula rasa implicit in the now rather discredited behaviourist approaches to learning and teaching. Knowledge is not directly transferred to students through teaching, which is an intervention into a continuous process of the student's knowledge-building activities.[11]

Hargreaves stated that the government's new 'personalisation agenda' was compatible with Piagetian theories of constructivism, and wrote approvingly of the ideas of Lev Vygotsky – a Soviet psychologist who died in 1934 and was a long-standing icon for progressive educationists. During his four years at the SSAT, Hargreaves produced 23 such pamphlets, while the government increased the funding of the organisation from £3 million to almost £50 million between 2001 and 2007.[12]

Another quango established by the Labour government was the National College for School Leadership (NCSL), a body accrediting prospective heads with the new, compulsory National Professional Qualification for Headship. Established in 2000 with an annual budget of £30 million, the NCSL was touted by figures such as Blair and Adonis as the 'Sandhurst for schools'. This vision was quickly lost in implementation, which was inevitably dominated by figures sympathetic to progressive ideas. In 2005, the NCSL published a report entitled *Learning-centred Leadership*, which endorsed all of the popular fads of the day such as 'personalised learning', 'learning styles', 'distributed leadership' and 'a student-centred approach to school organisation'. Typical of the disregard for clear expression common amongst educationists, one concluding sentence read: 'In short, learning-centred leaders who strive to personalise learning through the five components will be personalised learning-centred leaders.'[13] The NCSL also developed a residential programme for aspirant heads billed as '48 hours of intense experience'. Delegates were encouraged to imagine 'the school of the future', but warned that in the future the very concept of a school may become 'rapidly outdated'.[14] The headmasters' bootcamp seemed to be becoming more Shangri-La than Sandhurst.

Rare were the occasions where the government intervened to stop such developments. One occasion, for which we should be very grateful, was the government response to the 2004 Tomlinson Report. Mike Tomlinson had been Chris Woodhead's successor as Chief Inspector of Schools and in 2003 he was asked to chair a working group for the reform of examinations for 14-19 year olds after allegations of grade manipulation. His 2004 report set out a radical alternative which recommended scrapping GCSEs, A-Levels and vocational qualifications, and replacing them all with a single 'diploma'. Tomlinson's diploma would have been entirely modular, with pupils progressing at their own rate in mixed-age classes, being assessed throughout the year according to their own level of readiness. Assessments would have mostly taken the form of project-work and in-class assessment, with a significant reduction in the level of examinations. Tomlinson also proposed a compulsory, non-academic course in 'Common Knowledge, Skills and Attributes' covering areas such as 'communication skills' and 'family responsibilities'.[15] The report gained much support from the education establishment and it seemed a genuine possibility that Tomlinson's recommendations would be implemented. Mercifully, the Education Secretary Ruth Kelly made a stand, declaring: 'We won't transform opportunities by abolishing what is good.'[16]

Such vigilance in the face of dumbing down was exceptional. Observing from the Home Office, David Blunkett lamented the direction education policy took after his departure, in particular under Charles Clarke. In private he confided: 'They've taken their foot off the accelerator. They've gone soft. They've produced documents called *Excellence and Enjoyment*. The next one will be called *Smiley and Fun*.'[17] Blunkett was similarly dismayed when Clarke announced that the literacy targets in primary schools would be abandoned, and a school visit in 2004 prompted him to record the following in his diary: 'We were back to happy clappy, to children singing… Not once did they mention literacy and numeracy. Nobody offered to show me youngsters reading.'[18]

During this period, quangos and institutions that had originally been established to counter the ideas of the education establishment, gradually fell into their very hands. British schools now suffered the worst of both worlds – high levels of centralised bureaucracy and government agencies pushing progressive education. In June 2000, the *TES* primary editor Diane Hofkins summarised the significance of this development, pointing in particular to the appointment of Hargreaves at the QCA and the emergent focus on 'thinking skills':

> DUCK! Here comes the pendulum! It's swinging back again! You know, the one that sweeps back and forth between prescription and freedom, formal teaching and discovery learning, between trusting teachers (and children) and telling them exactly what to do… Maybe it is again possible to quote the 1967 Plowden Report.

Selling old rags for new

During the New Labour years, educationists found new monikers and justifications for child-centred teaching, perhaps due to the negative connotations the term had earned during the preceding decades. Two of the most influential were 'multiple intelligences' and 'learning styles', which together were used to justify the new fads of 'personalised' and 'independent' learning. Added to this was a millenarian conviction, based on little but proclamation, that the dawn of a new millennium and the rate of technological change necessitated a focus on '21st century skills'. It is impossible to read a report, initiative, or policy paper from between the years 2000 and 2010 that does not pay homage to one or more of these concepts. In terms of empirical or scientific justification, they were all built on sand.

Michael Barber was David Blunkett's most influential education adviser. A former teacher, NUT official and Labour Party parliamentary candidate, by 1996 he was a Professor at the Institute of Education and the author of the widely acclaimed programme for reform: *The Learning Game: Arguments for an Education Revolution*. In a chapter entitled 'The Millennium Curriculum', Barber declared that we had at last found 'a theoretical understanding of children and young people that will assist teachers in their task.' Who was responsible for this groundbreaking discovery? The answer was Howard Gardner, a Professor of Education at Harvard. Barber gave a lengthy explication of Gardner's 1983 book *Frames of Mind*, in which Gardner redefined human intelligence as not belonging to one uniform scale, but seven. These were spatial, linguistic, logical-mathematical, bodily-kinaesthetic, musical, interpersonal and intra-personal. Gardner dubbed this finding 'The Theory of Multiple Intelligences'. Gardner went on to revise the exact number of intelligences, adding at different points naturalistic, existential and moral intelligence, eventually bringing the number up to ten. In addition, he developed five 'doors' through which any school topic could be approached: aesthetic, narrative, logical/quantative, foundational and experiential.

Gardner's was an appealing message. He appeared to

demonstrate that pupils who did badly at school did so because their schools had a narrow, traditional approach that focused on linguistic and logical-mathematical intelligences at the expense of alternatives. Accordingly, Blunkett's adviser Michael Barber concurred that traditional teaching, with its focus on 'lecturing or textbooks', neglected 'students who are motivated to learn but whose own learning styles or profiles of intelligence are not in tune with prevailing instructional practices':

> One goal of policy would then be to ensure that each teacher had mastered the full repertoire necessary to open the room of learning, not just for an elite, but for everyone. In short, if we are to design a curriculum that can motivate and make possible success for all young people, it will need to recognise the full breadth of Gardner's seven intelligences and the importance of his five doors.

In essence, this was the same child-centred attack on teacher-led, whole-class instruction dressed up with a new pseudo-scientific justification.[19]

Gardner's ideas were embraced by educationists such as Barber, and heavily influenced teacher training, in-school professional developments and government agencies. His ideas even filtered through into the independent sector where a prominent public school head adapted Howard Gardner's theory into 'Eight Aptitudes', and had them displayed on a newly-built fountain in the school grounds. However, what was missing was any evidence to suggest that Gardner's groundbreaking 'theory' was valid. Clear criticism of the theory from within academia existed long before it overran British schools, from Robert Sternberg in 1983, Sandra Scarr in 1985 and Hans Eysenck in 1994. Even Gardner had said as much in his original work *Frames of Mind*, where he wrote: 'At present it must be admitted that the selection (or rejection) or a candidate's intelligence is reminiscent more of an artistic judgement than of a scientific assessment.' A decade later this remained the case. In a 2004 article co-authored by Gardner himself, he wrote there is 'little evidence to support Multiple Intelligence theory', but added he would be 'delighted were such evidence to accrue'. The emperor was openly telling his subjects that he wore no clothes.

So how did Gardner's pseudo-science, with its self-admitted lack of empirical evidence, become so wildly popular? Quite simply, it offered a new validation for some very old progressive prejudices against teacher-led lessons. The same can be said for another pedagogical epidemic of the New Labour years. Learning styles originated with a 1978 book by two American educationists entitled *Teaching Students through their Individual Learning Styles*. Various educationists during the succeeding decades took hold of the idea, and produced their own taxonomies of different learning styles. By the end of the millennium, most British adherents had coalesced around the acronym VAK, standing for visual, auditory and kinaesthetic learners. According to this theory, different pupils have varying cognitive profiles and are well suited to learn in different ways, either through sight, sound or movement. The implication was that all lessons should have activities that cater for such different 'styles'.[20]

This idea became a cornerstone of educational 'good practice' during the 2000s, with many schools insisting that every lesson plan demonstrate opportunities for visual, auditory or kinaesthetic learners. Just like multiple intelligences, it was a theory which appeared to prove that whole-class, teacher-led instruction was bad teaching which benefited only a limited number of pupils. Greg Brooks, an influential architect of the National Literacy Strategy, wrote in a DfES publication that '...it is possible that a few people's brains or preferred learning styles are so unsuited to learning by phonics that they would be impeded by it.'[21] The government utterly fell for this brave new world of teaching. The Education Department's *Five Year Strategy for Children and Learners* in 2004 endorsed the concept; David Miliband talked of 'unique learning styles' in a 2005 speech; and a DfES pamphlet of the same year declared: 'Through an understanding of learning styles, teachers can exploit pupils' strengths and build their capacity to learn.'[22] There was a corresponding boom in 'learning style' resources, with more than 70 different packages on the market for schools by 2005.[23]

These packages often included pupil questionnaires to help teachers diagnose their pupils' individual learning style. In his excoriating exposé of poor educational research, *Teacher Proof*, the *TES* columnist Tom Bennett compared such tests to a 'How sexy are you?' questionnaire in *Cosmopolitan*. He did so with good reason, as learning styles have no scientific validity whatsoever. The theory has been comprehensively shunned within academia for being both neurologically unviable and practically unsuccessful in improving student outcomes. Recently, Daniel Willingham, a cognitive scientist who writes extensively about education concluded that: '...teachers should be aware that, as far as scientists have been able to determine, there are not categorically different types of learner.'[24] In 2007, the neuroscientist and Director of the Royal Institution Baroness Greenfield wrote:

> The rationale for employing VAK learning styles appears to be weak. After more than 30 years of educational research into learning styles there is no independent evidence that VAK, or indeed any other learning style inventory, has any direct educational benefits.

Learning styles were discredited in academic literature as far back as 1987, and extensive reviews confirmed this conclusion in 1999 and 2004. In the latter review, Frank Coffield of the London Institute of Education found that all the independent evidence pointed towards learning styles being 'theoretically and psychometrically flawed' and, more worryingly, the only studies supporting learning styles were conducted by individuals promoting their own theories or specific products.[25] However, over the same period learning styles were repeatedly endorsed by the DfES. As Tom Bennett writes: 'Doesn't' that say something dark and terrible about the way in which bad ideas can lurch on ('zombie facts') for decades after their satanic birth, despite enormous evidence to suggest that there isn't any evidence available?'[26]

Learning styles and multiple intelligences were used to justify 'personalised learning', a concept that dominated Labour's education policy for much of the 2000s. It was presented as a pedagogical golden bullet and few could have entered a school during this period without hearing paeans to the virtues of 'personalisation'. In a 2004 speech, Schools Minister David Miliband claimed that personalised learning was 'the debate in education today', and promised that, if implemented, 'the prize is immense'.[27] Countless documents were published by government agencies proclaiming this new dawn. One, entitled *2020 Vision*, was written by the head of Ofsted, Christine Gilbert. It described personalised learning as follows:

> Learners are active and curious: they create their own hypotheses, ask their own questions, coach one another, set goals for themselves, monitor their progress and experiment with ideas for taking risks, knowing that mistakes and 'being stuck' are part of learning.[28]

What is not mentioned anywhere in the document is teacher teaching. Personalisation wasn't a theory of learning, or a programme for reform. It was a brand that sought to recast child-centred ideas in the suitably New Labour language of the market, with a focus on lesson 'customisation', the 'demands' of the pupils, and the role of the school as a 'provider'. The language was new, but the anti-teaching, child-centred ideas were decades old.

In 2007, the government agency in charge of training new teachers devised 33 'Professional Standards for Teachers'. Of the 33 standards, two were concerned with the need for 'personalised provision' and 'personalised learning'. However, in 2009, the Commons Select Committee held an enquiry into the state of the concept. Its key architect, David Hargreaves, was invited to give evidence, but the committee chairman complained that when Hargreaves spoke 'a fog seems to come up' leaving him 'totally confused'. Hargreaves meanwhile told the committee that personalisation 'has outlived its usefulness', and added that the government should 'simply drop' the whole idea.[29]

The last guise under which progressive education reinvented itself during the New Labour years was a breathless insistence on futurology and, in particular, the claim that the unprecedented speed of technological change meant traditional educational practices were becoming redundant. This argument was endlessly made, not through any evidence, but through the sheer force of unsubstantiated hyperbole. Almost always, the implication was that school curriculums defined by knowledge were outmoded, the rapid pace of technological change made deciding what to teach impossible, and that factual knowledge could now be outsourced to the grand repository of the Internet. Instead, the futurologists declared schools should focus on skills – more specifically, 21st Century Skills. In essence, this was the old progressive attack on subject content and discrete academic subjects, rebooted for the Internet age. A 2006 report for the Union ATL entitled *Subject to Change*, typified this thinking: 'A twenty-first century curriculum cannot have the transfer of knowledge at its core for the simple reason that the selection of what is required has become problematic in an information-rich age.'

Perhaps the most important example of this development was the RSA Opening Minds curriculum that was developed in 1999 and replaced a subject-based curriculum with one designed around five 'key competencies': Citizenship; Learning; Managing Information; Relating to People; and Managing Situations. It went on to be used in an estimated six per cent of British schools.[30] This revived enthusiasm for skills-based education was given full endorsement by central government in 2001, when the Department for Education and Employment was renamed the Department for Education and Skills. In 2004, the Education Minister Charles Clarke claimed:

> Over the last 60 years, a fundamental recasting of industry, employment, technology and society has transformed the requirement for education and training – not only driving the education system, but introducing new ideas about lifelong learning, personalised education, and self-directed learning.[31]

Such idle futurology has long been a hallmark of progressive education. A century ago, Dewey spent time pondering what *twentieth* century skills would be, and during the first wave of progressive education it was argued that the typewriter and the calculator had made handwriting and mental arithmetic redundant. By the millennium, educationists were arguing forcefully that the teaching methods peculiarly suited to the twenty-first century were the same teaching methods that had failed children and misled our education system since the 1960s. It was an exquisite case of the disease masquerading as the cure.

Just like Countesthorpe College during the 1970s, numerous schools of the 2000s implemented this child-centred vision only to see a rapid decline in pupil attainment. Perhaps the worst case has been in Knowsley,

Merseyside, where in 2009 the local council spent £157 million rebranding its seven schools as 'centres of learning'. These centres promised to 'rip up the rulebook': teachers were renamed 'progress leaders'; classrooms became 'homebases' and 'warehouses'; and a 'world class' education was promised for the pupils. The head of one school, Huyton Arts and Sports Centre for Learning, declared that they would not be teaching knowledge, as children can now 'sit on Google and find out anything at the push of a button'. Three years after the project began, four of the schools had received critical Ofsted reports and only 41 per cent of the pupils were securing five good GCSEs – the worst figure for any local authority in the country. One school, Christ the King Catholic and Church of England Centre for Learning, had a brand new £24 million building but only 381 of its 900 places were filled by July 2013. The school has since closed.[32]

Agents of coercion

One could be fooled into thinking that this revival of progressive education mainly took place in the fertile minds of educationists, but in actual fact it was very successfully disseminated through schools. Two forces allowed this promotion of the orthodoxy to be so strong and, ironically, both had been established by previous governments to curtail the excesses of 'trendy teaching'. They were Ofsted and the national curriculum.

In 2005 the QCA, which had been given responsibility for revising the national curriculum, appointed Mick Waters to be Director of the Curriculum. A former primary school teacher, teacher trainer and local authority official, Waters was previously the Manchester Chief Education Officer. He left his post in Manchester with GCSE results placing it 141st out of 150 in the country.[33] There was no secret as to the direction in which Waters hoped to take the curriculum. Two years after his appointment, he wrote the 'Introduction' to a report by the ATL union. He wrote that the curriculum can be made 'nourishing and appetising' by:

> ...seeing subject discipline as more vital than subject content, by seeing links between subjects, by seeing the world through important dimensions such as globalisation, technology or sustainability, we start to create a *sense of learning*.[34]

When Waters's revised national curriculum was introduced in 2007, it strenuously avoided any discussion of subject content. Instead, it focused on the skills and dispositions pupils should gain from their study. The three 'Aims' of the national curriculum were to create 'successful learners', 'confident individuals' and 'responsible citizens'. Each aim was elaborated with further details, ranging from the banal ('communicate well in a range of ways'), to the therapeutic ('are self-aware and deal well with their emotions'), to the quixotic ('can change things for the better'). Added to this was a framework of Personal, Learning and Thinking Skills (PLTS) such as 'self-management' and 'team-working', and a series of cross-curricular 'dimensions' to encourage breaking down subject barriers. These included 'healthy lifestyle', 'global dimension and sustainable development' and 'identity and cultural diversity'. Their tendentious nature requires no elaboration.[35]

Although subject distinctions were retained, they were emptied of subject content, and expressed in the language of interchangeable skills and dispositions. Each subject was introduced in terms of 'Concepts', then 'Processes', and then only in the third section a brief discussion of 'Range and Content'. The only specified topics for study in Geography were the UK and the European Union, and the only specified historical content was the World Wars and the Holocaust. When questioned by the *Guardian* about this, Mick Waters defensively explained that 'Anne

Boleyn will still be beheaded, the Pennines will remain the backbone of England and Romeo will still fall in love with Juliet'.[36] Such a claim was disingenuous: Anne Boleyn (plus Henry VIII), the Pennines and *Romeo and Juliet* were all left out of the history, geography and English curriculums respectively. The entire 2007 curriculum stands as a monument to the misdirection that education took during the New Labour years. As Phillip Hesner wrote in the *Independent*:

> Can the government really complain if the general public has the impression that education in schools nowadays appears to consist of a lot of pious nothing-in-particular? Nobody understands what their children are supposed to be learning, or how these ludicrous aims are supposed to be achieved.[37]

In 2010, the veteran education journalist Peter Wilby wrote in the *Guardian*: '[Mick Waters] has probably changed secondary schooling more profoundly than anybody in the past 20 years'.[38] Thankfully, at the time of writing, Waters's curriculum has been discontinued.

Even more powerful than the national curriculum as a tool of pedagogical uniformity was the schools inspectorate, Ofsted. It is an ongoing complaint within education that inspection judgements are based not on the academic success of a school, but on the progressive prejudices held by the inspectors. This has led to the risible situation whereby independent and grammar schools with excellent academic records are frequently given poor inspection reports for being too old-fashioned.[39] On stepping down from his role as head of Ofsted, Woodhead wrote in 2002 that: 'my single biggest doubt about Ofsted stems from the fact that some inspectors are unwilling or unable to jettison their progressive educational views.'[40] After Woodhead's departure, the progressive bias of inspectors went from something that was a concern to something that was actively promoted. By 2006, the Chief Inspector was Christine Gilbert, the author of the highly progressive government report *2020 Vision*. During the first decade of the new millennium, the Ofsted ideal of 'good practice' was unambiguously aligned with progressive teaching methods and the threat of a bad Ofsted rating became a significant motivation to embrace such practices.

Such a synergy between Ofsted and progressive teaching was demonstrated by the popular teacher handbook, *The Perfect Ofsted Lesson*, published in 2010. It triumphantly announced that the days of the 'latter-day witch-finder general Chris Woodhead' were over, and Ofsted was now looking for:

> ...a focus on learning, the development of thinking skills, opportunities for independent learning, a variety of strategies that take into account different elements of the individual learner's preferences, strengths and weaknesses, the use of positive emotions, great relationships, clear goals, metacognition, creativity and the willingness to take a risk or two...

According to the preface, due to the author's 'pioneering work on skills-based learning and what is known as the Competency Curriculum', she 'knows exactly what constitutes the sort of good practice that Ofsted is looking for these days'. The book condemned teacher-led lessons as 'superficial', and implied that the teacher who teaches from the front is simply an egoist. In conclusion, the author wrote: '...if you can implement at least some of it in your day-to-day teaching, that outstanding grade is within your reach'.[41]

The baleful influence of these inspections was a strong theme in Katharine Birbalsingh's controversial exposé of modern education, *To Miss With Love* (2011). Born out of Birbalsingh's anonymous blog about working in a South

London secondary school, *To Miss With Love* charted a year of teaching at 'Ordinary School'. Looming over the school is an impending Ofsted visit, so repeated staff training sessions are organised in preparation. Birbalsingh recounts one of them:

> 'Right.' Mr Goodheart reclaims everyone's attention. 'I'd like to remind everyone about our push on independent learning. Remember that this is what Ofsted will be looking for, when they finally get here.' He smiles in a way that suggests he doesn't really believe what he is saying. 'We simply cannot have a situation where teachers are teaching and children are listening.' I sit up in my chair, not entirely sure if I've heard correctly.

When Ofsted do arrive at Ordinary School in the summer term, they observe one of 'Ms Magical's' lessons. Ms Magical is a no-nonsense West Indian teacher in her fifties who has been teaching in inner-city London for 20 years. Her classroom is calm, her results are good, and she is fierce on discipline. However, Ofsted give her a poor grade. As Birbalsingh explains:

> Sure, she's a great teacher with fantastic results, but Ofsted isn't interested in that. She's too 'old-school' for them... She's a teacher who ignores the new fads in education and continues to teach and adapt her methods according to *choice* rather than the orders of some bureaucrat or politician.

Ms Magical is left demoralised by this negative assessment of her professional capabilities. Birbalsingh concludes: 'The eradication of the old-school teacher is the single most destructive "improvement" that is taking place in our schools today.'[42]

The educationist Daisy Christodoulou, an advocate of refocusing teaching on knowledge and subject content, painstakingly researched Ofsted subject reports for her 2013 book *Seven Myths About Education*. She broke down the subject reports for art, English, geography, history, maths, MFL, RE and science, and in all found references to 228 lessons. Almost every point of praise was directed at child-centred teaching methods while, when mentioned, teacher-led, knowledge-based lessons were nearly always criticised. Christodoulou observed that out of all 26 lessons covered in the art report, only one made any reference to explicit instruction from the teacher, in which a teacher explained the terms 'abstract' and 'expressionism'. This lesson was criticised for missing opportunities 'to engage students fully in their learning'. In the 34 English lesson reports that Christodoulou analysed, only one involved any teaching of grammar. On closer inspection, the lesson was in fact about stylistic devices (onomatopoeia and alliteration). As Christodoulou writes: 'the only grammar lesson Ofsted praise is not actually a grammar lesson.'[43]

The newly arrived Chief Inspector at Ofsted, Michael Wilshaw, has vowed that he will combat the prejudices of his inspectors, but their attachment to the progressive orthodoxy is proving particularly stubborn. This battle between the inspectors and their Chief has been doggedly tracked by the education blogger Old Andrew, who explained in February 2013:

> OFSTED remains the steadfast enforcer of the orthodoxies of progressive education, and it is OFSTED, not league tables or government policies, which most shapes our classroom practices... Careers will have been made or ruined on the back of the unofficial ideology enforced, through fear, by OFSTED. My view is that until OFSTED are abolished, or reformed beyond recognition, then our system will remain imprisoned by the progressive orthodoxy no matter what the politicians, or the chief inspector, happens to say.[44]

Between 1997 and 2010, influential figures within the Labour party would occasionally argue that no return to progressive education was taking place. Such claims were either disingenuous or naïve. During this period, there was an enormous emphasis placed on child-centred, knowledge-lite teaching that no classroom teacher could fail to have experienced. These ideas were often dressed in the contemporary idiom of modernisation, psychobabble or management speak, but such language was simply a veneer. What was being promoted was Progressive Education 2.0, a fact not lost on Matthew Taylor, the former Labour Policy Director and keen supporter of progressive education. Taylor became Chief Executive of the RSA in 2006 and helped develop their skills-based 'Opening Minds' curriculum for schools. In 2009, he wrote a piece for the *TES* proclaiming 'New progressivism is a cause to fight for':

> Yet behind the headlines there does seem to be a convergence of thinking among professionals and mainstream educationalists… A more flexible curriculum is advocated, balancing the acquiring of knowledge with cross-cutting capabilities and the goal of engaging pupils in understanding and designing the learning process. This approach might, for want of a better phrase, be termed 'new progressivism'.

A 2007 poll by the NUT and Teachers TV to find the ten most inspirational education books demonstrated that radical ideas die hard within the teaching profession. Four books were works of fiction, and one was a contemporary guide to classroom behaviour, but the remaining five had a distinctly progressive flavour – Vygotsky's *Thought and Language* (1934); Neill's *Summerhill* (1962); Holt's *How Children Fail* (1964); Freire's *Pedagogy of the Oppressed* (1968); and Donaldson's *Children's Minds* (1978).[45] The 'new progressivism' of the Labour years must have fallen on many receptive ears within the profession.

Academy converts

There was one development of the New Labour years that did, in some respects, run against the grain of a return to progressive education. It was pioneered by Andrew Adonis, a rather unorthodox figure amongst Labour's education reformers. Adonis, a former academic and member of the Social Democrat Party, joined Tony Blair's policy unit in 1998. He had been an education correspondent for the *Financial Times,* and like many education reformers before him, he was dismayed by the poor quality of schools in his home borough of Islington. However, unlike many in his party, Adonis was unsparing when it came to criticising state education. He later wrote: 'I saw failing comprehensive schools, many hundreds of them, as a cancer at the heart of English society.'

In *Education, Education, Education,* his account of his time as a schools reformer, Adonis writes of the formative experience he had as governor of George Orwell School, a comprehensive school on the Islington/Haringey border, shortly before he joined Blair's policy unit. The school was due to pass through the government's 'fresh start' scheme, which would give it a fund of money to refurbish its buildings, recruit new staff, change its name and develop a new curriculum. As he wrote: 'it was not a happy experience'. Islington council were able to influence many key decisions, the refurbishment was poorly managed, and the bloated governing body split into a 'moderate' and a 'left-wing' faction. Shortly after the school opened, there was a near riot with racial overtones, causing the arrival of the police and the closure of the school. Adonis learnt a valuable lesson about the difficulty of driving up standards through the existing bureaucracy of state education. As he wrote: 'The local authority which had allowed George Orwell School to fail so badly over so many years was hardly likely to be successful in managing its relaunch.'

Around the same time, Adonis had an altogether

different experience visiting Thomas Telford School in Shropshire, one of Ken Baker's original City Technology Colleges (CTC). Here he found a passionate head leading a school with an ethos 'akin to the best grammar schools'. There were sports teams, after-school activities, a technological curriculum and an excellent record of sending pupils to university. Adonis found similar stories of success at other CTCs, such as Emmanuel College in Gateshead and Harris CTC in Crystal Palace. Adonis analysed the data for the 15 CTCs and found that most of these schools, established during the late 1980s and free of local authority control, had been quietly prospering for the past ten years. Adonis concluded that the CTCs were successful due to their autonomy; the influence of sponsors from outside the education establishment; and their ability to forge a distinctive ethos and set high standards of behaviour and achievement. Taking this formula as his inspiration, the City Academies programme was born.

Adonis proposed that City Academies could replace failing schools, or be set up from scratch, and would be independent of local authority control. Instead, much of their governance would be in the hands of sponsors: individuals, or groups (such as charitable trusts) who were willing to pay £2 million towards the capital costs of establishing the school. In return, sponsors could make key decisions about the ethos and curriculum of the school. The City Academies programme was announced on 15 March, 2000 to the profound consternation of the education establishment. Refusing to contemplate this dilution of the 'comprehensive ideal', the teaching unions federated to create the Anti-Academies Alliance. Educationists such as Ted Wragg ridiculed Adonis in the national press and members of Adonis's own Labour party such as Neil Kinnock and Roy Hattersley openly attacked his plans. The politics surrounding the academies reform, in Adonis's own words, were 'toxic'.

The first three academies opened in 2002, with 12 more

in 2003 and 17 more in 2004. Sensing their initial success, New Labour's 'Five Year Strategy' proposed the target of 200 academies by 2009, giving the reform a considerable boost. In the end, New Labour established 197. Sponsorship came from an extraordinary array of sources, including school federations, wealthy philanthropists and charitable trusts. In 2005 Adonis, who had until then been a member of the Prime Minister's Policy Unit, was made a life peer so that he could be made Minister of State for Education and have continued control over the reform. In 2007, the first clear independent assessment of academies came from the National Audit Office, showing a significant improvement in examination results. The new schools were an unquestionable success, as Adonis writes: 'Academies which opened in 2002 have more than trebled their scores since opening, and those opening in the following three years have mostly doubled their scores, while the national average increased by barely a quarter.' What is more, further research showed that schools close to academies, driven by the arrival of new competition, tended to improve at a rate above that of the national average. In the public imagination, 'academies' soon became a hopeful alternative to the 'bog standard comprehensive', a phrase coined by Alastair Campbell in 2001.

Many new academies gained a reputation for success due to their 'back to basics' approach in areas such as assessment and pupil behaviour. Judging from his recent book, Adonis is no supporter of progressive teaching methods, and he seems to believe academies represent a break with such orthodoxies:

> ...academies are the 'new grammar schools', taking the best of the grammar school ethos and emphasis on rigour, qualifications and effort, including A-levels and sixth forms, but making it available to all children without selection.

For the very best academies, this is an accurate description. The most fêted of all was Mossbourne Academy in Hackney. Mossbourne was built on the site of Hackney Downs, one of the worst schools in the country until it closed in 1995. Infamously, the school's best GCSE results were gained in Turkish, a subject not even taught at the school. Hackney local Clive Bourne, who made his fortune in logistics, sponsored the new Academy, and it was opened in September 2004. The founding principal was Michael Wilshaw, a headteacher known for his uncompromising stance on pupil behaviour and school ethos. His philosophy of schooling was, to say the least, unusual within state education. In an interview with the *New Statesman* Wilshaw described the ethos at Mossbourne: 'We teach the children the difference between right and wrong, good and evil. They know that if they disrupt class or are rude to teachers, there will be consequences.' Each class began with pupils reciting the following mantra: 'I aspire to maintain an enquiring mind, a calm disposition and an attentive ear so that in this class and in all classes I can fulfil my true potential.' Lessons were challenging, testing was frequent, and no excuses were made on behalf of the pupils' backgrounds. Wilshaw even dubbed his new academy 'a grammar school with a comprehensive intake', words not heard in those parts of London since the days of Dr Boyson.

Critics derided Mossbourne for being a 'bootcamp', but the Wilshaw formula was extraordinarily successful. In 2009, pupils took GCSEs for the first time and their results, by far the highest in Hackney, placed Mossbourne in the top one per cent nationally for schools of a similar student makeup. In 2011 the first A-level results were recorded. Nine students won places at Cambridge, with two to read medicine. In all, seventy students won places at Russell Group Universities. This had all been achieved at a school where 40 per cent of the pupils were eligible for free school meals, compared with 18 per cent nationwide.[46]

Other academies that employed the same 'no excuses' approach recorded similar results. Burlington Danes Academy, which serves the deprived White City estate in Shepherd's Bush, emulated the rituals and routines of a private school with a house system, extra-curricular activities and (controversially) class rankings. In 2013, 77 per cent of their pupils gained five good GCSEs including English and maths, compared with 31 per cent of pupils when the academy was founded in 2006.[47]

However it would be wrong to imply, as Adonis perhaps does, that a 'grammar school ethos and emphasis on rigour' is a defining feature of academies. These schools were established whilst the winds of the progressive renaissance were blowing hardest, and such winds filled the sails of many newly launched academies. The SSAT, led by the arch-progressive David Hargreaves, was the main government agency providing 'thought leadership' for academies at the time. One group of academies in Kent, named New Line Learning, was amongst the many that fell under this spell. Their executive head Dr Chris Gerry once co-authored a pamphlet with Hargreaves and described the philosophy of New Line Learning as follows:

> There is a need to move away from traditional approaches, to involve students in more choice and the opportunity to work independently. Project Based Learning offers a route forward here and, in particular, the use of meta questions that span traditional subject areas, for example, 'Is all violence wrong?', 'Will science save us?' 'Is truth always necessary?'

The schools introduced 'learning plazas' for 90 pupils to be taught simultaneously by teams of teachers. There was to be a decreased focus on exams, textbooks were to be replaced by a personal computer for every pupil, and teachers were retrained to work 'less as subject specialists and more as mentors and guides for students'.[48] In 2008, the *TES* reported that Dr Gerry was designing a curriculum around 'emotional intelligence', and had sent 16 teachers to Yale University to learn how to become 'emotional intelligence coaches'.[49] However, by 2010 it was being reported that the flagship New Line Learning Academy had the worst truancy record in the entire country, with 27 per cent of pupils regularly absent from school. In 2013, the school had more than 40 per cent of its year 7 places vacant for the start of term in September.[50]

Despite the misguided approach taken by some academies, the overall policy did demonstrate a valuable lesson: positive school transformation is best achieved outside of the existing structures of state education. Schools such as Mossbourne and Burlington Danes demonstrated that breaking from the tired orthodoxies of state education is best achieved by breaking from the institutions, such as local authorities, that have traditionally been the guardians of such ideas. What is more, sponsors from outside the education establishment provided academies with a new breadth of ambition. Paul Marshall, the hedge-fund manager and co-founder of the remarkable Ark Academies chain, explains their philosophy as follows:

> Collectively, as a chain, we have sought to implement a model of schooling which truly transforms the life-chances of disadvantaged children. We have sought to do so by implementing a distinctive model (no excuses for poor behaviour, high aspirations, depth before breadth, high emphasis on data assessment and pupil tracking, schools within schools) which has worked elsewhere and is now demonstrably working in the UK.[51]

At the beginning of New Labour's reforming drive, they stuck to the principle of 'standards, not structures'. However, driving up standards from central government proved impossible within the confines of existing structures. Academies demonstrated that only once the structures of state education had been challenged could a drive on standards really begin.

Improved behaviour?

Mossbourne generated an inordinate amount of press attention, as many could not believe that such outstanding academic results could be achieved in one of Britain's most deprived boroughs. Towards the end of the 2000s, its 'no excuses' approach to behaviour was spreading to many other schools, particularly in London. However, for the most part, the picture of behaviour in British schools remained steadfastly shocking. In 2010, a secondary school English teacher called Charlie Carroll took to the road in a VW camper van to write an account of life as a supply teacher in inner-city schools. He witnessed a pupil stabbed in Nottingham, a girl who passed around vodka in history lessons in Birmingham, a pupil who dealt weed in IT lessons in Sheffield, and a 13-year-old boy who bullied him out of a school in Yorkshire:

> I cannot count how many times I have been told to fuck off by a student – from the faltering and nervous 'fuck *off*' of the young school bully uncertainly flexing his muscles, to the casual and jokey '*fuck* off' of the older student for whom swearing has become an everyday part of vocabulary.[52]

In his conclusion, Carroll was damning of the Labour government's record on behaviour during their 13 years in government, in particular their promotion of an 'inclusion' policy which made expulsion of poorly behaved pupils prohibitively difficult.

Carroll's experiences were not unusual, as teacher surveys about behaviour in British schools repeatedly bore out (see Chapter 8). This persistent reputation of

British schools for disorder did untold damage to teacher recruitment, which remained a concern for the duration of the 2000s. At points, university teacher training courses for 'shortage subjects' such as maths, physics and foreign languages could not even fill their places, and in 2001 it was reported that around 40 per cent of teacher trainees in their final year did not even become teachers.[53] Open vacancies, defined as an advertised job that is not filled for at least one term, rose to 2,200 in 2006 with 180 of them being for headship positions. In 2001, the vacancy rate in London was 3.8 per cent. Such a situation called for drastic measures, and teachers from abroad were permitted to work at schools for four years before having to gain a British qualification. Unqualified 'instructors', with the requisite specialist knowledge, were even allowed to be employed where it was impossible to find qualified teachers.[54] Young Australian teachers on short-term contracts became a much-commented on sight in inner-city schools. One recorded her experiences in the *Observer* in 2001:

> The first day in a class I leaned over a desk and got a pencil shoved up my bottom from behind. Later I had a dog mess in my bag and my friend got a black eye from another kid. I quickly learnt that the laid-back Australian way was not going to work here.[55]

This difficulty in recruiting teachers was closely related to the daily chaos that characterised so many British schools, as national surveys repeatedly showed that poor pupil behaviour was amongst the top reasons why teachers quit their jobs, and graduates often listed it as the main deterrent preventing them from entering the profession. Despite this, many heads refused to abandon their permissive, lenient approaches towards school discipline, greatly to the detriment of pupils and staff alike.

The government commissioned a report into behaviour in schools – an indication that little real action was going to be taken. Published in 2005, the 'Steer Report' (officially titled *Learning Behaviour*) endorsed many of the hobbling dictums that had got schools into such a troublesome position in the first place. The report declared it was in agreement with the equally meek Elton Report of 1989, which stated 'bad behaviour in schools is a complex problem which does not lend itself to simple solutions'. The report promoted the progressive view that poor behaviour is simply a consequence of poor teaching, and if lessons were made relevant and fun, bad behaviour could be eliminated. It claimed: 'Respect has to be given in order to be received... pupils and teachers all need to operate in a culture of mutual regard.' The report also recommended that lessons be made 'appropriate' and 'accessible' for pupils to prevent them from misbehaving, a sure route to dumbing down.[56]

Worst of all, the Steer report denied there was even much of a problem. Whilst accepting that some examples of bad behaviour did exist, it wrote that overall standards of behaviour should be seen as 'good'. To support such a judgement, the report referred to the Ofsted Annual Report from 2010, which judged behaviour to be good or outstanding in 89 per cent of primary schools and in 70 per cent of secondary schools. However, in the same year, a survey by the Teacher Support Network found that only 20 per cent of teachers in Britain thought behaviour in their schools to be good. As if to ram home the point, teachers in a school in Lancashire later that year took strike action against persistent pupil misbehaviour, citing pupils challenging teachers to fights, pushing and shoving staff, and constantly swearing. In June 2010 Ofsted had visited this same school and judged the standard of behaviour to be 'good'. It appeared that the inspectorate perhaps needed to raise its own expectations.[57]

Slipping standards

Those who bemoaned Labour's lack of progress in reforming England's schools were frequently referred to the remarkable improvement in GCSE results by way of rebuttal. In 1997, the proportion of pupils gaining five GCSEs from A* to C sat at 45 per cent. This improved year-on-year, rising to 60 per cent in 2007 and then rapidly to 76 per cent in 2010. These rises led to the recurrent summer debate over 'grade inflation'. The implied accusation was that examinations were becoming easier and pass marks were being lowered, so that schools could meet their improvement targets and the government could demonstrate their reforms were succeeding.

Each time this August bank holiday ritual played out, the education establishment reacted with righteous indignation, claiming that grade inflation was a myth and such accusations cruelly detracted from the hard work of students. In 2009, Ed Balls attacked the shadow education secretary Michael Gove, who had made accusations of dumbing down, for attempting to 'rubbish the achievements of young people'.[58] Unfortunately for the likes of Balls, grade inflation was an objective fact. Professor Robert Coe of the Durham University Centre for Evaluation and Monitoring (CEM) is a specialist in examination grading. By comparing pupils' GCSE results against an annual benchmark aptitude test ('Yellis score'), he has shown that a D grade at GCSE in 1996 was, by 2011, worth a C grade. In addition, internationally benchmarked assessments of pupil performance, such PISA and TIMSS studies, show pupil attainment in Britain was flat lining during this period of supposed improvement:

> Even half the improvement that is entailed in the rise in GCSE performance would have lifted England from being an average performing OECD country to being comfortably the best in the world... The question,

therefore, is not whether there has been grade inflation, but how much.[59]

Grade inflation was particularly pronounced at the top end of GCSE exams, with a trebling in the number of pupils gaining 10 or more A*s between 2002 and 2012.[60] Coe's research has empirically proven what teachers and pupils have known for years – dramatically rising GCSE results were a Stakhanovite illusion. As Katharine Birbalsingh said when she addressed the Conservative Party conference in 2010: 'We have a situation where standards have been so dumbed down that even the children themselves know it. When I give them past exam papers to do from 1998, they groan and beg for one from 2006 because they know it will be easier.'[61]

What is more, the increasing popularity of vocational courses such as GNVQs and BTECs at key stage 4, greatly skewed the 'five good GCSEs' figures. These courses, known as 'equivalences', could count for up to four GCSEs. Without counting equivalencies, the amount of pupils gaining five good GCSEs in 2010 would not have been 75 per cent but 56 per cent, meaning only a four per cent rise since 2005. As these courses were generally accepted to be far less challenging than GCSEs, equivalencies became immensely popular amongst schools looking to boost their levels of achievement artificially .[62]

Grade inflation was more dramatic at A-level. Professor Coe's research from 2008 showed that sixth-fomers awarded a C grade in the late 1980s would now, at the same ability level, receive an A grade. Independently administered aptitude tests showed students were no brighter, but their average results had improved by two grades in most subjects. In mathematics, the improvement was three-and-a-half grades.[63] Tests conducted by independent academic bodies, such as the Royal Society of Chemistry and the London Mathematical Society, have repeatedly corroborated this verdict.

Many different forces contributed to grade inflation. Examinations were gradually becoming easier in a host of different ways: history A-levels saw a departure from the more challenging chronological overview papers; foreign language papers increasingly tolerated inaccuracies at GCSE; and science GCSE saw the introduction of multiple choice questions. More seriously, whistleblower examiners often spoke to the press about the pressure they were under to mark exams in a more lenient fashion. Many exam boards simply dropped their grade boundaries. For one GCSE English exam, the mark required for a C grade dropped from 65 per cent in 1997, to 46 per cent in 2002. Pupils also shied away from challenging A-levels and towards more undemanding choices. The number of pupils taking French dropped from 21,446 in 1997 to 12,486 in 2004 and there were similar drops in subjects such as German and maths. Meanwhile, the number of pupils taking media, film and TV studies rose from 8,967 to 20,997.[64] In 2004, the academic Colin MacCabe wrote a stinging open letter to the Education Secretary Charles Clarke in the *Observer*, reflecting on their one-time friendship as undergraduates at Cambridge University:

> If anybody had told me that in three decades you would be Minister of Education in a Labour government, I would have been delighted that our shared socialist goal of all being educated to the best of their ability was in the most capable of hands. Instead you are presiding over a potential catastrophe… Nobody who teaches A-level or has anything to do with teaching first-year university students has any doubt that A-levels have been dumbed down, to use the pejorative term, or democratised, to use a more positive description.[65]

Unfortunately, Labour ministers were intensely relaxed about this drop in standards, preferring to preserve the public misconception that a rise in pupil attainment was taking place.

The same phenomenon could be seen in vocational qualifications, long a weak point within British education. In 2011, the economist Alison Wolf wrote *Review of Vocational Qualifications,* also known as the Wolf Report. It argued that vocational qualifications such as BTECs and GNVQs, which were intended to serve as an alternative route for less academic pupils, were insufficiently rigorous to be respected by employers. Wolf wrote: 'The staple offer for between a quarter and a third of the post-16 cohort is a diet of low-level vocational qualifications, most of which have little to no labour market value.' She made a call for vocational qualifications characterised by 'quality' and 'rigour', instead of well-meaning calls for 'parity of esteem'. The *Wolf Report* contained a truth that has long been ignored by British educationists: a vocational education is not an alternative to an academic education but an extension of it. Post-16 vocational qualifications can only be useful if they are based upon a certain level of academic attainment, particularly in English and mathematics.[66]

David Blunkett arrived in office promising to raise standards. However, over the 13 succeeding years, Labour ministers tolerated, and even encouraged, a steady decline in the academic value of examinations. Genuine improvement was sacrificed for the expedience of perceived political progress.

The final battle of the Reading Wars

The 2000s saw the last major conflict in a war that had by then been raging for almost fifty years. When the National Literacy Strategy (NLS) was unveiled in 1998, *The Daily Telegraph* hailed it as a 'Return to Phonics', but such a hasty judgement was incorrect. The NLS was an essentially whole-word approach, with just a smattering of phonics. Campaigners had long argued that, for the effects of the phonics method to be beneficial, it must be taught 'first, fast and only'. So, they said, only once pupils have learnt the different letters and sounds in the alphabet, and are capable of blending simple words, are they able to move on to reading words and texts. However, the NLS promoted an essentially 'mixed methods' approach to teaching literacy, where phonics were to be taught gradually and alongside practice in whole-word recognition and graded readers. As the reading specialist Tom Burkard wrote: 'To give an example of the dilatory pace of the NLS, the spellings 'er' and 'or' are not taught until the second term of year 2. Synthetic phonics pupils will learn these before their first half-term break.'[67]

NLS guidance contained many of the old recommendations popular amongst 'look-say' adherents, such as using clues from context (rebranded as 'searchlights') to guess the meaning of a word. Confusingly, this approach was disingenuously dubbed 'analytic phonics', forcing phonics campaigners to rebrand their style of teaching 'synthetic' phonics. The NLS ultimately prioritised appeasing all camps in the reading wars over promoting successful teaching methods. Consequently, it had an unsystematic nature that may explain why the initial bump in national attainment quickly petered. By the mid-2000s, 20 per cent of pupils were leaving primary schools each year without having reached a satisfactory level of literacy.

The 'mixed methods' of the NLS were called into serious question in 1999, with events occurring north of the border amongst a small group of primary school children in Scotland. A controlled trial conducted by Professor Rhona Johnston and Dr Joyce Watson had produced some startling results. Johnston and Watson took 300 year one pupils in the deprived area of Clackmannanshire and divided them into groups taught using either synthetic phonics or a mixed methods approach similar to the NLS. After just 16 weeks of instruction (the time taken to complete the phonics course), the pupils in the phonics groups were seven months ahead of the comparison groups in reading age, and eight to nine months ahead in spelling. Unusually, the gap in performance between pupils from socially disadvantaged and advantaged backgrounds was negligible, and boys were outperforming girls. *The Scotsman* hailed the results as 'The Holy Grail in Education', and the *TES* wrote: 'A radical way of teaching children to read has easily outperformed the Government's preferred literacy strategy.'[68] In reality, there was nothing radical about the methods used. They were simply a rebooted version of the phonics method that had been spurned by the teaching profession from the 1960s onwards. The headteacher at Abercrombie Primary School, Joyce Ferguson, admitted:

> The scheme might have been contrary to my educational philosophy, but very quickly we were impressed by the results for the less able as well as the able. The children have developed remarkable listening and concentration skills as well as confidence and self-esteem.[69]

Critics argued that the early phonics advantage in Clackmannanshire would be 'washed out' as the alternative methods were given time. The Education Department did not pay much attention to the Clackmannanshire results, and calls to stipulate phonics in the NLS went unheeded.

So, the trial was followed up in 2005 to see how the two different groups had fared. Far from being 'washed out', the early advantage of the phonics pupils had compounded over the six years. By the time they were at the end of year 7, pupils who had been given 16 weeks of phonics instruction in their first year of school were three years and six months ahead of their chronological age in word reading, one year and nine months ahead in spelling, and three-and-a-half months ahead in reading comprehension.[70] Such results were staggering, and the superiority of phonics, which had repeatedly been ignored from the formation of the national curriculum onwards, was now too clear to be disregarded. In 2005, the primary specialist Jonathan Rose criticised the 'mixed methods' employed by the NLS, and promoted synthetic phonics 'first and fast'. Ruth Kelly took note of Rose's suggestion and became the first Education Secretary to recommend explicitly the phonics method for all primary schools.

In the years that followed, public awareness of this seemingly arcane area of pedagogy grew, with national newspapers dedicating news stories, columns and features to the subject. 'Rejoice, rejoice,' wrote Minette Marrin in *The Sunday Times* in June 2005, heralding a major victory 'in the long war against institutionalised prejudice'. Marrin singled out for praise Ruth Miskin, a primary school head who for years had been achieving startling results at Kobi Nasrul school in Hackney to the wilful ignorance of the education establishment.[71] In 2007 Miskin featured in 'Last Chance Kids' on Channel 4, a programme described by Minette Marrin as 'one of the few documentaries that have made me cry'.[72] Miskin developed her phonics lessons into commercial teaching schemes which began to filter into primary schools over the following years, as did fellow phonics advocates Sue Lloyd and Irina Tyk.

However, the convincing victory in Clackmannanshire did not bring an end to the battle. The *TES* was full of articles and letters complaining of this new push for phonics, with headlines such as 'Phonics myopia is poor prescription' and 'Don't buy this phonics snake oil'.[73] In spite of its empirical success, many within the teaching profession still believed phonics to be unforgivably teacher-led, and even 'right-wing'. Once again, entrenched orthodoxies were trumping objective evidence.

The centre cannot hold

The centralised direction at the Education Department

that began under David Blunkett reached a new level of hyperactivity from 2007 onwards under the reign of Ed Balls. New Labour education secretaries displayed an almost comical conviction that the brute force of increased funding could engineer any number of changes, with millions of pounds emanating from Whitehall targeting areas as diverse as bullying, emotional intelligence, increased IT provision, careers advice, healthy eating and staff training for interactive whiteboards. Much of this was due to the ever-expanding reach of the primary and secondary National Strategies, which saw central government directing myriad features of school life, from lesson planning to provision for 'gifted and talented' pupils. Notoriously, nearly £1 billion was spent on school initiatives to reduce truancy over a period during which truancy actually rose.[74]

In this environment of impetuous legislation and spending, schools were left floundering but the education establishment enjoyed a significant boom: at one point, the head of the QCA had a salary of £328,000.[75] By 2008, the 11 largest education quangos had a combined annual budget of £1.2 billion, with many enjoying annual budget increases of between 10 to 15 per cent.[76] These windfalls meant that progressive educationists, to whom implementation of these initiatives inevitably passed, enjoyed a greatly enhanced influence. Tony Blair had promised Britain a 'world-class education system', but his government entrusted the delivery of this promise to people signed up to the very ideologies that had made Britain's schools 'bog standard' in the first place.

Throughout the 13 years of New Labour, annual government expenditure on education reached £89 billion, almost doubling in real terms from 1997 and coming to constitute 6.2 per cent of Britain's total GDP.[77] The Education Department was twice overhauled and renamed, first as the Department for Education and Skills, then as the Department for Children, Schools and

Families (DCSF). It was noted that the word 'education' no longer appeared in the departmental title and Andrew Adonis dubbed it the 'Department for Curtains and Soft Furnishings'.[78] A House of Lords committee report, entitled *The Cumulative Impact of Statutory Instruments on Schools*, recorded that, in 2006-7, the Education Department and its agencies produced over 760 documents for schools, more than two per day not discounting holidays, with no apparent concern for how frenzied teachers might keep up.[79] All the while, there was no real improvement in pupil attainment. The whole education profession appeared to be peddling very fast in a very low gear.

In 2010, New Labour's educational campaign came to an end. Few were willing to label it a success. An early bump in primary school literacy and numeracy levels had petered out, and the public were distrustful (with good reason) of the gains made at GCSE and A-level. There were a few reasons to be cheerful: the academies programme had produced some exceptional success stories; the 'Building Schools for the Future' programme had given many schools a much needed sense of renewal; and increased pay and the Teach First programme were slowly transforming the prestige of the profession. However, the general landscape of state education had not been transformed.

The extent of New Labour's underperformance in education has more recently been laid bare by the OECD's international rankings for literacy, numeracy and science. These results show that Britain, despite being the world's sixth largest economy, is currently placed 26th in the world for maths, 23rd for reading and 21st for science.[80] More shocking than these rankings, but less commented upon, was a finding contained in the OECD's 2013 adult skills survey which showed England/N. Ireland to be the only country in the developed world where literacy and numeracy levels amongst 16-24-year-olds are no higher than amongst 55-65-year-olds.[81] So much for David

Miliband's promise in 2004 that children of the Blair years would be 'the best educated generation in our nation's history'.[82] In the wake of such underachievement, New Labour education reforms are now mocked by their own Panglossian slogans: 'excellence in cities', 'fresh start', 'building brighter futures', 'every child a reader', 'achievement for all' and so on.

Such findings cannot be disentangled from the education establishment's longstanding attachment to progressive education. For decades, these ideas have dictated how our teachers teach and how our schools are run. In 1997, there was an early promise that David Blunkett would overturn them, but rhetorical commitment soon foundered in the face of political reality. By 2000, government agencies were actively promoting these orthodoxies. Far from transforming Britain's schools, the government's indiscriminate approach to reform poured billions of pounds into propping up the very ideas that had already been causing schools to fail.

PART II

PEDAGOGY

6

The Child-centred Orthodoxy

Children learn best when they are having fun. Lessons should be made relevant to the interests of the child. A child will never learn something if forced to do so. Learning by doing is better than learning by hearing or seeing. Such commonplaces can still be heard repeated in university seminars and teacher training days across the country, and at their heart lies the pervasive creed of child-centred teaching.

The premise of child-centred teaching is that learning is more likely to occur if a pupil finds something out for himself or herself. Perhaps the most oft-repeated quotation within education is the proverb attributed to Confucius: 'I hear and I forget. I see and I remember. I do and I understand.' This principle is held as an article of faith within the education establishment, where an aversion to 'teacher talk', and a reverence for 'independent learning' is a longstanding orthodoxy. When I trained to be a teacher, one tutor told me never to exceed the 'five-minute limit' of teacher-talk whilst conducting a lesson. With a spurious level of accuracy, another tutor told me that a pupil could only listen to a teacher for as many minutes as their year group, minus two. It remains accepted within many of today's schools that, to quote the 1967 Plowden Report: '"Finding out" has proved to be better for children than "being told"'.[1]

Despite the efforts of the present Chief Inspector Michael Wilshaw, schools still believe that they risk a poor inspection rating from Ofsted if they do not cherish the child-centred faith. Judging by the most recent Ofsted subject reports, they have good reason to do so. The report on Religious Education classified 'weak' lessons as those in which 'the teacher controlled the pace and nature of the work and scope for independent learning and exploration of ideas was limited'.[2] Similarly, the report on the teaching of mathematics criticised lessons in which 'pupils often spent a substantial part of such lessons listening to the teacher and, in secondary lessons, copying down worked examples'.[3] In the most recent Ofsted inspection handbooks, 'outstanding' teaching is axiomatic with independent learning. In 'outstanding' geography lessons:

> Pupils show exceptional independence; they are able to think for themselves and take the initiative in, for example, asking questions, carrying out their own investigations and working constructively with others.[4]

Similarly, in English lessons 'outstanding' achievement means:

> Pupils have learnt to be effective independent learners, able to think for themselves and to provide leadership, while also being sensitive to the needs of others.[5]

It is little wonder that under such guidance, today's teachers are led to believe the less teaching they do, the better they are.

This re-conceptualisation of children as drivers of their own learning implies that pupils will only learn if they make the autonomous decision to do so. Any learning achieved through the gently coercive furniture of formal school life (tests, homework, practice exercises, memorisation) is somehow seen as 'superficial'. Instead, teachers are charged with imbuing pupils with an intrinsic motivation to learn: lessons should be made fun and enjoyable; subject content should be relevant to the existing interests of the child; and the child's enquiries should determine the course of a lesson. Although 'independent learning' is the most popular current moniker, child-centred ideas lie at the root of discovery learning, active learning, incidental learning, personalised learning, group work and project work. One psychologist has speculated that this diverse terminology exists because each time child-centred learning is discredited, it has to reinvent itself under a new guise.[6]

Child-centred education has made numerous attempts to bolster its claims with the evidence of modern science, in particular psychology, but its animating force has always been a romantic conviction in the self-educating powers of the child. This was recognised by Robert Skidelsky in 1969 when he wrote a sceptical account of Britain's independent progressive schools, focusing in particular on Summerhill. With an insight which remains just as true today, Skidelsky wrote: 'The important point is that whereas the progressives have to some extent been pioneers of a "scientific" approach to teaching and learning, science for them has always been subservient to metaphysics.'[7]

Generations of teachers have been encouraged to believe that freeing the child from the yoke of a teacher gives them the best opportunity to learn. They have taken on the language of the radical Californian psychologist Carl Rogers, who wrote in *Freedom to Learn*: 'As I began to trust students... I changed from being a teacher and evaluator, to being a facilitator of learning.'[8] This child-centred orthodoxy would be unproblematic were it effective, but it is not. There is now overwhelming evidence that it is both empirically unsuccessful and psychologically flawed, and such evidence deserves a greater awareness within the teaching profession.

John Hattie, Direct Instruction and Project Follow Through

Empirical research within education has long been hampered by the fact that almost any teaching method can be shown to *work*. According to Professor John Hattie from the University of Melbourne, teachers need to be more discerning when faced with 'evidence' for a successful teaching method. When faced with a new intervention, teachers and schools should not ask whether it works, but whether it has an *above average* impact. In applying such scrutiny, Hattie has become one of the world's most influential educationists, and certainly one of the most controversial. His 2009 book *Visible Learning* took on the gargantuan task of giving coherence to the blizzard of educational research blowing from university departments. He synthesised 800 meta-analyses of academic research in order to judge the impact of 138 different teaching methods and school interventions. *Visible Learning* is, if you will, a meta-meta-analysis that brings together some 50,000 individual research articles, involving an estimated 240 million students.

In order to compare different 'influences', Hattie assigns each influence an 'effect size', calculated by working out the average improvement in pupils' academic outcomes and dividing this by the spread or standard deviation. Hattie then ranked the effect sizes of 138 different 'influences', ranging from 'use of calculators' to 'pre-term birth weight'. The average effect size was around 0.4, so Hattie defined this as the 'hinge point': he suggests that only interventions with an effect size higher than 0.4 should be considered as effective, and those with an effect size over 0.6 highly effective. Published in 2009, the *TES* labelled Hattie's work the 'Holy Grail' of educational research, and his findings have proven controversial. They challenge many of the education establishment's most cherished ideas.

Hattie's book contains the following table, comparing

the teaching methods based on the teacher as an 'activator' with a high sense of agency over pupil learning, and those based on the constructivist view of the teacher as a 'facilitator'. The outcome is stark:

Teacher as Activator	***d***	**Teacher as Facilitator**	***d***
Reciprocal teaching	0.74	Simulations and gaming	0.32
Feedback	0.72	Inquiry-based teaching	0.31
Teaching students self-verbalisation	0.67	Smaller class sizes	0.21
Meta-cognition strategies	0.67	Individualised instruction	0.20
Direct Instruction	0.59	Problem-based learning	0.15
Mastery Learning	0.57	Different teaching for boys and girls	0.12
Goals – challenging	0.56	Web-based learning	0.09
Frequent/effects of testing	0.46	Whole language – reading	0.06
Behaviour organizers	0.41	Inductive teaching	0.06
Average activator	*0.60*	*Average facilitator*	*0.17*

Hattie is duly critical of the 'constructivist theory of teaching', which is the psychological school that underpins child-centred practice. This is not to say he promotes an alternative of pure didacticism: Hattie's proposed model of 'visible learning' sees the teacher is in charge of what happens in a lesson, but also attending keenly to the progress being made by the pupils, and adjusting their teaching accordingly. Nevertheless, he emphasises that far from being 'facilitators', teachers must see themselves as 'directors of learning':

> Constructivism too often is seen in terms of student-centered inquiry learning, problem-based learning and task-based learning, and common jargon words include "authentic", "discovery", and "intrinsically motivated learning"... These kinds of statements are almost directly opposite to the successful recipe for teaching and learning.

Later on in the book, Hattie confronts the dominance of empirically unsuccessful constructivist ideas in teacher training. He explains the effectiveness of Direct Instruction, a structured and unapologetically teacher-led method of teaching that originated in 1960s America. Despite being shunned by the American education establishment, Hattie's analysis shows that Direct Instruction has one of the largest effect sizes (0.59) for any teaching programme:

> Every year I present lectures to teacher education students and find that they are already indoctrinated with the mantra 'constructivism good, direct instruction bad'. When I show them the results of these meta-analyses, they are stunned, and they often become angry at having been given an agreed set of truths and commandments against direct instruction.

Little wonder then that in an interview in 2012, Hattie said that educationists spend most of their time discussing things that 'don't matter', and attacked teacher training as 'the most bankrupt institution I know'.[9]

When one looks a little deeper at Hattie's ranking of effect sizes, the contradiction of the dominant ideas of child-centred teaching is remarkable. Take for example the reading wars, perhaps the bloodiest of all pedagogical disputes over the past century. Phonics instruction, as measured in 14 meta-analyses covering 425 individual studies, has an effect size of 0.6. On the other hand, whole language teaching, which for decades was exclusively promoted in teacher training, has an effect size of 0.06 as measured in 64 individual studies. Some meta-analyses even showed that when whole language programmes are taught with no supplementary phonics, they can result in a negative effect size – actively making young readers worse.

Repetitive practice in subjects such as mathematics and languages to achieve fluency or 'automaticity' has long been disdained by progressive educators as 'drill and kill'. Yet Hattie shows it has an effect size of 0.71. Similarly, 'worked examples' which tend to be discouraged in mathematics education as passive and superficial, have an effect size of 0.57. A high quality of teacher clarity, as defined by teacher organisation, explanation, examples and guided practice, has one of the largest effect sizes at 0.75. Yet it is an aspect of the job that is often ignored in teacher training for fear of encouraging didacticism. Direct Instruction, the most teacher led of all methodologies studied, scored a 0.59 rating. In comparison, studies in 'student control over learning' scored just 0.04 – barely more effective than not being taught at all.[10]

Hattie is not the first person to spot the positive results gained by Direct Instruction, a teaching programme that began with Siegfried Engelmann at the University of Illinois in 1964. As a former advertising executive, Englemann was an outsider to the educational 'thoughtworld' in America, so he avoided the pervasive influence of Dewey and Piaget. Instead, he developed a series of highly structured and scripted lessons, each of which followed the same seven stage structure: explain learning intentions; explain success criteria; build engagement; present the lesson; guided practice; closure; independent practice. Although Direct Instruction has since spread to other areas, Engelmann's first courses were accelerated reading and numeracy programmes for struggling or disadvantaged pupils.

Direct Instruction stood in stark contradiction to the dominant modes of teaching within American schools, and shortly after it was developed, Engelmann's programme was offered a unique opportunity to prove its worth. Launched as part of President Johnson's War on Poverty, Project Follow Through was, and remains, the largest educational experiment in history: a controlled, longitudinal study that aimed to put the competing claims made by rival teaching methods finally to rest. It cost half a billion dollars, involved 10,000 low-income students in 180 different communities, and tested nine different teaching models. Two of the models (one being Direct Instruction) were teacher-led, one was bilingual teaching, and the other six were all to varying degrees progressive, child-centred programmes inspired by the likes of Piaget, Montessori and Dewey. Once taught, pupils were tested in reading, language, maths and spelling, and 'affective' measures such as pupil self esteem. These results were compared against each other, and against control schools in similar circumstances where the teaching had continued as normal.

Direct Instruction achieved first place in virtually every measured outcome. In terms of academic skills, Direct Instruction was the only method that did significantly better than its control groups, far outstripping all other methods. Five of the methods actually achieved lower results than their control groups, with the worst being the Piagetian 'Cognitive Curriculum' and the highly progressive Open Education Model. Direct Instruction even outperformed the child-centred models on their own turf of 'affective' measures, with pupils scoring higher self-reported levels of self-esteem.

One would have hoped that this proven success of Direct Instruction would have spurred a turn away from the ideology of progressive education in America, but it did not. Instead, the education establishment disputed the study, arguing that the control groups were not well chosen, the models had been wrongly implemented, and that Direct Instruction students still lacked the ability to think independently. Project Follow Through was written out of the history books of educational research by academics who found its conclusions too much of a challenge to their child-centred faith.[11]

The most expensive educational research project ever conducted and the most ambitious meta-analysis of current educational research have both demonstrated that teacher-led instruction is the most effective basis for teaching. This does not mean that the current dominance of child-centred ideas should be replaced by a new dominance of didacticism. However, it does mean that the disapproval of teacher-led pedagogy must end. Currently in Britain, teachers entering the profession are encouraged by their training, Ofsted, and senior staff to teach ineffectively, and discouraged from teaching in a way that would secure the best results for their pupils.

Metropolitan Achievement Test Percentile Score for Five Models

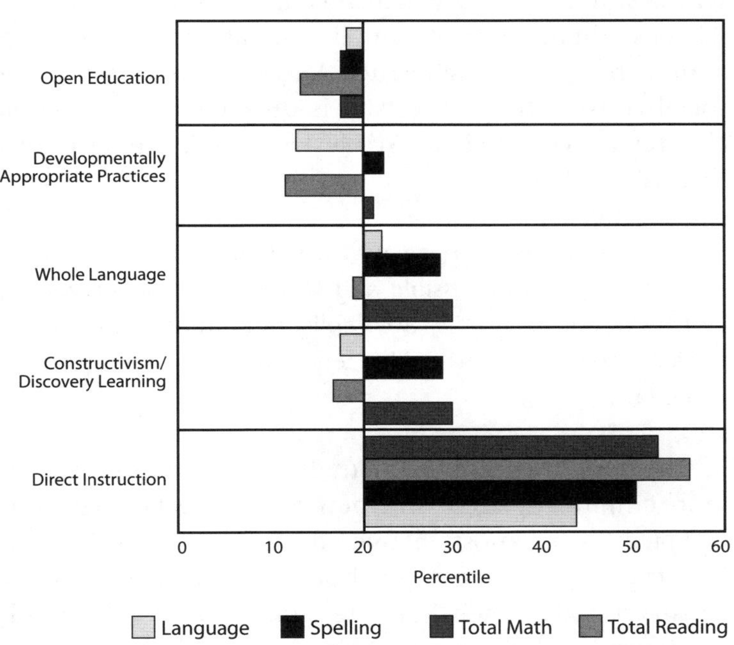

Source: Becker, et al, "The Direct Instruction Model", in *Encouraging Change in America's Schools* (New York: Academic Press, 1981)

The constructivist teaching fallacy

The dominance of child-centred teaching is upheld by the constructivist theory of teaching. Developed by the Swiss psychologist Jean Piaget, constructivism states that humans learn new information by habilitating it with their already existing knowledge. From this, a constructivist theory of teaching emerged which states that such a process works best when pupils drive their own learning. An influential variant of constructivism has been 'social-constructivism', developed by the Russian psychologist Jean Vygotsky, which suggests that learning should be mediated through discussion and interaction with one's peers.

As a trainee teacher, I was encouraged to read the widely used text book *Learning to Teach in the Secondary School.* It introduces a chapter on 'Ways Pupils Learn' with a summary of constructivism, which concludes that Piaget's 'theory implied an investigative, experimental approach to learning'. Once Piaget is dealt with, the social-constructivist Vygotsky is duly covered. A whole chapter is dedicated to 'Active Learning', which quotes Vygotsky's claim that:

> Practical experience also shows that direct teaching of concepts is impossible and fruitless. A teacher who tries to do this usually accomplishes nothing but empty verbalization, a parrot-like repetition of words by the child...[12]

The book includes, incidentally, no chapter on the far more empirically successful method of 'Direct Instruction'.

Piaget was most active during the 1960s, and Vygotsky was a Soviet psychologist who died in 1934. Unsurprisingly, their theories have been repeatedly challenged and superseded since. So why does a textbook published in 2009 cling to two such outmoded and contested psychological theories? The answer can be provided by the book itself, which declares that Piaget and Vygotsky have 'common denominators as a child-centred approach'. Within teacher training, child psychology is less an academic pursuit than a convenient ancillary for progressive pedagogical orthodoxies. During my training, the pressure to conform to these orthodoxies was profound: my lesson observations were judged according to the level of 'active learning' that took place; and the essays questions I was set were essentially catechisms, with grades assigned according to one's willingness to enter child-centred fold.

Three educational psychologists in a recent joint paper concluded that the constructivist theory of teaching is both 'widespread and incorrect'. They argue that whilst constructivism is a generally accepted theory of learning, it is not a valid theory of teaching. The way in which educationists have latched onto constructivism as evidence that students must 'construct' their own knowledge with minimal guidance from a teacher is entirely erroneous. One psychologist has dubbed this the 'constructivist teaching fallacy'. Much of this relates to the commonly made distinction between 'active' and 'passive' learning. It is commonly argued within education that, for example, reading through *Of Mice and Men* in an English lesson and having a teacher-led discussion of its content is 'passive', as the pupils will be inactive and most probably bored. Far better, a class should engage in 'active' learning, with tasks such as dressing up and performing scenes from the novel. Such arguments rely on a simplistic view of 'active learning' requiring behavioural or physical activity. However, contemporary cognitive science has shown that mental activity is the royal road to learning, as the aforementioned paper argues:

> In fact, the type of active cognitive processing that students need to engage in to 'construct' knowledge can happen through reading a book, listening to a lecture, watching a teacher conduct an experiment while simultaneously describing what he or she is doing, etc. Learning requires the construction of knowledge. Withholding information from students does not facilitate the construction of knowledge.[13]

Daniel Willingham, a cognitive scientist from the University of Virginia, is perceptive on this point. In his invaluable guide for teachers, *Why Don't Students Like School?*, he writes that our minds are programmed to remember information that we think about, especially on more than one occasion. Based upon this, Willingham has devised a cognitive principle to guide teaching: 'memory is the residue of thought'. Though this may seem like a truism, it contradicts the implicit assumption behind much child-centred practice, which works from the premise that memory is the residue of play, activity, experience or discovery. If we really want our pupils to learn, lessons should aspire not to be fun or active, but to be interesting.

Child-centred activities can be effective when they reliably result in a particular and powerful thought process, but this is rarely the case. Willingham offers the example of an American history lesson about the Underground Railroad (the name given to the routes used by American slaves escaping the Deep South for the free states in the north) in which pupils baked biscuits according to the recipe used by the slaves. Such a lesson would be promoted by child-centred educators as an engaging and memorable way to learn about a difficult historical topic, but Willingham is not so sure. He writes: '…students probably thought for forty seconds about the relationship of biscuits to the Underground Railroad, and for forty minutes about measuring flour, mixing shortening, and so on'. To return to the previous example, getting pupils to dress up as characters from *Of Mice and Men* and act out scenes may encourage pupils to think about period dress and their own acting skills, but not necessarily about the content of the novel. As such, child-centred activities frequently serve as a distraction, drawing the pupils' cognitive processing away from the subject in hand and leading to a shallower grasp of the subject.

Cognitive science is now demonstrating that many methods that have been cast aside by child-centred educators are in fact valuable parts of the teacher's arsenal. For example, repeated practice of procedures (such as times-tables in mathematics or verb endings in French) is an important way of achieving what cognitive scientists term 'automaticity'. It has long been argued that exercises such as practising verb endings in French are boring and inhibit further learning, but an understanding of cognitive science shows that the opposite is the case. Repeated practice renders the simple task of verb conjugation automatic and can speed up a pupils' progress towards more complex forms of communication. The cognitive scientist Daniel Willingham observes that 'drilling has been given a bad name' but adds: 'it is virtually impossible to become proficient at a mental task without extended practice.'[14] Likewise, testing has for decades been disdained as a cruel measuring instrument inflicted upon unwilling pupils by insensitive teachers. However, the psychologist Robert Bjork has demonstrated that the process of retrieving a memory can reinforce its place in one's mind and increase its longevity. Used correctly, testing can be in itself an effective learning activity.[15]

This is not to say that pupil-led activities have no place in the classroom. Used judiciously, they can be a useful means of building engagement, avoiding monotony and applying knowledge already learnt. What they are *not* is a superior means of acquiring initial knowledge. As Hattie has written, the entire premise of discovery learning is 'flawed and incorrect'.[16] For a pupil uninitiated in subject content, the guidance and instruction of a teacher is indispensible. Granting pupils independence may seem enlightened, but it is too much to expect every one of our pupils to be their own Galileo, their own Newton and their own Darwin. As implemented in most classrooms, discovery learning becomes failing-to-make-a-discovery learning.

The Lazy Teachers' Handbook

It is often argued that, despite the talk of child-centred practice, if you spend time in one of today's schools you are unlikely to witness repeated examples of well-orchestrated independent learning (unless, perhaps, if Ofsted are visiting). This is true: what you are likely to see is even worse. The most destructive effect of child-centred education's orthodoxy is the veneer of legitimacy given to slack, ineffective teaching. Endemic within today's schools are aimless 'projects' that lasts for weeks; 'group work' lessons where pupils talk off topic to their friends; computer research lessons where pupils idly surf the internet; and endless purposeless poster making. In each case, the fact that pupils are 'learning independently' serves as a convenient justification for teachers who are essentially not doing their job. This is an unsurprising outcome of the child-centred philosophy. If the instruction of the teacher is deemed inferior to the discovery of the pupil, there is little wonder that teachers are tempted to renege on their responsibility to ensure that learning occurs. Such a view was clearly expressed in the 1992 'Three Wise Men' report, which criticised the dominance of child-centred methods in primary schools:

> The ideas and practices connoted by words like 'progressive' and 'informal' had a profound impact in certain schools and LEAs. Elsewhere they were either ignored, or – most damagingly in our view – adopted as so much rhetoric to sustain practice which in visual terms might look attractive and busy but which lacked any serious educational rationale... The real problem was not so much radical transformation as mediocrity.[17]

Nowhere have I seen this development better demonstrated than in the popular teaching guide *The Lazy Teacher's Handbook: How Your Students Learn More When You Teach Less* (2010). The book was published by an influential educational consultancy and endorsed by Mick Waters, the architect of the 2007 national curriculum. It proposes that by neglecting to take an active role in their lessons, teachers can improve the education that their pupils receive. The guide suggests an array of different 'lazy' lessons, which include: inviting pupils to teach the lesson; turning the content of previous lessons into TV shows; pondering nonsense questions to improve 'thinking skills'; and making PowerPoint presentations. As the handbook says: 'The use of technology in the classroom is a gift for the Lazy Teacher'. Quite.

What is so alarming about this book is not that it depicts a child-centred approach as 'lazy', but that it genuinely believes such methods to be effective. As the author claims in the introduction: 'The combination of independent learners and lazy teachers is *the* outstanding combination that every school should be striving for... It's Ofsted friendly too, especially in light of the fact that nearly every initiative coming from central government at the moment seems to revolve around individualised, personalised and independent learning.'[18]

When a teacher grants pupils responsibility for their own learning, they also grant them responsibility for their own failure. In few areas are the baleful effects of this clearer than in learning to read in primary school. Those pupils who are not able to achieve literacy through the child-centred methods used by many primary schools, or who do not receive the additional support at home, are judged to have Special Educational Needs (SEN). Thus, what is in fact the outcome of poor teaching, is instead pathologised as the 'condition' of the pupil. How else has the UK arrived at a situation where 21 per cent of all UK pupils are diagnosed with having SEN – five times the EU average?[19] Many have observed that if a pupil cannot read in South Korea (where eight per cent of 15 year olds are poor readers) it is concluded that they have been taught poorly, whereas if a pupil cannot read in the UK (where 17 per cent of 15 year olds are poor readers) it is concluded that they have Special Educational Needs.

Done well, child-centred teaching requires superhuman reserves of energy and time from the teacher, and still may only just approximate the successes of more formal methods. Done poorly (as it almost inevitably is) child-centred teaching results in hours of directionless activities, wasted time, confusion and tedium. However, within modern education, formal methods of teaching are invariably assumed to be boring and passive. There is no reason why this should be the case. When delivering a lesson with passion and careful planning, a teacher is the single most effective presence in the classroom for encouraging pupils to think and learn about a topic. This was a truth not lost on the philosopher Michael Oakshott, who understood that the defining feature of any classroom, and what makes a school a school, was the presence of a teacher:

> To teach is to bring about that, somehow, something of worth intended by a teacher is learned, understood, and remembered by a learner. Thus, teaching is a variegated activity which may include hinting, suggesting, urging, coaxing, encouraging, guiding, pointing out, conversing, instructing, informing, narrating, lecturing, demonstrating, exercising, testing, examining, criticizing, correcting, tutoring, drilling and so on – everything, indeed, which does not belie the engagement to impart an understanding.[20]

The assumptions of child-centred education are for many at variance with common sense, but they are also contradicted by cognitive science. The overriding message from experts such as Hattie and Willingham is that learning is and should be difficult, and therefore requires the guidance of teachers, the diligence of repeated practice and sustained effort in order to be achieved. Whilst humans are naturally curious, they avoid thinking unless the cognitive conditions are favourable, and it is the job of teacher to make them so. The romantic conviction that a child should self-educate is doomed to fail as all children have to struggle to succeed. As the cognitive scientist Steven Pinker has written, it is evolutionarily illogical to expect humans to acquire knowledge naturalistically, when it is the historically contingent creation of civilisation. Pinker gives the example of mathematics:

> ...constructivism has merit when it comes to the intuitions of small numbers and simple arithmetic that arise naturally in all children. But it ignores the difference between our factory-installed equipment and the accessories that civilisation bolts on afterward. Setting our mental modules to work on material they were not designed for is *hard*.

Bitter roots bring sweet fruits

Hard work is not a fashionable concept in today's schools. The expectation is that all learning can be made fun and easy, but this only leads to dumbed down lessons and pupil underachievement. Such an idea may be at odds with the sympathies of many Western-liberals, but children require the guidance, the structure and even the coercion of an authoritative teacher.

Such a process is clear in the memoirs of renowned historian Tony Judt, written just before his death in 2010. Judt was from a modest background – his parents ran a hairdresser in South London – but his scholarship to a Direct Grant school in Battersea set him on course for a brilliant academic career. In *The Memory Chalet,* Judt describes his favourite teacher, Paul Craddock, who taught German. Known as 'Joe', he was the short-tempered survivor of some unspecified wartime experience, but was nonetheless a 'deeply human person':

> In just two years of intensive German study, I achieved a high level of linguistic competence and confidence. There was nothing mysterious about Joe's teaching methods. We learned by spending hours every day on grammar, vocabulary, and style, in the classroom and at home. There were daily tests of memory, reasoning, and comprehension. Mistakes were ruthlessly punished: to get less than eighteen out of twenty on vocabulary tests was to be 'Gormless!' Imperfect grasp of a complicated literary text marked you 'Dim as a Toc-H lamp!' (a World War II reference that still meant something – just – to a cohort of teenagers born around 1948). To submit anything short of perfect homework was to doom yourself to a roaring tirade from a wildly gyrating head of angry grey hair, before meekly accepting hours of detention and additional grammatical exercises... By halfway through my second year of German, Joe had us translating with consummate ease and real pleasure from Kafka's *Die Verwandlung*.

There could be no better illustration of the dictum that 'the roots of education are bitter, but the fruits are sweet'. Judt remarked that 'Joe would be impossible today'.[21] He was correct, and the absence of such rigorous teaching from the state sector is much to the detriment of Britain's schoolchildren. So long as schools continue to hold onto the scientifically unfounded and empirically unproven conviction that learning is best when independent of teacher instruction, pupils will continue to fall short of their potential.

7

Empty Vessels and the Neglect of Knowledge

During my time as a trainee teacher, I visited the school in which I was due to spend my first year teaching. With the summer holidays approaching, the Deputy Head asked me how I planned to spend the break. I replied that I intended to bone up on my historical knowledge. The Deputy Head looked at me askance and said: 'History is a skills-based curriculum. You should really be able to teach it without knowing anything at all.'

It was my first exposure to, in a rather extreme form, the widespread aversion within British schools to the teaching of knowledge. The perception of a school's mission as the transfer of knowledge is deeply mistrusted by today's profession. Such a standpoint is seen as unforgivably old-fashioned and draws comparisons with Thomas Gradgrind in Charles Dickens's *Hard Times*. Dickens describes the classroom of (the less imaginatively named) teacher Mr M'Choakumchild in an industrial town, in which pupils were 'arranged in order, ready to have imperial gallons of facts poured into them until they were full to the brim.' The analogy of knowledge-based teaching with filling a receptacle is a favourite of the progressive educator, the most quoted example being the aphorism: 'Education is not the filling of a vessel, but the lighting of a fire.' Such thinking has entered the received wisdom of the modern teaching profession, where it is generally assumed that focusing lessons on 'mere knowledge' and 'rote learning' is poor practice, whilst developing greater powers, such as critical thinking, transferable skills or creativity is good practice.

With a few exceptions, subject knowledge tends to be ignored during teacher training courses in favour of the dismal science of pedagogy. Textbooks, which should store the academic content that is at the heart of good lessons, are synonymous with poor, unimaginative teaching. Woe betides the teacher who takes the textbooks out of the store cupboard during an Ofsted inspection. The 2011 TIMSS international survey suggested that this aversion to textbooks is an entirely English phenomenon: in Germany, 86 per cent of teachers surveyed reported using textbooks as the basis of science instruction for ten-year-olds; in Korea the figure was 99 per cent; and in Sweden the figure was 89 per cent. In England, with its enduring legacy of progressive education, the figure was ten per cent.

There have been many different arguments marshalled to defend the anti-knowledge position over the past century. Today, the most frequently cited is the '21st Century Skills' argument, which suggests that in a time of fast-moving technological change it is pointless to base a curriculum on a stable body of knowledge. Educationists, such as the highly influential Guy Claxton, often claim that instead of content, a modern school curriculum should be concerned with 'learnacy', or 'learning to learn' – as detailed in Claxton's own 'Building Learning Power' programme:

> The well-rehearsed economic argument says that knowledge is changing so fast that we cannot give young people what they will need to know, because we do not know what it will be. Instead we should be helping them to develop supple and nimble minds, so that they will be able to learn whatever they need to.[1]

Tom Bentley, one of Tony Blair's key advisers on education, would have agreed. He even suggested in a 1999 report entitled *The Creative Age* that academic knowledge is an impediment to creative thinking:

> Because of the premium on new ideas and flexibility, people who have built up detailed knowledge over time find themselves at a disadvantage if they do not know how to apply what they know in different ways.[2]

There is nothing peculiar to the twenty-first century about the rhetoric that lies behind 21st Century Skills. One hundred years ago, Dewey pondered what new skills would be needed for the twentieth century. In 1966, during the 'white heat' of Harold Wilson's technological revolution, a headteacher wrote in the comprehensive school journal *Forum* that: 'the subject-based curriculum is clearly inadequate in view of the knowledge explosion... The idea that our schools should remain content with equipping children with a body of knowledge is absurd and frightening.'[3] Such a view is now mainstream within the profession.

The adoration of skills and the embargo on knowledge reached its apogee in 2007 when the by-now named Department for Education and Skills developed its skills-based national curriculum (see Chapter 5). The attempts by the current Secretary of State Michael Gove to reform this document have proven controversial, but a reorientation of schools towards the teaching of knowledge is keenly needed. Daisy Christodoulou has made this case eloquently in her recent book *Seven Myths About Education,* which convincingly disassembles the pseudo-science and faulty logic that underpins the proscription against teaching knowledge in schools:

> It is not simply a matter of saying that we have got a few bits of obscure theory wrong... What we are looking at here is something far worse. The fundamental ideas of our education system are flawed.[4]

Knowledge and memory

The virtues of teaching knowledge can be promoted on two fronts – one scientific, the other idealistic. Firstly, cognitive science has demonstrated that 'higher order thinking', so prized by today's schools, is not an alternative to knowledge but entirely dependent upon it. Secondly, the unwillingness to place academic knowledge at the core of the school curriculum has led to a palpable dumbing down in subject content. Though noble in intent, the ideals of progressive education consign many of its recipients to a state of ignorance, excluded from partaking in the conversation of mankind.

Complete the sum 43 × 6. If you have a rough idea of your times-tables, you will be able to do so with relative ease. Your mental processing will be something along the lines of calculating 40 × 6 equals 240, then calculating 3 × 6 equals 18. You may then calculate 18 + 240, and arrive at the final answer of 258. For cognitive scientists, such a mental calculation neatly demonstrates the interplay between 'working memory' and 'long-term memory' that characterises human thought. Working memory, which manipulates new information, is very limited in space: as a general rule it can hold between five and seven new pieces of information before experiencing 'cognitive overload'. Therefore, in order to achieve complex cognition on any given subject, a sufficiently large amount of subject knowledge needs to be established in your long-term memory to free space for your working memory. In the case of mathematics, your ability to carry out a simple double-digit calculation depends on the fluency of your times-tables. If single digit multiplications are stored in your long-term memory and occur to you as automatic mental reflexes, then you will have sufficient space in your working memory to calculate more complex sums. For this reason, our ability to think about new problems invariably relies upon the furniture of our long-term memory, known in cognitive psychology science as 'schema'.

For this reason, a proficiency at simple mental arithmetic still lies at the heart of mathematicians' ability to consider complex problems. This was demonstrated by the famous story of the Hardy-Ramanujan number. Srinivasa Ramanujan was a gifted mathematician, and the first Indian to be elected as Fellow of Trinity College, Cambridge in 1918. Ramanujan died aged 32. His colleague, the British mathematician G. H. Hardy, recalled visiting him in hospital:

> I remember once going to see him when he was ill at Putney. I had ridden in taxi cab number 1729 and remarked that the number seemed to me rather a dull one, and that I hoped it was not an unfavourable omen. 'No,' he replied, 'it is a very interesting number; it is the smallest number expressible as the sum of two cubes in two different ways.'[5]

The routine mental mathematics stored in Ramanujan's long-term memory allowed him to perform complex mental calculations (in this case $1729 = 1^3 + 12^3 = 9^3 + 10^3$), and gave him the mental dexterity to see patterns where others did not.

This relationship between working memory and long-term memory, illustrated through mathematics, applies to all areas of human cognition. It is widely agreed amongst cognitive scientists that thinking and learning are 'domain specific', so one's ability to think is always contingent upon one's previous knowledge of the given subject, or 'domain'. Just because a doctor is proficient at evaluating causation when it comes to early onset Alzheimer's, it does not follow that he or she will be proficient at evaluating the causes of the French Revolution. This is why the idea of 'transferable skills', popular amongst modern educationists, is so misguided: skills such as 'resourcefulness' or 'problem solving' are overwhelmingly domain specific. A legendary demonstration of this came from the Dutch psychologist Adriaan de Groot during the 1940s. De Groot recorded the ability of chess players to memorise a chess position from an actual game, with twenty-five pieces left on the board, in the space of five to ten seconds. Grand masters could recall the position with 100 per cent accuracy, masters with 90 per cent accuracy, and novices could only place five to six of the pieces accurately. De Groot then repeated the experiment, but instead of giving the participants positions from an actual game, he placed the twenty-five pieces randomly across the board. When retested, grand masters, masters, class A players, and class B players all performed the same as novices, placing only five to six of the pieces correctly.

The experiment demonstrated that what are often thought to be discreet mental skills, in this case recall, are bound to prior knowledge. It is estimated that grand masters store around 50,000 chess positions in their long-term memory, so their ability to recall chess positions in de Groot's experiment was bound to their existing familiarity. Such results were replicated with similar studies in other 'domains', such as algebra, physics and medicine. The conclusion each time was that, when it comes to thinking, knowing stuff is vital. As Willingham has written:

> Data from the last thirty years lead to a conclusion that is not scientifically challengeable: thinking well requires knowing facts, and that's true not simply because you need something to think *about*. The very processes that teachers care about most – critical thinking processes such as reasoning and problem solving – are intimately intertwined with factual knowledge that is stored in long-term memory.

This may seem to be (as psychology is often accused of being) the academic extrapolation of common sense. However, it is a message that is wilfully overlooked in the world of education, which retains an idealistic hope that schools can bypass the, as it is so often characterised, joyless accumulation of knowledge.

Those who argue for more knowledge-acquisition in teaching are frequently accused of establishing 'false dichotomies'. As a result, many educationists present themselves as mediators in the debate, and argue that education is not a question of choosing knowledge *or* skills but combining knowledge *and* skills. To adopt such a position misses the point. Cognitive science does not teach us that we should focus on knowledge *over* skills, nor that we should focus on knowledge *and* skills, rather that we should focus on knowledge *then* skills. The teaching of any topic is essentially a question of process, and knowledge must come before complex cognition. A Harvard educationist is often quoted for his observation that:

> ...far from thinking coming after knowledge, knowledge comes on the coat-tails of thinking. As we think about and with the content that we are learning, we truly learn it... Therefore instead of knowledge-centred schools, we need thinking-centred schools.

Such a view is mainstream thought within education. However, it is hard to think of a statement more at variance with the conclusions of cognitive science. Perversely, the more we focus on inculcating thinking skills, the more we distract pupils from learning the knowledge that will actually allow them to think.

As a result, many of our contemporary teaching practices are ineffective because they are back-to-front. Some early literacy teachers still believe that through reading whole words and real books, pupils will develop their knowledge of letter sounds. It should be the other way around. Likewise, many teachers in early numeracy still falsely believe that by setting pupils real life maths problems, their sense of number and basic calculation will emerge. History teachers try to give pupils a sense of the past by encouraging them first to analyse historical sources, but do not realise that any source is impossible to understand without a pre-existing knowledge of the period. Similarly, much modern language teaching focuses on building vocabulary and grammatical awareness though communication, and good science teaching is thought to allow knowledge to emerge through experimentation. In both cases, a pupil's cognitive capacity would be greatly aided by having the order reversed. Learning by doing is an impoverished philosophy: learning then doing is the principle that should guide teachers.

This defence of knowledge should not be mistaken as a declaration that, in the words of Thomas Gradgrind from *Hard Times*: 'Facts alone are wanted in life. Plant nothing else, and root out everything else.' Critical thinking, reasoning and independent thought should still be the ultimate aims of school education. However, there needs to be greater appreciation that in order to achieve 'everything else', pupils require knowledge first. The 2007 national curriculum included an overlay of Personal Learning and Thinking Skills, which schools were encouraged to teach throughout the curriculum. Under the heading 'Independent enquirers', the guidance stated that schools must create young people who 'plan and carry out research', 'consider the influence of circumstances' and 'analyse and evaluate information'. All worthy aims, but entirely meaningless when not related to a specific domain. Most 11-year-old pupils will be able to analyse and evaluate what they ate for breakfast, but unless they have had a remarkable primary education, they will find it difficult to transfer this skill to analysing and evaluating, say, the Bretton Woods system of international finance.

In British schools, critical thinking is routinely attempted amongst pupils who have not built up sufficient knowledge to perform it adeptly. Consequently, what one so often sees in today's classrooms is an imitation of thinking as opposed to thinking itself. With well-constructed writing frames, teachers can encourage pupils to write 'analytical' statements, convincing themselves that if a conclusion contains the word 'because', evaluation is shown, or if a paragraph begins with the word 'whereas', a comparison has been made. Such a style of teaching is encouraged by examination assessment criteria that are overwhelmingly concerned with pupils demonstrating 'skills', and pay little heed to knowledge. As a result, teachers spend hours focusing upon the mechanics of demonstrating particular 'skills' in an answer, at the expense of learning content, and produce a style of teaching just as formulaic and boring as the oft-ridiculed 'rote-learning' of old.

More generally, the aversion to teaching knowledge in schools sets lessons on a clear trajectory towards dumbing downward. When 'thinking skills' are encouraged in the abstract, the content of what is being thought about is seen as immaterial. Subject content is perceived to be merely a vehicle for the pupils' cognitive development. Therefore, pupils are asked to complete generic activities to develop 'skills' for which teachers have to resort to the lowest common denominator of shared pupil knowledge: 'make a presentation about your friends'; 'organise a campaign against school uniform'; 'write a review of your favourite TV programme'. A typical such lesson was reported when a journalist visited a Birmingham school, where the curriculum was being delivered almost entirely through IT:

> The pupils were designing web pages, which meant writing something – typically about cars, pop stars or sport – and illustrating it with pictures downloaded from the internet... few had written more than a poorly spelt paragraph or two.

Such a scene is not untypical. This lack of concern over content is reflected in the English Language GCSE which aims to assess 'understanding and producing non-fiction texts'. The examination is often hampered by the pupils' inability to understand the content of the chosen text, which is assumed to be common knowledge by the author. To avoid such a fate, recent GCSE examinations from one examination board have invited pupils to analyse texts on Tinie Tempah, Michael Caine, Gordon Ramsay, Johnny Depp and Jamie Oliver.

Educators of all stripes believe that schools should produce pupils who are independent minded and take an active interest in the world. However, progressive educators are wrong to assume that pupils are able to become so without first mastering a solid basis of knowledge. To light the fire, you first have to fill the vessel.

Cultural Literacy

This principle was realised during the late 1970s by a Professor of English Literature at the University of Virginia called E. D. Hirsch. He was conducting research into the comprehension of texts amongst pupils from two nearby, but very different, institutions: the University of Virginia and Richmond Community College. Hirsch presented pupils from each establishment with two texts: one was a general passage on 'friendship', and the other a more domain-specific passage about the Generals Ulysses S. Grant and Robert E. Lee from a popular history of the American Civil War. The community college students were mostly African-American, and had been educated at local public schools. Hirsch's research showed that they tended to have the same reading ability as their wealthier peers when it came to the passage on friendship, but read the passage about the American Civil War far slower, and with a lower level of comprehension. These community college students were bright and literate – they had no trouble understanding vocabulary such as 'burdensome' and 'reassurance' – but their schooling had left them with insufficient knowledge of American history to make sense of the second text. Most of them did not even know who Grant and Lee were, despite the fact that Lee had surrendered to Grant only a few miles from where they were sitting, let alone understand the significance of Lee being from Tidewater Virginia, whilst Grant was the son of a tanner on the western frontier.

Hirsch was 'shocked into educational reform', as he came to believe that an aversion to teaching knowledge within American schools was causing educational failure, and actually fuelling social inequality. He formulated the concept of 'cultural literacy', and wrote a book of the same name in 1987. It struck a nerve with the American public and stayed on the *New York Times* bestseller list for 26 weeks. Hirsch argued that the greatest failing of American schools was their unwillingness to provide pupils with 'core knowledge', the assumed reference points that allows educated individuals to partake in a national conversation. In a recent book, Hirsch explained that, in any given issue of *The New York Times*, there will be around 2,700 occurrences of 'unexplained references' to events, people, ideas or institutions which it is assumed the reader should understand. Schools, Hirsch argues, should equip pupils with the cultural literacy to do so. Over the years Hirsch has devised a 'Core Knowledge' curriculum designed to do this, and despite much opposition it has spread to around 1,000 schools in the United States, many of which are charter schools.

In 1993, Massachusetts established a state-wide knowledge-based curriculum inspired by Hirsch and the state became a test bed for the Hirsch philosophy. Today, Massachusetts consistently outperforms all other American states in national test scores and has also narrowed the achievement gap between ethnic minority students and their more advantaged peers. According to the 2012 PISA test scores, America was ranked 17th in the world for reading, 23rd for mathematics, and 20th for science. Were Massachusetts its own country, it would be ranked 4th, 7th and 10th respectively. However, despite the clear success of Hirsch's Core Knowledge curriculum, he remains an outsider to the American education establishment. His suggestion that all pupils should be taught a prescribed core of knowledge leaves Hirsch, a liberal University Professor and Democrat, repeatedly dismissed as a scary right-winger by the teaching profession. The idealistic sentiments of educationists still stand in the way of them acknowledging the objective evidence of successful teaching.

Hirsch recognised that the African-American students at Richmond Community College had been left with a knowledge deficit that made them unable to engage in the national conversation. The ability to engage with intelligent debate is an outcome much neglected in schools today, which tend to be more concerned with a pupil's 'workplace skills', 'creativity', 'critical thinking' or 'self esteem'. However, engagement with the world around you is vital for leading a fulfilled life. Knowledge should be seen as a good in itself, and schools should foster a spirit of a disinterested curiosity in the world, irrespective of any material benefits or practical outcomes. When discussing the teaching of classics in 2003, the Labour Education Secretary Charles Clarke labelled the ideal of education for education's sake 'a bit dodgy', and declared the study of medieval history 'ornamental'. He was expressing a strong contemporary philistinism that crosses party lines, and judges all education according to its practical or vocational value. One of Blair's education advisers wrote in 1998:

> The most detailed formal knowledge is without value unless you can understand what it is for and what you can do with it. Conventional school-based learning,

> it seems, too often fails to mesh the knowledge of the curriculum with the contours of wider experience.

The conclusion that the great lives and events of history, profound achievements in literature, and the revelations of science and mathematics are 'without value' unless they can be given some direct, real-world application is bleak indeed.

There needs to be no further justification for the content of a knowledge-based curriculum than granting students the ability to participate in what Oakeshott dubbed 'the conversation of mankind'. People discussing a specialist subject, it is often remarked, sound as if they are communicating in a foreign language. This is the sensation gained when you hear Americans talk about a sport, as Hirsch demonstrates by writing the simple sentence, 'Jones sacrificed and knocked in a run'. To Americans, this is an everyday explanation of baseball tactics, but to a British listener it is meaningless. Now, imagine if every conversation, television programme or news article you encountered, which covered history, economics, literature, politics, world events or science, left you with the same sensation. Condemned by your un-ambitious schooling, the common reference points of the well informed would forever be a foreign country.

This argument is often said to be redundant in the age of the Internet. You may not understand everything in a newspaper article, it is argued, but you can always look it up. 'Why bother knowing something if you can just Google it?' has become a familiar refrain in education circles. A report from a union conference in 2012, included in Christodoulou's book, told the following story of a speech given by one of the delegates:

> [He] asked the delegates to find Mozart's birth date using their smartphones. The answer – 27 January, 1757 – was shouted from the floor in seconds... We are no longer

> in an age where a substantial 'fact bank' in our heads is required, he said. We need to equip our young people with skills; interpersonal skills, enquiry skills, the ability to innovate.

Such an argument does not stand up to scrutiny. Although a smartphone is more convenient than leafing through Denis Diderot's encyclopaedia, reference books have existed for 250 years and they have not yet made the value of human knowledge redundant. With little knowledge stored in your long-term memory, the repeated need to refer to the Internet to work out the meaning of texts would be extremely tiresome, and assimilating so much new information would significantly burden your working memory. To return to the example of Mozart, consider the following extract about him from a popular history of music:

> For all his grumbles, Franz Joseph Haydn lived and died a loyal servant of his patron. Wolfgang Amadeus Mozart famously did not. His emancipation from Colloredo, deemed by some to be nothing less than 'a declaration of war between the new bourgeois world and the old regime of artistic production', demonstrated emphatically that he did not find the bars on his cage to be gilded in the slightest.

Some knowledge of eighteenth century European history is vital for understanding this passage. A Google search will give you some idea who Haydn was, who Colloredo was, and what is meant by 'bourgeois'. However, no amount of Internet searching will allow you to understand the implication, in the allusion to the *ancien régime*, that Mozart's career somehow foretold the French Revolution (which occurred two years before his death). A 'fact bank', however hazy, proves eminently more useful than 'enquiry skills' for passing with pleasure through such a text.

It should be qualified that Hirsch's concept of Core Knowledge need not be interpreted in a rigid fashion. No school can aspire to give their pupils a universal, comprehensive coverage of the major disciplines, such that no reference will ever pass them by unnoticed. The constant pushing forth of the frontiers of human knowledge over the course of the twentieth century has made the canonical ideal of a classical curriculum, in its nineteenth century guise, untenable. During the nineteenth century, the biologist Thomas Henry Huxley was fond of defining an educated person as someone who knows 'something about everything, and everything about something'. During a period when around 5,000 new titles were published each year in Britain, this may have been a reasonable aspiration. Today, when around 150,000 new titles are published each year, such an aspiration is not so easy. Many knowledge denialists conclude that, in the face of such a 'knowledge explosion', we should dispense altogether with knowledge-centred curriculums. This view is misguided in the extreme: even though schools cannot teach pupils everything, they still must aspire to teach them something.

The benefits of this are clearly demonstrated in what Hirsch, amongst others, has described as the 'Matthew Effect'. The name comes from a passage in the New Testament, Matthew (25:29), which states 'for to all those who have, more will be given, and they will have an abundance; for from those who have nothing, even what they have will be taken away.' When it comes to an individual's knowledge accumulation through life, the rich become richer, and the poor become poorer. This has been demonstrated by cognitive psychologists in the area of vocabulary acquisition, as the more words that one knows at a young age, the more words one can come to learn through reading independently later in life. A text can generally be understood if 95 per cent of the language is familiar, and the remainder can be worked out through understanding the 'gist'. Therefore, vocabulary learnt directly in school empowers pupils later in life to learn more vocabulary indirectly as a reader, creating an exponential growth in reading ability.

The same is true in terms of knowledge. Skills are often referred to as 'transferable', but the transferable nature of knowledge is much underappreciated. A school should give pupils the multiple schemata of long-term memory, in which new knowledge can be habituated throughout the rest of their life. For example, if one has a general understanding of the British Industrial Revolution from school, one has a frame of reference for understanding current industrialisation in the developing world. If one studies *Hamlet* at school, one will have a greater confidence in appreciating *Macbeth* at the theatre. If one studies exponential functions in mathematics, one will stand a chance of understanding compound interest as an adult. Knowledge begets knowledge, and a 'lifelong learner', to use a phrase currently popular amongst educationists, cannot be created by a school that neglects to teach an essential basis of knowledge. This principle was understood by the celebrated Eton schoolmaster Arthur Christopher Benson. In his 1902 teaching guide, he wrote that school should give a child an 'intellectual life', such that their free time is not simply 'beguiled with billiards or bridge'. He wrote: 'My idea of an intellectual person is one whose mind is alive to ideas; who is interested in politics, religion, science, history, literature; who knows enough to want to know more…'[18]

The irrelevance of relevance

In education debates, the question of whether knowledge should be taught is closely followed by the question over what knowledge is taught. Particularly in the humanities, the selection of curriculum content is a much contested and politically charged process. In 2012, Gove encountered criticism for his history curriculum full of 'patriotic stocking fillers', whilst the 2007 Labour version was suffused with the language of political correctness: its history curriculum mentioned 'diversity' on 12 occasions but 'religion' only once. This is an enormous debate, and beyond the scope of this chapter. However, one misnomer that must be dispatched is the child-centred idea that topics should be chosen on account of their 'relevance' to pupils' lives. The former head of Ofsted, Christine Gilbert, wrote in 2006: 'Pupils are more likely to be engaged with the curriculum they are offered if they believe it is relevant and if they are given opportunities to take ownership of their learning.'[19]

This obsession with pupil 'relevance' is yet another under-challenged truism that bedevils British schools. It is commonly assumed that curriculum content should appeal, or be made to appeal, to the existing interests of the child. In English, pupils are often given literature with contemporary, adolescent themes at the expense of more established works, with titles such as *2die4, Blade* or *Wasted*. In Religious Education, the study of world faiths or religious texts is subordinated to contemporary issues and the exploration of pupils' personal feelings. In science, there has been a move towards an awareness of science in public debates, and in geography learning about the world is overlaid with contemporary themes such as 'shopping' and 'tourism'. In my own subject, history, a significant number of pupils still study a GCSE course entitled 'The American West' which was devised during the 1970s to appeal to pupils' love of cowboys and Indians films – demonstrating just how quickly 'relevance' can date.

Where academic content is retained, it is often delivered in a 'relevant' fashion that robs it of any of its original value. In such a spirit, I have witnessed Shakespeare translated into 'ghetto grammar', pupils designing a facebook page for Jesus of Nazareth, and the story of Henry VIII and his six wives re-enacted as an episode of Blind Date. Such an approach robs academic subjects of the majesty that makes them worthy of study in the first place. This is not to say the outside world should be absent from the classroom. Making a well-judged allusion, analogy or comparison with the present day is an important part of teaching, and can be of great interest for the pupils. However, the wholesale sacrifice of an academic subject at the shrine of contemporary relevance undermines its intrinsic interest.

These calls for 'relevance' in the curriculum are symptomatic of the transferral of authority from the knowledge of the adult to the interests of the pupil. However, if schools merely mirror what is already relevant to a pupil's life, then why do these institutions need to exist in the first place? It is precisely because schools introduce something that runs ahead of the immediate interests of a child, something that lies beyond their existing horizons, that schools are necessary. Once again, the romantic belief that the seed of education lies within every child and simply needs to be nurtured in order to flower lies at the root of this misconception. Kingsley Amis recognised this in 1969, when he wrote in the first *Black Paper*:

> A student, being (if anything) engaged in the acquiring of knowledge, is not in a position to decide which bits of knowledge it is best for him to acquire, or how his performance in the acquisition of knowledge can most properly be assessed, or who is qualified to help him in this activity... Who can understand the importance of Roman law, or anatomy, or calculus, if he has not mastered them?

Schools should foster an ethos that sees knowledge as a good in itself. Adults so often lament 'I wish I had seen the value of school when I was a child', but it is too much to expect a child to make judicious choices over the content of their own curriculum. Instead, the teacher should be the better angel of the child's nature, guiding the child through what is in its own best interest to learn. A good teacher, Oakshott suggests, encourages pupils to answer questions that it would not otherwise have occurred to them to ask. He writes that schooling, by definition, should move pupils away from their existing concerns:

> Thus, an educational engagement is at once a discipline and a release; and it is the one by virtue of being the other. It is a difficult engagement of learning by study in a continuous and exacting redirection of attention and refinement of understanding which calls for humility, patience and courage. Its reward is an emancipation from the mere 'fact of living', from the immediate contingencies of place and time of birth, from the tyranny of the moment and from the servitude of a merely current condition...[21]

Restoring knowledge

If the general public truly knew how far mainstream educational thought has moved from the premise that education is based upon the transfer of knowledge, they would be shocked. The fact that today's schools produce pupils who do not know a great deal is often blamed on troubled teens, neglectful parents and poor teachers. It is not sufficiently appreciated that the education establishment is complicit in this neglect of knowledge. This situation must change.

Progressive educators have defended their aversion to knowledge with pseudo-science, sociological attacks on 'elitism', and the supposedly unprecedented pace of technological change. However, at the root of these arguments remains a sentimental aversion to the idea that schools should be defined by anything so hierarchical as the transmission of knowledge from the teacher to the child.

Cognitive science has shown that this attitude leads to a wrongheaded approach to the learning process, as complex cognition is impossible without a solid grounding in factual knowledge. However, there remains a greater question at stake. Schools must rediscover the conviction that some knowledge about the world, be it scientific, artistic or historical, is an invaluable inheritance to pass on to any pupil, irrespective of their social background. Through pursuing a school curriculum that is unashamedly irrelevant, and pays little heed to a child's immediate concerns, an education based on knowledge encourages pupils to look beyond the temporal and geographical parochialism of their own existence and understand their life within the greater story of mankind's performances and capabilities. An education based on skills does not.

8

Discipline, Character and Moral Education

When I first decided to become a teacher in 2010, friends and family would often say 'you must be brave'. I found it remarkable that bravery had become a commonly acknowledged trait required to teach in Britain's schools, but such reactions did prove apt. Once I began teaching, I wrote an article about pupil behaviour for *Standpoint* magazine under the pen-name Matthew Hunter:

> Halfway through my first year as a history teacher at an inner-city comprehensive in England, I am reeling from the volley of abuse and misbehaviour that makes up my daily grind. I can be sure that at some point in my day I will be aggressively confronted, blithely disobeyed, and probably sworn at. Restless nights are common, and nervousness ongoing. Still, talking to my friends from teacher training, I feel I'm having a comparatively easy ride. I have not yet been physically assaulted, and so far I have avoided the much-feared mid-lesson breakdown.[1]

Today, it is seen as normal that popular books for the teaching profession should have such titles as *Getting the Buggers to Behave* or *I'm a Teacher, Get me Out of Here!* Poor behaviour in our state schools has long been a depressingly consistent feature of national life, commonly blamed on the social deprivation of the children who attend them. However, some inspiring schools, which are standing up to these low expectations by introducing 'zero tolerance' behaviour policies, are being rewarded with transformative improvements. Such schools demonstrate that the endemic discipline problems that have characterised state education since the 1970s are not inevitable. In reality, they are self-inflicted. Progressive education, which seeks to free pupils from the constraints of adult direction, has been more destructive in school behaviour and ethos than in any other area.

Statistics reveal that my experience of teaching was not unusual. A 2010 survey by the Teacher Support Network found that 80 per cent of teachers believed their ability to teach to be reduced by pupils' poor behaviour, and 92 per cent of teachers believed that behaviour had worsened over the course of their career. The proportion of teachers who reported being deliberately distracted or having their lessons disrupted by pupils on a daily basis over the previous year numbered 57 per cent. More seriously, in 2010 there were 44 teachers hospitalised due to pupil attacks.[2] Similar results were found in 2011 from a survey of the *Guardian* Teacher Network, where 40 per cent of the respondents reported having been bullied by pupils.[3]

One cannot underestimate the dysfunction that poor behaviour creates in a school. Teachers feel continually prevented from doing their job properly, as the fire-fighting of low-level disruption becomes an overriding concern. When teachers could be marking, lesson planning or providing extra-curricular activities, they instead spend hours every week breaking up fights, following up incidents, and engaging in 'behaviour conversations'. In classrooms where a large portion of each lesson is spent settling the class to the point where they are ready to learn, the opportunity costs are enormous. In an unfortunate paradox, those schools that do not stress the importance of good discipline find themselves having to worry about it far more than those that take a more robust approach.

Behaviour is perhaps the most commonly commented upon problem in British schools, but it is also the area where the most positive changes have recently been seen. Many schools, particularly in London, have taken a stand against poor behaviour and are blazing a trail of improvement that few others can ignore. It is now accepted that in failing schools, poor behaviour is almost always the greatest impediment to learning, and the first thing a failing school must solve in order to improve. The most celebrated demonstration of this transition came courtesy of Mossbourne Academy under the leadership of Michael Wilshaw, who was duly made Chief Inspector of schools in 2012 (see Chapter 5), but hundreds of other schools have made the same journey.

In 2007, Stanley Technical High School in South Norwood had been rated as 'failing' by Ofsted and had numerous reports of pupils in possession of weapons and drugs. In one report, a pupil found with a knife had simply been sent home for the day without even having the weapon confiscated. In 2006, only 24 per cent of the Stanley pupils were achieving five good GCSEs including English and maths. That year, the school was taken over by the Harris Federation, an academy chain that currently runs 27 schools in South London and is well known for its strict disciplinary model. Harris schools have a smart school uniform; escalating sanctions moving from subject detention to Saturday detention; permanent exclusion for more severe incidents; an 'inclusion unit' to support persistent misbehavers; a system dubbed 'Vivo Miles' to reward good behaviour; and a traditional house structure providing pastoral care. Once this model was introduced to Harris Academy South Norwood, the subsequent improvement was immense. In the space of three years, 60 per cent of pupils achieved five good GCSEs, and Ofsted graded the school 'outstanding', reporting that 'learning takes place in a calm and orderly way'. In 2012, 80 per cent of the pupils received five good GCSEs, placing Harris Academy in the top one per cent of schools nationwide for pupil progress. Parents are now so keen to send their children to the school, Harris Academy's catchment area has shrunk from 8 miles to 0.8 miles.[4]

The measures introduced at Harris Academy were not radical; they were simply the same structures with which good schools, in particular independent schools, have operated for generations. However, such structures have historically been absent from many state schools due to the legacy of progressive education, with its aversion to adult authority and its romantic faith in the innate goodness of the child. The result was the freewheeling, chaotic comprehensive of the 1970s (as detailed in Chapter 2), casting a long shadow over our state schools that still envelops many today.

The effect that a strict approach to school behaviour had on Harris Academy's academic record should not be surprising: good behaviour is the *sine qua non* of good lessons. However, schools should encourage good behaviour for reasons greater than just academic success. During the New Labour years, a common phrase in schools, popularised by the government's National Strategies, was 'Behaviour for Learning' (trendily abbreviated to B4L). As a Religious Education teacher pointed out to me, the phrase has a morally reductive implication, that suggests the only reason schools should enforce good behaviour is to improve learning. However, many voices – particularly in America – are calling for a wider appreciation of why schools should increase their efforts to foster good behaviour in pupils. Institutions such as schools invariably develop amongst their inhabitants either good or bad habits, and over time these habits come to shape their character. Researchers in fields as varied as neuroscience, psychology and moral philosophy are coming to recognise that 'character formation' should be an integral aspect of schooling. This new direction in academic research is reviving debates about the relationship between education and character that seem redolent of the days of Dr Arnold.

In Britain, a revived focus on character formation was given impetus by the 2011 August riots, which led many public figures to demand that schools play a greater role in nurturing a sense of civic responsibility amongst their pupils. Speaking in the House of Lords after the emergency recalling of Parliament, the Archbishop of Canterbury pointed the finger of blame at an 'educational philosophy' which over the last two decades has become 'less and less concerned with a building of virtue, character and citizenship – "civic excellence" as we might say.'[5] In May 2012, the Master of Wellington College, Anthony Seldon, wrote in *The Daily Telegraph* that: 'Character, and specifically its neglect, is the number one issue of our age.'[6] Tellingly, the famously strict Mossbourne Academy is situated right next to the riot-struck Pembury Estate in Hackney, but not one of its pupils was involved in the disturbances.[7]

There is a gathering recognition that the laissez-faire ethos that characterised our schools for the last half-century has failed. In granting children the freedom to develop without restraint, schools have neglected the role they should play in nurturing children through their formative years. Children are not independent rational agents; they are vulnerable and impressionable, and require the benevolent authority of adults and institutions. This is the message that schools such as Harris Academy and Mossbourne Academy are bearing out. In America, where a similar emphasis on character and discipline can be seen in high-performing charter schools, one commentator has labelled this new direction in schooling the 'New Paternalism'. Whatever term is used, it is at last being recognised that children are social beings, whose mores, habits and ultimately character are shaped by the institutions they attend. How the majority of schools in Britain respond to this recognition is yet to be seen.

Terroring

Behind every statistic demonstrating poor behaviour in schools, there are individual teachers being worn down by the enervating stress that working in such conditions induces. As a result, poor behaviour has had a pronounced, long-term effect on the recruitment and retainment of good teachers in Britain. It is often lamented that in this country teaching is a low-status profession, but the role that poor school discipline has played in creating this problem is not sufficiently recognised. Of the graduates who begin teacher-training, 43 per cent leave the profession within five years, with pupil behaviour often cited as the main reason for departing.[8] Were the behaviour crisis in all British schools to be solved, staff recruitment and stability in schools would improve dramatically.

One of the most memorable accounts I have read of teaching in chaotic schools came courtesy of *On The Edge* (2010) by Charlie Carroll. He did a brief stint of supply work at a Nottingham school given the name 'Varka School', where he recounts being bullied and threatened by a disruptive pupil named Ralph. This pupil would interrupt his classes with contributions such as 'Mr Carroll stinks of shit' and 'Sir's a virgin', and would refer to him as 'the posh cunt' whilst he was still in earshot. The senior management at the school were unwilling to do anything about Ralph's behaviour. The situation became more serious when Ralph threatened Mr Carroll with physical violence, and the school still did nothing to address the situation. Carroll recounted his fear at returning to work the next day:

> That night, I barely slept. The scene ran around and around my head, infiltrating my fitful dreams. The following morning, during the drive into work, I thought myself into near-hysteria, getting to the point where I feared Ralph might bring a knife into school to use on me. Every time I saw him over the following two days –

> and especially when he would walk past my classroom on his way to John's maths lesson and, in a sing song voice, call out, 'dickhead!' – I felt sick.

When the school continued to take no action against Ralph's aggressive behaviour, Carroll concluded:

> I knew right at that moment that I had to leave Varka. Ralph had finally disempowered me. He knew he could speak to me how he liked and knew that I would always back down. That was enough, because – and here's the thing – I had become scared of this 13-year-old boy. I am deeply embarrassed to admit it, but it is the truth. Around Ralph, I did not feel safe, and this robbed me of my confidence which, in turn, stripped me of my professionalism. I could already see what was happening: Ralph, with the cause-effect mentality of a thug, was beginning to bully me.[9]

Many British teachers bear the scars of similar encounters. A word has even developed within the lexicon of British schoolchildren for bullying a teacher to the point that they quit their job – 'terroring'. For those who have not been 'terrored', it is hard to imagine the indignity felt by being thrown into such a disturbed state by a 13-year-old child. Sadly, many school heads remain so wedded to their permissive philosophy on pupil behaviour that they refuse to introduce stricter rules and sanctions to prevent such goings on. They believe that orderly behaviour is fundamentally ensured by teachers establishing a good relationship with their pupils and even blame staff for being insufficiently 'positive' in doing so.

For this reason, pupil behaviour is a significant factor in teacher attrition. In 2011, the *Guardian* Teacher Network survey revealed that just over half of the teachers were thinking about quitting teaching, and pupil behaviour was the second most common reason to do so, behind excessive government meddling in schools.[10] In 2008 a report from Policy Exchange, which was focused on getting more good teachers into the classrooms, surveyed over a thousand university undergraduates. It found that the most significant factor in deterring them from entering the profession was not salary, but 'feeling unsafe in the classroom'.[11] Similarly, a large-scale survey undertaken by the GTC and published in 2009 found that amongst PGCE students training to be teachers, the most prominent concern, more prominent than salary, mastering the curriculum or managing the workload, was maintaining discipline in the classroom. In addition, respondents noted that their teacher training generally ignored the topic of classroom discipline despite it being their prime concern.[12] Such surveys demonstrate that from the perspective of teacher recruitment and retention alone, schools must take seriously the issue of pupil behaviour if Britain is ever to achieve a world-class education system.

The abnegation of adult authority

How did this longstanding problem with pupil behaviour in schools come about? To answer such a question, one has to take a historical perspective. During the 1960s and 1970s, when comprehensivisation was at full tide, British society was experiencing a crisis in adult authority. The legacy of fascism and World War II, and the liberationist rhetoric of the counter-culture, had thrown the very idea of institutional authority into doubt. Publications such as *The Authoritarian Personality* by Theodor Adorno, and studies such as the Milgrim experiment (where participants famously inflicted electric shocks on other volunteers when ordered to do so by an 'authority figure'), led many to conclude that obedience to authority was not a necessary feature of a functioning society, but the wellspring of fascism and genocide. In addition, radical psychoanalysts such as Wilhelm Reich suggested that the strictures placed on children by adults caused them to grow up neurotic and depressed. This spurred a move towards romantic childrearing, where children would be nurtured free of constraints, and even a movement against the family unit itself.

Institutions can embody the temper of the period in which they are created long after their birth. In this way, the outlook of many public schools is still shaped by the muscular Christianity of the nineteenth century, whilst the destructive idealism of the 1970s lives on in many comprehensive schools today. This rejection of adult authority and the embracing of liberated childhood was evident in the infamous schools of the period, such as Summerhill School, Risinghill Schoool, William Tyndale, Faraday Comprehensive, Creighton Comprehensive and Countesthorpe College (see Chapters 1 and 2). In such schools, sanctions and uniforms were rejected; school rules were reduced to the bare minimum; rituals such as assemblies and prize-giving were stopped; and heads actively renounced their role as the moral arbiter of the school community. Those who tried to defend a more old-fashioned view of school discipline were routinely greeted with hysterical accusations of Nazism, revealing the anti-authoritarian impetus that lay behind this new permissive approach.

A. S. Neill, the prophet of liberated childhood, summed up such an approach in his bestselling book *Summerhill*. 'I believe,' he wrote, 'that to impose anything by authority is wrong. The child should not do anything until he comes to the opinion – his own opinion – that it should be done.'[13] To this day, many schools in Britain remain uncomfortable with the idea of strong adult authority. In 1993, a lecturer who went on to become a senior academic at the Institute of Education wrote:

> Doing what is right cannot be a matter of doing what one is told . . . When exposed to a little more teaching

> of history, perhaps, this pupil will see that by such an argument the values of slave states and Nazi states would have to be endorsed.[14]

Similarly, Tony Blair's top education adviser, Tom Bentley, wrote in his 1998 book *Learning Beyond the Classroom*:

> As adults and guardians, we have the power to control much of what young people are allowed to do. But we do not necessarily have the authority, and when power and authority come apart, the result is eventually alienation, hostility and rejection... expecting young people automatically to accept someone's authority because they are in a position of power is unrealistic, as well as unhealthy.[15]

Schools that take such a principled stance against adult authority try with desperation to find alternative means of 'behaviour management'. Progressive educators base their faith upon the innate goodness of the child, and this leads them to believe it is their role to be tough on the causes of misbehaviour, not misbehaviour itself. This leads to the common assumption that poor behaviour is the result of poor teaching, as expressed in the 2005 Steer Report which claimed that: 'By engaging pupils more effectively, standards of behaviour improves [sic]'.[16] Of course, poor teaching can lead to poor behaviour, but the premise that a well-taught lesson can eliminate bad behaviour is a fantasy, and one that causes new teachers undue levels of stress. They are encouraged to blame their own teaching for the failings of their school, and apply an endless number of 'behaviour management' strategies, in the vain hope that one will prove to be a golden bullet. This may be gimmicks such as playing music in the classroom, rewarding good behaviour with sweets, or applying scripted 'behaviour conversations' with misbehaving pupils.

More often, behaviour management results in teachers being encouraged to make lessons 'fun' and 'accessible' – euphemisms for dumbing down and a style of teaching that aspires not to educate pupils but to placate them. On a school-wide level, behaviour management translates into a galaxy of fads, such as pupil interventions; CCTV surveillance; behaviour tracking; child therapists; more assessment; less assessment; motivational training; bribes; and even bouncers. It all amounts to a merry-go-round of 'cutting edge' methods trying in vain to compensate for the abdication of adult authority in the classroom.

Applying political principles such as freedom to the organisation of children in schools is clearly damaging, but unfortunately such rhetoric remains seductive to modern ears. Today, a speaker at an education conference will still be greeted with warm approval if they talk of empowering pupils, granting them independence and encouraging self-expression. They will be greeted with toe-curling silence if they stress the need for pupil compliance, the fulfilment of obligations and the observance of school rules. However, such structures are vital in building the sort of orderly school community within which freedom and self-expression can ultimately emerge. If you visit schools such as Harris Academy or Mossbourne Academy, you will realise that confident and fulfilled pupils are not created through granting adult freedoms to children prematurely. As Michael Wilshaw stated in an interview with the *New Statesman*:

> It's just common sense. Kids can't learn unless there is order in the classroom. Kids can't learn if they don't respect adults or teachers. This is non-negotiable. If you come here, you respect the adults. These people are here at six o'clock in the morning and leave at nine o'clock at night. They work long hours. Respect them.[17]

Today, too many schools grant children freedoms for which they are not yet ready. When pupils need guidance, they are given independence; and when pupils need clear rules, they are given shades of grey.

Moral education

The question of school discipline is inseparably bound to the question of moral education. Many people today intuitively recoil from such phrases as 'moral education' and 'character formation', as they associate such language with the priggish, hypocritical morality of a Victorian schoolmaster. However, the idea of nurturing pupil character has not been absent from the recent history of British schools. Quite the opposite, in fact. The tail end of the New Labour years saw a surfeit of reforms aimed at creating a certain type of 'responsible citizen', particularly through the botched introduction of Citizenship lessons and the Social and Emotional Aspects of Learning (SEAL) National Strategy. In addition, much of the 2007 national curriculum covered what one could term 'moral education', though it was more often expressed in the non-judgemental language of 'social competencies' or 'skills'.

Most of these initiatives from central government turned out to be embarrassing failures. The SEAL programme, for example, was born out of the enormous success of Daniel Goleman's 1995 book *Emotional Intelligence*. It was launched as a National Strategy in 2005 and cost around £10 million a year, with £60 million earmarked for the last three years of Labour government. The programme devised a taxonomy of what constitutes a good person, outlining in painstaking bureaucratese fifty different 'outcomes' for emotionally healthy pupils. These included: 'I can work out how people are feeling through their words, body language, gestures and tone and pay attention to them', or, 'I can use my experiences, including mistakes and setbacks to make appropriate changes to my plans and behaviour.' The National Strategy provided schools with training and a range of resources for teaching and assessing the 'emotional competence' of pupils.[18] Five years after the introduction of SEAL, the Department for Education commissioned a report on its impact. Its conclusion must have made for uncomfortable reading for all those involved:

> In relation to school-level outcome data, our analyses indicated that SEAL (as implemented by schools in our sample) failed to have a positive impact... Analysis of school climate scores indicated significant reductions in pupils' trust and respect for teachers, liking for school, and feelings of classroom and school supportiveness during SEAL implementation. Additionally, qualitative data around perceptions of impact indicated a feeling that SEAL had not produced the expected changes across schools.[19]

Similar initiatives to teach pupils how to be good citizens have played out in personal, social and health education (PSHE), citizenship lessons, and the Every Child Matters programme. All have been met with underwhelming results. It is worth asking the question, why if 'moral education' and 'character formation' are seen as such vital areas of schooling, have these attempts to provide them so consistently failed? The answer can found in the underlying philosophy behind the moral education as practised in schools today. British schools have been heavily influenced by the theory of 'moral rationalism', which suggests that instilling good conduct and behaviour in pupils through rewards, sanctions and school ethos is misguided. Instead, it seeks to give pupils objective information in decision-making areas ranging from going to university to the dangers of underage drinking, so that they can make, independently and in a rational fashion, informed judgements on their life choices. Such a practice means that the lesson content, teacher and school all remain morally neutral – a preferable situation for our relativistic age. Ever fond of a rhyme, the motto devised by educationists to guide this style of moral education is 'teach, don't preach'.

The 'moral rationalist' approach to childrearing was developed during the 1960s by Lawrence Kohlberg, a protégé of Jean Piaget, founder of the constructivist school of child development. Kohlberg sought to demonstrate that children construct their moral beliefs through experience and rational assessment, not through environment and social influences. He divided a child's moral development into three stages and suggested that children would be most proficient at making moral decisions once they reach the final 'post-conventional' stage if they had been nurtured through childhood to resolve moral problems for themselves. Kohlberg's ideal was a world populated by independent moral reasoners, each developing their own ethical systems. Such thinking proved extremely popular during the 1960s as it leant weight to those who wanted to see society move away from traditional morality and embrace a more individualistic approach to human ethics. As the psychologist Jonathan Haidt recently wrote:

> Kohlberg's timing was perfect. Just as the first wave of baby boomers was entering graduate school, he transformed moral psychology into a boomer-friendly ode to justice, and he gave them a tool to measure children's progress toward the liberal ideal.[20]

Today, Kohlberg's ideas remain influential within education. I first encountered them as a trainee teacher whilst reading a chapter of my stipulated course textbook, *Learning to Teach*. Explaining Kohlberg's work, the authors endorse the moral rationalist orthodoxy, writing: 'mature moral judgement is dependent on a capacity to reason logically: it develops as children's reasoning ability develops.'[21]

Such a philosophy could also be seen underlying much

of New Labour's literature on teaching. When applied to the classroom, the general conduct of such lessons is well established. Pupils will be taught the necessary information about, for example, the dangers of Class A drugs, the benefits of higher education or the impact of racial diversity on Britain. They will then be given an activity such as devising a role-play, designing a poster or engaging in a group discussion, which will allow them to develop their own opinions on the issues. The Californian psychologist Carl Rogers first devised such an approach during the 1960s and it was later termed 'values clarification'. He hoped that schools would no longer impose society's normative *virtues* on pupils but instead allow pupils independently to develop their own personal *values*.[22] Unfortunately, today PSHE lessons are notorious in schools for their poor quality, and values clarification lessons have an unimpressive track record in both America and the UK for having any positive influence on pupil conduct. For example, a review of 26 randomised controlled trials into school-based sex education published in the *British Medical Journal* in 2002 found that these strategies have had no effect at all on delaying the initiation of sexual intercourse, the use of birth control, or the rate of pregnancies amongst adolescent girls.[23]

Thanks to the latest conclusions of moral psychology, we can better understand why a moral rationalist approach does not work. In his recent book *The Righteous Mind,* the psychologist Jonathan Haidt established that the rational part of one's mind remains largely dormant whilst moral decisions are made. However, the automatic, subconscious part of one's mind is highly active. Haidt explains that deliberative moral reasoning amongst humans is nearly always a post hoc justification for conclusions already reached through intuitive cognition. Brain scans run by the Harvard cognitive scientist Joshua Greene have even demonstrated that the prefrontal cortex, the area of the brain associated with deliberative reasoning, remains largely unlit whilst humans answer difficult moral questions. Put simply, humans rarely 'think rationally' when they make most moral decisions. For this reason, Haidt has dubbed Kohlberg's theory 'the Rationalist Delusion'.[24]

What does all this have to do with moral education at schools? Many schools over the past few decades have prized themselves on being morally neutral institutions, and one does not need the work of a moral psychologist to see that this approach is bound to fail. Go to many secondary schools and you will not find a Utopia of Immanuel Kants 'constructing' their individual modes of moral reasoning. You will see PSHE lessons informing pupils about the health dangers of smoking cannabis whilst the same school turns a blind eye to pupils arriving at lessons visibly stoned. Similarly, you may see a school teach lessons on the need to have a positive work ethic, yet still passively tolerate lazy, disengaged behaviour in the classroom. Children cannot be taught how to be good citizens in a classroom setting: they must be nurtured towards such a goal through a morally assertive school environment.

Of good character

Within the English public school tradition, it remains a fundamental assumption that schools should not be concerned merely with their pupils' academic outcomes, but also with the development of good habits and character. Much of the traditional furniture which makes up life at public schools – prize-giving, competitive sports, prefects, mottos, hymns, assemblies, traditional rituals, rewards and sanctions – are designed to instil virtues which such schools unapologetically promote. The founder of this tradition was Dr Thomas Arnold, the celebrated headmaster of Rugby School during the 1830s, whose concern for the moral development of his pupils was immortalised 20 years later by former pupil Thomas Hughes in *Tom Brown's School Days*. In 1864, the Clarendon Commission into England's nine leading public schools commented on the positive effect Arnold had had in changing the culture of English education: 'The principle of governing boys mainly though their own sense of what is right and honourable is undoubtedly the only true principle; but it requires much watchfulness, and a firm, temperate and judicious administration, to keep up the tone and standard of opinion.'[25] Such a tradition carries on in many independent schools today. The headmaster of Eton recently addressed a 'character and resilience summit', explaining how schools can build character and develop well-rounded pupils.[26]

Character formation was once a tradition towards which all sectors of British education, not just independent schools, aspired. In 1937, the Board of Education's Handbook stated that: 'The purpose of the Public Elementary School is to form and strengthen character', and suggested the virtues which schools should cultivate were industry, self-control, duty, respect for others, good manners, fair play and loyalty.[27] However, the arrival of progressive education put paid to this tradition in the state sector, as the idea of a morally assertive school was called into question. It was accused of fostering obedient pupils who were unable to question authority, or of creating pupils who were repressed or neurotic. In addition, 'virtues' traditionally promoted by schools were attacked for being, amongst other things, middle-class, anglocentric and elitist. Consequently, the Arnoldian tradition came to be seen as risible in an age of moral relativism. A. S. Neill typified this repudiation of moral education during the 1960s when he wrote: '*I believe that it is moral instruction that makes the child bad. I find that when I smash the moral instruction a bad boy has received, he becomes a good boy*… There is no case whatever for the moral instruction of children.'[28]

Today, more than ever, Neill's position should be seen as unsustainable. Insights into child-psychology from across the Atlantic have shown that character and habit, so long neglected by schools, are in fact crucial determinants of success in life and in education. An experiment that has achieved almost mythical status in this field is the 'marshmallow test'. During the 1960s and 1970s, Professor Walter Mischel of Stanford University conducted a series of experiments to find out the methods children used to delay gratification. Children were left in a room with one marshmallow, and told that if they could resist eating the marshmallow for 15 minutes, then they would be rewarded with two marshmallows. Only a minority of children had the self-control to complete the task. By 1990, the original participants were in their mid-twenties and Mischel tracked them down. He found that those who resisted the marshmallows showed greater levels of success in an astounding array of life outcomes: they were more popular, less likely to do drugs, and on average had scored 210 points higher in their SATs. Such evidence shows that characteristics such as self-control can have a pronounced effect on a pupil's life outcomes.

The research of Angela Duckworth, a former student of Mischel's and now Professor of Psychology at the University of Pennsylvania, has further established character as a vital component of educational success. Duckworth devised a series of willpower tests that quantify the self-discipline of school pupils and used them in a study of 164 eighth-graders at a high school in Philadelphia in 2005. When the self-discipline scores were compared against future academic achievement, the correlation was remarkable:

> Highly self-disciplined adolescents outperformed their more impulsive peers on every academic-performance variable. Self-discipline predicted academic performance more robustly than did IQ. Self-discipline also predicted

> which students would improve their grades over the course of the school year, whereas IQ did not... Self-discipline has a bigger effect on academic performance than does intellectual talent.[29]

Duckworth's research has since found that high measures of self-discipline also correlate with a high grade point average among Ivy League undergraduates, the likelihood of completing West Point Military Academy training and ranking in the National Spelling Bee. Duckworth does not seem to share the indulgent attitude towards child-development that is common amongst English and American educationists. She believes that learning is and should be difficult, and if pupils are to prosper they should not be sheltered from this. She has even given a name to the characteristic that so often correlates with success – 'grit'.

There are many who would interpret the conclusions of Mischel and Duckworth in a deterministic fashion, assuming that if you are not blessed with characteristics such as the ability to defer gratification, you are consigned to a life of underachievement. However, such an interpretation would be misguided. As Duckworth has written, character is not immutable, and there is a great deal that schools can do to affect character development in their pupils. Of course, the most powerful determinant of a child's character will always be their family background, but good schools should aspire to come a close second.

In America, this has been demonstrated by the astounding success of the Knowledge is Power Programme (KIPP) chain of charter schools, which have achieved miracles serving the country's most deprived urban areas since their formation in 1994. The American journalist David Whitman profiled the KIPP Academy South Bronx, and five other high-performing American schools in his 2008 book *Sweating the Small Stuff*. What united all six schools was their robust approach to pupil behaviour and character formation, which Whitman termed 'The New Paternalism'. This label was greeted with some disagreement, as many of the schools featured in the book admitted discomfort with the idea of being called 'paternalistic'. More so than in Britain, 'paternalism' has preachy, authoritarian overtones in America, and is historically associated with the harsh American Indian boarding schools of the nineteenth century. However, Whitman defends his label:

> The new paternalistic schools profiled in this book look and feel very different… They are highly prescriptive institutions that often serve *in loco parentis*; they are morally and culturally assertive schools, which unapologetically insist that students adhere to middle-class virtues and explicitly rebuff the culture of the street; they are rigorous both about academics and instilling character; and they are places where obligation trumps freedom – they compel students to act according to school standards and pre-empt misbehavior, much in the manner of a watchful parent.

The KIPP joint philosophy of academic attainment and character formation is neatly summed up by their four-word slogan, 'work hard; be nice', and their methods of achieving this have become famous. Before the school year begins, KIPP run a three-week summer school in which pupils are acclimatised to the school routines. They arrive at school at 7:45 am in impeccable uniform or else their parents are immediately contacted, and are taught how to stand in line – 'SILENT, STRAIGHT and SERIOUS'. They drill standing in line and walking to lessons in silence, until they can do it perfectly. Any pupils who are off-task or not wearing correct uniform during the day have to apologise publicly in front of their class. Pupils are even instructed on how to conduct themselves in lessons, with the mnemonic SLANT, standing for sit up; listen;

ask and answer questions; nod your head; and track the speaker. Right from the beginning of school, pupils are encouraged to set their sights on attending college, with classrooms often named after the college that the teacher attended. All pupils also play an instrument in the school orchestra, and KIPP concerts have been performed in the Lincoln Centre, Carnegie Hall and Apollo Theatre.

At KIPP schools, sanctions will be issued for infractions as minor as tapping a pen on a desk. Such an ethos has earned KIPP the nickname 'Kids in Prison Programme', but such a description is unfair. As Whitman writes, there is nothing Spartan or nasty about these schools: on the contrary, they are pervaded by a sense of loving concern and the pupils often refer to them as their 'second home'. As one journalist wrote for a *New York Times Magazine* cover story in 2006, this new generation of American schools exhibit a 'counterintuitive combination of touchy-feely idealism and intense discipline'. They are also immensely successful. In the KIPP Academy in the South Bronx, with pupils from one of the most famously deprived boroughs in America, 87 per cent met or exceeded the New York standard test in mathematics in 2007. This compared with five per cent, 15 per cent, and eight per cent at the three most demographically similar neighbouring schools.

KIPP South Bronx is not *sui generis*. There are currently 141 KIPP schools in 20 states across America, with many more set to open. These schools take on the most deprived pupils in American society, with 86 per cent enrolled in the federal school meals programme and 95 per cent from African-American or Latino backgrounds. However, at the end of 8th Grade, 96 per cent of KIPP classes outperform their local districts in reading, and 92 per cent do so in maths. So far, 83 per cent of KIPP students have enrolled in college, compared with 45 per cent of low-income pupils nationally. The co-founders of KIPP, Mike Feinberg and Dave Levin, have been fêted by Presidents Bush and Obama, and in 2008 were awarded the Presidential Citizens Medal.[30] Due in no small part to the success of KIPP, left-leaning school reformers in America are becoming increasingly interested in the role of character in education, a revealing shift seeing that the topic has long been seen as the preserve of conservatives, particularly Ronald Reagan's one time Secretary of Education William Bennett.[31]

KIPP schools create an environment in which positive character traits can be forged. The school day is filled with chants, mottos, routines and rituals, such that many observers complain that they seem 'cultish' and accuse them of 'brainwashing' their pupils. However, such an accusation is naive, as all institutions, for better or for worse, can have a profound effect on the type of people their inhabitants become. The important question is what sort of effect will this be. In his impressive synthesis of recent research into human behaviour, *The Social Animal*, David Brookes writes:

> As we go through life, we travel through institutions – first family and school, then the institutions of a profession or a craft. Each of these comes with certain rules and obligations that tell us how to do what we're supposed to do. They are external scaffolds that penetrate deep inside us... In the process of absorbing the rules of the institutions we inhabit, we become who we are.[32]

Whether educating the sons of the British elite at Eton, or the deprived South Bronx children at the KIPP Academy, good schools that imbue their ethos with clearly defined virtues have a powerful influence on their pupils' characters. However, most schools remain uncomfortable with this idea, as it requires a high degree of moral assertion. For this reason, the moral rationalist approach, which gives pupils the requisite information to reach their own moral decisions whilst schools remain morally neutral, has been dominant. However, this approach does not work. An increasing number of academic fields are confirming that a young child's moral code is caught, not taught, and it is the running of the school and not the content of its curriculum that is decisive in moral education. This was a truth recognised by the renowned criminologist James Q. Wilson. Wilson demonstrated the effect that environment has on social behaviour with his 'broken windows' theory of crime, which argued that if 'petty' urban crimes such as graffiti, public urination and breaking windows were targeted, the more salubrious urban environment would encourage fewer people to commit more serious crimes. During the 1990s, the Mayor Rudolph Giuliani applied Wilson's theory to New York, achieving a precipitous and lasting fall in crime. In his book *The Moral Sense,* Wilson applied this thinking to American schools:

> A moral life is perfected by practice more than by precept; children are not taught so much as habituated. In this sense the schools inevitably teach morality, whether they intend to or not, by such behaviour as they reward or punish. A school reinforces the better moral nature of a pupil to the extent it insists on the habitual performance of duties, including the duty to deal fairly with others, to discharge one's own responsibilities, and to defer the satisfaction of immediate and base motives in favour of more distant and nobler ones.[33]

British schools need a renewed confidence in affirming the virtues expected of their pupils. Of course, lively debates should be had about precisely what virtues these should be, but few could argue with a school that seeks to imbue their pupils with diligence, honesty, politeness, tolerance and self-control. However, this can only be achieved by placing pupils in structured environments where such virtues are upheld by the staff, and repeatedly practised by the pupils. As Aristotle wrote: 'we are what we repeatedly do. Excellence, then, is not an act but a habit.'

Freedom's orphans

In 1915 D. H. Lawrence wrote *The Rainbow*, drawing inspiration from his own lack of success as a schoolteacher. In the novel, the sprightly, idealistic young Ursula Brangwen becomes a teacher and expects to be able to teach without 'compulsion', depending on force of personality alone. Ursula has a gruelling experience of teaching, and Lawrence explains the failure of her project:

> Children will never naturally acquiesce to sitting in a class and submitting to knowledge. They must be compelled by a stronger, wiser will. Against which they must always strive to revolt. So that the first great effort of every teacher of a large class must be to bring the will of the children into accordance with his own will. And this he can only do by an abnegation of his personal self, and an application of a system of laws, for the purpose of achieving a certain calculable result, the imparting of certain knowledge.[34]

Such language would repel most modern teachers, but it is ultimately true. Progressive education relies on the twin premises that children are naturally effective learners, and that they are innately good. Although admirable in their idealism, both beliefs are misguided. Children are not born perfect, and any institution that attempts to function as if they are will only exacerbate their imperfections. This is what has happened in so many British schools from the 1960s onwards. Had it not been for the crisis in adult authority that took place during this period, the poor behaviour that has characterised British schools for almost half a century since could have been avoided.

However, it does at long last seem the tide is turning.

Schools in both the United States and Britain have shown what can be achieved when adults reprise their role as authority figures and create a school ethos that encourages pupils to work hard, practise good habits and develop a sense of right and wrong. There is still a long way to go. In his 2013 annual report for Ofsted, Wilshaw observed that many schools are still characterised by a 'casual acceptance' of misbehaviour and a tolerance of low-level disruption.[35] It will take time before these vestiges of progressive education completely disappear, but if they do, the positive effect for children, teachers and schools will be immense. If they do not, disorderly, morally relativistic schools will continue to produce, in the words of child-psychologist Aric Sigman, 'freedom's orphans'.

9

The Soft Bigotry of Low Expectations

> However specious in theory the project might be of giving education to the labouring classes of the poor, it would, in effect, be found to be prejudicial to their morals and happiness.[1]
>
> *Davies Giddy MP, 1807.*

> The academic, subject-based curriculum is a middle-class creation… the effect of the [1988 national curriculum], if not its intention, has been to make it difficult for many children not from a middle-class background to adjust to a highly academic school culture.[2]
>
> *Professor John White, 2007.*

Although two centuries divide these two quotations, they are united in an important sense: both deny the ability of poor children to benefit from an academic education. The first quotation comes from a Tory MP speaking against the 1807 Parochial Schools bill. The second comes from a man at the heart of today's education establishment, an emeritus professor at the London Institute of Education. His is a different sort of snobbery, one that comes with the gentle inflection of liberal sympathy, but is no less socially damaging. Due to the perverse logic of sociological theory, much of today's education profession has come to adopt a deep pessimism about the extent to which schools can succeed in educating disadvantaged children.

How has this happened? Over the past forty years, it has become an accepted truism in education debates that the overriding determinant of a child's success will be their socio-economic background. So dominant is the effect of a pupil's home background, argue many, that schools only ever have a marginal impact on the life chances of their charges. Such an outlook – we might call it 'the sociological view' – has created a mindset whereby pupil underachievement is seen as an unfortunate but predictable result of their socially determined life trajectory. It is this that so many politicians, both Labour and Conservative, have correctly diagnosed as a 'culture of excuses' in our schools.

The origins of this mindset can be traced to the 'new sociology of education' that developed during the 1970s, and in particular the work of Michael Young and Basil Bernstein, whose 1970 essay famously declared 'Education cannot compensate for society' (see Chapter 2). Young and Bernstien's work hardened over the following decades into Educational Sociology, an academic discipline dispensed to generations of trainee teachers. In 1999, a professor at the Institute of Education declared:

> ...in the same sense that Michel Foucault (I've forgotten where) declared that we are all Marxists now, all of us in the field of educational studies at the close of the twentieth century inhabit a world that has been profoundly influenced by the thinking of Basil Bernstein. We are all, in some respects, Bernsteinians now.[3]

Having adopted the sociological view, educationists and teachers could deflect any discussion of educational underperformance in Britain to wider questions of social inequality. It is futile, they would argue, to expect the schools to improve in an iniquitous society where success is defined by the dominant social elites. One critic of the sociological view termed such a stance 'revolutionary defeatism', as it implied that solving educational failure was impossible without sweeping social change. For one year, I worked as a part-time teaching assistant in a high school in a deprived part of West Philadelphia. There, such thinking had found longevity in the motto, 'you can't solve education until you solve poverty'.

This idea is still rife in debates over education reform. A friend once recounted to me the content of a university seminar he attended for a master's degree in education. The professor launched into a tirade against the current Education Secretary, and demanded to know how he expected schools to raise standards while belonging to a government that was 'making the poor poorer'. In a recently published book, the same professor wrote: 'Social variables are too significant to be ignored and there can be no hope of improving education until we have understood and found ways to deal with the pernicious problems of poverty and social disadvantage.'[4] In 2007, the *TES* visited a struggling primary school in an impoverished former pit town near Worksop, Nottinghamshire. It had ranked as one of the worst primary schools in the country, making the national press in 1996 when teachers staged a walkout due to pupil violence against staff. This resulted in the appointment of a new head, but he informed his chair of governors not to expect a quick fix. He told the *TES*: 'If you can't fix the community, you'll never fix the school.'[5] The school has since closed.

Such pessimism about the potential for school improvement can also be found in the mainstream press. In October 2013, the veteran education commentator Peter Wilby wrote an open letter in the *Guardian* to the recently appointed Labour Shadow Education Secretary, Tristram Hunt, offering the following advice:

> Start from a premise which, to anybody who studies the evidence (as I know you will), should be beyond dispute. The best way of improving standards across the board is to reduce poverty and inequality. Poverty has such a powerful effect on children's capacity to learn that,

> when they start school, many are already hopelessly behind. Yes, schools can make a difference, sometimes a large one, but family background remains the biggest single influence.[6]

To the lay reader such an opinion may seem reasonable, if a little depressing. However, once internalised by schools and teachers, the implications drawn from it are highly damaging. The first is that schools can have little impact on the academic success of their pupils in the face of wider socio-economic forces. Such a defeatist outlook has been of great use to progressive educators, as it deflects attention away from debates concerning the relative success of different teaching methods. Thus, negative effects caused by progressive methods – such as poor behaviour and low literacy rates – are blamed on the social disadvantage of the pupils instead. Worse still, the sociological view produces a mindset that sees the low academic attainment of certain pupils as somehow permissible, and schools set their sights for what disadvantaged pupils can achieve before they have even entered the classroom. It was the American speechwriter Michael Gerson who coined the phrase to describe this mindset 'the soft bigotry of low expectations'.

Thankfully, an increasing number of excellent schools are embarrassing the 'soft bigots' of the education establishment into revising their opinions. There is no denying that socio-economic background has a effect on educational outcome, but the only decent response from educators is to strive to overcome this pattern, not to capitulate to it. As the current head of Ofsted Michael Wilshaw has observed:

> There are a growing number of schools producing fantastic results in areas of deprivation, because of the effort they are putting in and the high aspirations of the children... It can be done. We've got to stop making

excuses for background, culture and ethnicity and get on with it.[7]

Deprivation is not destiny

The percentage of pupils who qualify for free school meals (FSM) is used as a marker of child poverty: to qualify, a pupil's parents must have a combined income lower than £16,190 per year. The poor attainment of such pupils is significant; only 36 per cent of FSM pupils gained five good GCSEs in 2012, compared with 59 per cent of non-FSM pupils. As pupils move upwards through their education, this gulf persists: in 2011, four per cent of pupils on FSM aged 15 end up going to a Russell Group university, compared with nine per cent of non-FSM pupils.[8] Research by the Sutton Trust in 2010 found that private school pupils are 22 times more likely to go to a top-ranked university than FSM pupils, and 55 times more likely to go to Oxbridge. Westminster, a top independent school, regularly sends more pupils to Oxbridge in a year than the entire FSM population of Britain.[9]

However, the relationship between child poverty and educational failure is a broad correlation, not a mark of certain destiny. FSM pupils are proportionately more likely to leave British schools without five good GCSEs, but over three-quarters of those who suffer such a fate are non-FSM pupils. It is an important fact to realise that, as the chair of ARK Schools Paul Marshall recently noted, the great majority of school failures in Britain are not poor.[10] In addition, the correlation between poverty and school failure in Britain varies significantly across schools and regions. In the worst local authorities, only one in five FSM pupils leaves school with five good GCSEs, whilst in the best local authorities that figure is four in five.[11] Equally, in 2012 there were 440 secondary schools, around one in nine, where FSM pupils score a higher average GCSE point score than the average for all pupils nationwide. Such schools and local authorities prove that deprivation need not be destiny.[12]

International comparisons offer a similar conclusion. Compared to other nations in the developed world, there is nothing unusual about inequality in Britain that can explain its unusually poor educational outcomes. Commentators who adopt the sociological view exaggerate the extent to which British society is characterised by child poverty and inequality. In his collected journalism about British education, *The School Report* (2000), *Guardian* reporter Nick Davies dismissed the idea that poor educational achievement could ever be due to 'bad teachers' or 'trendy teaching methods'. Instead, he wrote, 'you cannot make sense of why some schools fail and some succeed without taking account of the corrosive impact of child poverty', and later explained: 'Our levels of pupil failure are higher than in most of the rest of the developed world, but our levels of child poverty are also higher than in most of the rest of the developed world.'[13] Christine Blower, the General Secretary of the National Union of Teachers, recently made the same causal argument in response to the PISA rankings:

> Social segregation is greater in England than in almost all other OECD countries. It is regrettable but a plain fact that child poverty is the biggest factor limiting children's potential. Life outside of the classroom does impact on the ability to learn and is an issue that this and future governments must address.[14]

Are these claims correct? No. This idea that the poor record of Britain's pupils can be blamed on unusually high levels of child poverty is a persistent canard that must be refuted. The PISA rankings compile a measure of 'economic, social and cultural status' of pupils, based on measures ranging from parental occupation to the number of books in the house. According to this measure, 15 per cent of children in OECD countries are 'disadvantaged'. The figure in Britain is just six per cent and only five countries in the world have a better, or the same, track record. They are Canada, Finland, Denmark, Norway and Iceland. So, according to PISA, Britain has an enviably *low* proportion of disadvantaged children.[15] That is absolute child poverty dismissed, but what about relative child poverty? UNICEF completes an annual index of relative child poverty, defined by children living in a household in which disposable income, when adjusted for family size and composition, is less than 50 per cent of the national median income. Amongst the 35 wealthy nations surveyed, Britain came 22nd. This is not a good result, but it is by no means an outlier: Canada, Poland and Japan all scored worse in this measure of relative child poverty, but rank higher than Britain in the PISA tables – as would, one assumes, the South Asian nations which are not included in the UNICEF study.[16]

Nor can Britain's poor educational record be blamed on social inequality. It is well known that Britain has one of the highest levels of social inequality amongst developed nations: the second highest in Europe, behind only Bulgaria, according to the Gini coefficient measure. There are many, including myself, who see this as a grave national problem. However, it would be intellectually dishonest to claim that if it were solved, that other national problem of educational failure would also disappear. Despite the claims of commentators such as Peter Wilby in the *Guardian*, there is no proven correlation between success in the PISA rankings and social equality. South Korea, China, Singapore and Hong Kong all have much higher levels of social inequality than Britain, but comprehensively beat us in the PISA rankings.

During the 1980s, it would have perhaps been plausible to blame educational failure in Britain on underfunded state schools. Such an argument is also no longer tenable: PISA have shown Britain to be the eighth highest education-spending nation in the world, with numbers adjusted for purchasing power parity. Of the 25 nations with higher PISA mathematics results than Britain, 21 spend less money on their schools.[17] The research conducted by PISA since 1997 has done an invaluable job in discrediting many of the sociological arguments historically used by apologists for British state schools. Underfunded schools, uniquely high levels of child poverty, and social inequality are not valid explanations for the relatively poor performance of British schoolchildren. As Andreas Schleicher, the coordinator of PISA at the OECD, has said, their work 'debunks the myth that poverty is destiny'.[18] If our education system is to catch up with the best in the developed world, it is the schools themselves that will have to change.

The gospel of defeatism

In 2006, a *Guardian* story covering a study into educational outcomes in Britain drew the following conclusion: 'This unprecedented project has revealed that a child's social background is the crucial factor in academic performance, and that a school's success is based not on its teachers, the way it is run, or what type of school it is, but, overwhelmingly, on the class background of its pupils.'[19] Having been a teacher, I find it hard to think of a sentiment that does more to undervalue the profession.

This idea that pupils' cards in life have been dealt before they even enter the classroom is not only defeatist; it is also incorrect. Extensive levels of research, particularly in the United States, have shown the significant impact that individual teachers have on pupil attainment. A recent synthesis of academic research conducted by the Sutton Trust estimated that pupils from disadvantaged backgrounds taught by effective teachers (those in the 84th per centile according to value added scores) gain 1.5 years worth of learning in a year, whilst pupils taught by the least effective teachers make only 0.5 years of academic progress. The report estimated that if the lowest performing 10 per cent of teachers in Britain were brought up to the standard of average teacher performance, Britain's OECD ranking for reading could move up 14 places over the next five years.[20]

Good teachers make a difference, but so do good schools. Were education unable to compensate for society, rapid school improvement without a corresponding change in school demographic would be unheard of. However, such transformations are going on all around us. In 2012, the Department for Education named 100 primary schools where the number of pupils reaching an acceptable level of literacy and numeracy by the age of 11 had increased by 30 per cent or more over the previous three years. The two most improved, Thornhill Primary School in Southampton and Henry Fawcett Primary School in London, had moved the proportion of pupils achieving a Level 4 in English and Maths from 24 per cent to 88 per cent and from 36 per cent to 97 per cent respectively, without any corresponding change in their proportion of FSM pupils. These schools demonstrate that poverty should never be used as an excuse for illiteracy.[21] In the secondary sector, schools such as Perry Beeches in Birmingham and the Sir John Cass Foundation School in East London have recorded meteoric improvements in GCSE results. If even half of our failing schools were to take the same steps as these beacons, the benefits to British society would be unimaginable.

Despite such inspiring examples, the media continue to perpetuate the myth that schools are powerless in the face of greater, socio-economic forces. This assumption underlay a documentary produced for BBC Radio 4 entitled 'Do Schools Make a Difference?', aired in 2012. The presenter, Fran Abrams, gave the following introduction:

> You see, the problem with our education system isn't that the teachers aren't good enough, or that we haven't got the right curriculum, or that we haven't given schools enough freedom from local authority control. It's much more fundamental than that. The problem is we've been expecting schools to rid us of social inequality.

Later in the documentary, an academic leant Abrams the dubious statistic that of all of the factors accounting for a child's academic success such as parents, peer group and social class, the 'school effect... maybe accounts for 10 percent'. The programme concluded by stating that schools could do little to change the life chances of their pupils, but saluted the 'hopeless optimism' of the teaching profession for still trying anyway.[22] If taken on by educators, the sociological view becomes a gospel of defeatism.

There is a dogmatism to this outlook, which wilfully refuses to entertain the idea that pupil results could be majorly effected by *what is actually happening inside the classroom*. Those who hold dear to the sociological view prefer to see all change, positive or negative, in the simplistic terms of crude, socio-economic materialism. For this reason, Michael Gove has labelled them 'the enemies of promise'. He courted controversy for doing so, but Gove is not the first politician to make such an accusation. In 1999, Tony Blair spoke to a conference of headteachers and in words almost indistinguishable from Gove's, he stated that 'the forces of conservatism' in education come not only from the right:

> ... we must also take on what I call the culture of excuses which still infects some parts of the teaching profession. A culture that tolerates low ambitions, rejects excellence and treats poverty as an excuse for failure. These too are outdated views holding our nation back. They have no place in modern Britain.[23]

As Blair found out, and Gove is no doubt discovering, there is little that an elected government can do to change the mindset of a profession. However, if good schools are able to flourish, an increasing number of teachers and school leaders will realise they do not have to be passive handmaidens in the reproduction of social inequality. They can be agents of social change themselves.

The inverse snobbery of sociology

A particular subset of the sociological view manifests itself in attacks on the traditional, subject-based curriculum. Working from the assumption that an academic curriculum is a middle-class creation bound to alienate working-class pupils, educators have long attempted to devise alternatives. Few such attempts have been met with success, and many have been patronising. In 1973, during the first flush of sociological theorising, Brian Jackson wrote in *New Society* that boredom and misbehaviour in state schools could be overcome if the curriculum was fitted to the existing interests of the pupils:

> Spend any time in a decaying back street, and you'll see how important television or football pools are. Or chalking on walls. Or pulling a motor bike to pieces. Or a group of girls dolling up each other's hair. Why isn't the education there, putting on children's chalking competitions, building runnable cars out of junk, dress-making, street theatre, 'holiday at home' weeks?[24]

Such inverse snobbery persists to this day, with the most notorious recent example coming courtesy of the ATL teachers union. Their pamphlet *Subject to Change* was published in 2007 with the intention of influencing the redrafted national curriculum. It was subtitled 'New Thinking on the Curriculum', but in reality it was a reheated version of 1970s educational sociology. The author, Martin Johnson, argued that:

> We need a bit of honesty in this analysis. Most people are not intellectuals... Yet throughout the world, education systems are based on the considered superiority of the abstract over the real, of thought over action. This is because mass education systems developed in the twentieth century copied the curriculum considered necessary for social elites; leisured classes who could afford and valued such attitudes.

Such an analysis may seem reasonable, until you read what Johnson proposed for those pupils not belonging to 'social elites'. He wrote that schools should teach 'dance, different forms of sport and crafts... physical skills such as walking, and digging, should be practised as they are close to the essence of humanity... a comprehensive curriculum recognises humanity as physical beings... we should all know how to plant, grow and harvest wheat.'[25]

In the same year, Professor John White published his essay 'What Schools are for and why', quoted at the beginning of the chapter, to add to the national curriculum debate. He wrote that 'the academic, subject-based curriculum is a middle-class creation', speculating that it has been designed to give the middle-class a 'competitive advantage' in society. White suggested for comprehensive schools a curriculum based around general life 'aims', as opposed to academic knowledge, as it would appeal to the whole of society and not just the middle class. The 'aims' that White put forward covered topics such as 'become discerning and critical consumers', 'relate to and communicate with other people appropriately in various contexts', and 'critically examine how wealth is created and distributed, nationally and world-wide'.[26]

These claims demonstrate the extraordinary reversal in attitudes that has taken place within state education since its inception in 1870. Originally, the provision of an elite education for all was seen as an egalitarian, even noble aim. However, during the second half of the twentieth century, it came to be seen as an elitist, middle-class imposition. During the early twentieth century, figures on the political right such as T. S. Eliot argued that learning and high culture would be wasted amongst the vulgar masses. It is deeply ironic that today, due to the inverse snobbery of sociology, many who see themselves as being on the left make the same argument.

A telling example of this came in 1992, during the debates over the teaching of standard English and 'the canon' thrown up by the first national curriculum in English. Printed in *The Times* in 1992, the letter was drafted by the Marxist Professor of English at Oxford University, Terry Eagleton, and was co-signed by no fewer than 576 English dons. It attacked the government's preoccupation with 'sound grammar and spelling', writing of the proposed curriculum:

> ...its evident hostility to regional and working-class forms of speech in the classroom betrays a prejudice which has little or no intellectual basis, and which is seriously harmful to the well-being and self-esteem of many children. We are all committed to the study of Shakespeare; but to make such study compulsory for 14-year-olds, as the minister intends, is to risk permanently alienating a large number of children from the pleasurable understanding of classical literary works.[27]

It is important to consider the implications of Eagleton's argument, as many schools have historically followed this line of reasoning. If a school does not value standard English, it neglects the fact that the rest of society, in particular professional life, still does. Working-class pupils taught in a way that protects their 'self-esteem' will encounter a far greater hit to their self-esteem once they attempt to apply for a job. Having been taught by teachers who believe that the difference between 'its' and 'it's' is pedantry, and that 'we was' should be protected as a noble part of working-class vernacular, their life prospects will have been significantly reduced. In addition, if Eagleton really had such a low opinion of a 'large number' of 14-year-olds that he does not believe they could be taught Shakespeare without suffering alienation, then such teenagers will simply be consigned to a lifetime of ignorance about Britain's greatest literary figure. By presupposing what pupils can and cannot achieve on account of their background, the sociological view becomes a self-fulfilling prophecy.

An elite education for all

Inspiration for an alternative to this modern philistinism can be found by looking back to the original implementation of state education. The animating spirit behind the nineteenth-century push for universal education was a belief in 'liberal education', a much-neglected term which, despite what one may assume, is very much distinct from progressive education. Liberal education, as explained by David Conway in his book *Liberal Education and the National Curriculum* (2010), originated in Ancient Greece and was concerned with preparing young men for a 'liberal' life: one in which they enjoyed leisured pursuits and a political voice. As Aristotle wrote: 'Clearly then there is a form of education which we must provide for our sons, not as being useful or essential but as elevated and worthy of free men.'[28]

The 1870 Forster Act introduced universal state education to Britain. It is no coincidence that the Act was passed three years after Benjamin Disraeli granted the vote to Britain's urban working class for the first time. Democracy was dawning and political leaders realised, as the Liberal MP and education reformer Robert Lowe is said to have commented, 'we must educate our masters'. It was hoped that this would be achieved by providing an elite education for all, and the original plans for state schooling show an admirable belief in the elevating power of education. A significant figure in this movement was the poet Matthew Arnold, the son of the great public school headmaster Thomas Arnold, who in 1851 was appointed Her Majesty's Inspector of Schools. In his work of social criticism, *Culture and Anarchy* (1869), Arnold wrote the definitive Victorian description of liberal education:

> It does not try to teach down to the level of inferior classes; it does not try to win them for this or that sect of its own, with ready-made judgements or watchwords. It seeks to do away with classes; to make the best that has been known and thought in the world current everywhere; to make all men live in an atmosphere of sweetness and light, where they may use ideas, as it uses them itself, freely, – nourished, and not bound by them.[29]

The Victorian board schools that followed universal education are now caricatured as scenes of Dickensian oppression, but that is not how they were remembered by former pupils. Although provision was patchy, a good board school offered a strong grounding in literacy and numeracy, and often a great deal more. During the 1960s, two historians carried out an oral history survey interviewing the first generation of children to be educated in these schools. Now nearing the end of their lives, the great majority, 66 per cent, had positive memories of school life. One historian, who has done much to rehabilitate our views of the Victorian school, has speculated: 'one may well wonder whether children living in poverty today, in Britain or the United States, would give their schools such high marks'.[30]

The 1904 Elementary School Code was a precursor to the national curriculum, and it established what children up to the age of 13 would learn during their compulsory education. This included English, geography, history, foreign languages, mathematics, science, physical exercise and drawing. The 'Introduction', authored by the civil servant Robert Morant, was a classic demonstration of the liberal education's egalitarian ideal. He wrote that elementary schools should instruct all pupils:

> ...carefully in habits of observation and clear reasoning, so that they may gain an intelligent acquaintance with some of the facts and laws of nature; to arouse in them a living interest in the ideals and achievements of mankind, to bring them some familiarity with the literature and history of their own country... and to develop in them such a taste for good reading and thoughtful study as will enable them to increase that knowledge in after years by their own efforts.[31]

Whilst it would be wrong to say that the schools that followed the 1870 Forster Act constituted a 'golden age' in education, they did perhaps at least follow a golden ideal.

Spurred on by universal education, the late Victorian period in Britain saw an effervescence in working-class intellectual life, well documented in Jonathan Rose's history *The Intellectual Life of the British Working Classes*. Armed with high literacy rates, these decades saw the development of the Workers Educational Association, factory reading clubs, university settlements and the Everyman Library. When the first Labour MPs entered Parliament in 1906, the journalist W. T. Stead surveyed them about their reading habits. The results, covering the likes of Adam Smith, William Shakespeare, Charles Darwin and John Stuart Mill, gave evidence of an educated and widely read community within the working class. Rose's history contains a panoply of extracts from working-class memoirs, all of which pay testament to a lively intellectual culture that crossed social divisions. Many memoirists credited their board schools with first introducing them to the world of ideas. To give just one example, Elizabeth Blackburn was a Lancashire weaver born in 1902, who later in life recalled:

> I left school at thirteen with a sound grounding in the basic arts of communication, reading and writing, and I could 'reckon up' sufficiently to cope with shopping and domestic accounts and calculate my cotton wages... I had gained some knowledge of the Bible, a lively interest in literature and, most important, some impetus to learn.

Blackburn continued to lead a lively intellectual life, reading voraciously and studying commercial arithmetic at a technical college, classical music with the WEA, and Esperanto at an adult school. She became a published author, and in her memoirs Blackburn wrote: 'To a State school and its devoted teachers, I owe a great debt, and I look back on it with much affection.'[32]

Today, one rarely hears talk of a liberal education, except in disparagement. However, there are some lone voices beckoning for its egalitarian spirit to return. One such voice is the writer and broadcaster Lindsay Johns, who is also a youth leader in Peckham, South London. The organisation with which he works, Leaders for Tomorrow, is a rather unusual youth scheme. Their children are taken to theatres, art galleries, and museums. They are encouraged to read the literary classic that their schooling neglects and taken to top universities in order to foster a spirit of aspiration. Participants in John's scheme have won scholarships to top public schools such as Westminster and Winchester, graduated from Russell Group universities, and won competitive City internships. Lindsay Johns has found common cause with Michael Gove's drive to raise the academic expectations in British schools and to combat the culture of low expectations:

> I'm so tired of the vacuous PC educationalists and the hand-wringing liberals that take great offence at Michael

> Gove's championing of a bunch of dead white men and what they perceive to be arcane, difficult books. Books which they claim have no relevance whatsoever to modern multicultural Britain and to the lives of Tommy, Dwayne, Abdul or Nadeen in the inner cities... To deny kids in the inner cities access to such mind-expanding, life-affirming and potentially life-changing authors is not only undeniably selfish and wrong but is actually positively nefarious.[33]

Unfortunately, Johns' message is rarely heard amongst those who work in today's schools. The soft bigotry of low expectations means that educators are far more likely to pander to the existing interests of their pupils, rather than challenge them to break new ground.

Teacher agency

There is no denying that in the broad averages of large-scale longitudinal studies, social background does correlate with educational success. But schools deal with individuals, not averages. It is a school's responsibility to do all it can to iron out such differences, and not to treat them as a foregone conclusion. When teachers and schools take on the belief that certain social groups can only be expected to achieve so much, such crude assumptions inevitably fulfil themselves in reality. Teachers cannot spend their whole careers waiting for family breakdown, social inequality and unemployment to end, whilst underestimating their own potential to be agents of change.

Conclusion:

How Freedom to Learn Became Freedom to Fail

Over the course of the last half-century, progressive education has triumphed in winning over the minds of British educators. It has done so not through proven effectiveness but due to its intuitive appeal to our modern sympathies: for the idealistic teacher, it seems axiomatic that granting our pupils more freedom, more independence and more autonomy will result in improved learning. However, this victory in the intellectual battle has been matched only by failure in practice. In international comparisons, Britain and America are the two nations with the richest histories of progressive schooling, but both now share an unfortunate combination of high education spending and poor pupil results.

Reflecting on the revolution that had taken place in American schools, the political philosopher Hannah Arendt wrote: 'the crisis in American education, on the one hand, announces the bankruptcy of progressive education'. That was in 1954. Arendt, a German émigré, was perceptive in diagnosing the fundamental error of this new philosophy. She wrote that the freedoms and rights of modern America, whilst beneficial in governing politics and public life, would wreak havoc if applied to the realm of a child's education. This was for the simple reason that children are of a pre-political age and still require the structures and hierarchies that had so rapidly been surpassed elsewhere in American society. Arendt clearly stated that, whilst praiseworthy in adult life, ideals such as freedom and individual autonomy had little place in the classroom:

> The problem of education in the modern world lies in the fact that by its very nature it cannot forgo either authority or tradition, and yet must proceed in a world that is neither structured by authority nor held together by tradition. We must decisively divorce the realm of education from the others, most of all from the realm of public, political life, in order to apply to it alone a concept of authority and an attitude toward the past which are appropriate to it but have no general validity and must not claim a general validity in the world of grown-ups.[1]

Accordingly, Arendt concluded that 'conservatism, in the sense of conservation, is of the essence of the educational activity'. She did not believe this because she was a political conservative, quite the opposite: she argued that it is because children needed to be prepared for existence in a free democracy that their schooling should be didactic. To return to the language of liberal education, a child's schooling should be a preparation for freedom, not freedom itself.

Such thinking runs against the grain of today's practices. In many schools, it is the autonomy of the child, not the authority of the adult, that defines the institution. This applies equally to the realms of pupil behaviour, curriculum content and teaching methods. Disorderly schools, dumbed down curriculums and aimless lessons are the result. If our education system is to improve, such a philosophy has to change. In his analysis of British education, *Wasted: Why Education isn't Educating*, the sociologist Frank Furedi laid the blame for our failing schools with a wider crisis in adult authority. The terms 'authority' and 'discipline' traditionally have a double meaning within education, applying both to the teacher's role in ensuring good pupil behaviour and providing a specialism in the subject they teach. It is this perception of the teacher as an authority that needs to be reaffirmed.

There are currently two education systems in Britain. One is respected and replicated the world over; the other is a persistent source of national embarrassment. They are the independent sector and the state maintained sector. Any comparison between the two sectors usually gets dismissed out of hand in education debates: it is argued that independent schools are simply better funded and have wealthier pupils with a higher level of cultural capital, so are bound to do well. However, research carried out by Professor David Jesson in 2005 using data supplied by the DfES showed that high-achieving pupils who are at exactly the same level of ability aged 11, are three times more likely to gain three As at A-level if they are educated in an independent school than if they are educated in a state school.[2] It is not just the profile of the pupils who go to independent schools that makes the difference, it is how they are taught once they get there that matters.

This gulf in achievement has as much to do with philosophy as it has to do with finance. Independent schools have by no means been impervious to progressive education, but compared to the state sector, they have withstood the wilder extremes of the movement. Most remain institutions where academic subject content, hard work, accuracy and formal testing are focused upon in the classroom, whilst competition, good behaviour and character formation define school life. Whilst progressive education has dominated the state sector for decades, it is the relative conservatism of Britain's independent schools that has allowed them to prosper. It is heartening that many academies have already recorded significant improvements through emulating those features traditionally associated with the independent sector.

However, progressive education in the state sector is

remarkably difficult to dislodge. It cannot be boiled down to an institution, a list of practices, or even a set of clearly defined ideas. It has become more of a temperament, or a mindset, which dictates the numberless interactions and decisions made every day by teachers across Britain Reading the work of previous generations who have criticised progressive education, it is notable how many employ the language of religion to explain its hold. Within the progressive church, child-centred teaching is an article of faith, upheld by the unchallengeable orthodoxy of constructivism. The temples of child-centred teaching are the university departments, staffed by former teachers who reinvent themselves as academics, but are really Sadducees protecting the authority of their temple's doctrine. School inspectors are the inquisition, ensuring that once sent out to classrooms, teachers do not stray from the fold. Each tenet of progressive education is promoted with a subtle moral force, and traditional approaches are depicted as not only incorrect, but iniquitous. There is little room for dissent.

That is, until recently. When New Labour came to office in 1997, their manifesto vowed to focus on 'standards not structures', but it soon became clear that an improvement in standards would be impossible whilst retaining the existing structures. For progressive education to be overturned, change could not be directed through the established channels of the Blob. Instead, exemplar schools had to be given the freedom to do things differently and blaze a trail of success along which other schools could follow. It took the dedicated and often deeply unpopular work of a steadfast reformer in the shape of Andrew Adonis to produce the Academies movement – the one New Labour reform that challenged the education establishment and has since borne fruit. Academies were a counter-current in the general trend of the New Labour years, which otherwise saw the Blob grow at an unprecedented rate.

However, since Michael Gove came to power in 2010, the Blob has experienced a sustained attack. The Education Secretary has taken the time to understand the institutional weight that sustains progressive education and, in so far as the power of office enables him to do so, he is challenging it. Just two months after the coalition came into office, the Academies Act received royal assent, giving all schools the option to convert to academy status and gain independence from local authority control. To date, 3,689 schools have taken up this offer, including the majority of secondary schools. Local authorities have been weakened as a result, and the days in which local authority advisers could dictate how schools were run are quickly becoming a thing of the past.

In addition, much of the giant quangocracy that grew up during the New Labour years has been slain. By Gove's own count, nine quangos have been scrapped since the 2010 election, and the steady stream of propaganda in favour of fads such as 21st Century Skills and independent learning has been largely stemmed. In addition, university education departments, the temples of progressive education, are in the process of being, if not cleansed, significantly challenged. The newly established school-centred initial teacher training schemes mean that trainee teachers can bypass the traditional university-based PGCE and train in the classroom as apprentices to experienced teachers instead. Indoctrination in child-centred ways at a university department is no longer a prerequisite of becoming a qualified teacher.

However, the most significant step of all has to be the Free Schools movement. A Free School is the same as an academy, with all the same freedoms from local authority control, but instead of converting from an existing school it is set up from scratch. Under such a definition, Adonis claims to have established 20 Free Schools during the New Labour years. Free Schools could have a transformative effect on British education as they are wresting power from the existing education establishment. Faith organisations, philanthropists, academy chains and groups of parents and teachers now have the power to design alternatives to the status quo, and have the chance to override the tired, failed nostrums of progressive education. Many Free Schools are currently mirroring the established consensus on teaching, but a significant number are doing things radically different.

There is now a clutch of free schools, in existence or in development, that are offering a style of education unimaginable during the age of bog-standard uniformity. In Hammersmith, the West London Free School is billing itself as a 'comprehensive grammar', offering a liberal education to all irrespective of social background. It has opened one secondary school, and has three primary schools in development. In Newham, an academically rigorous sixth-from free school established in 2012 has just seen six pupils secure places at Oxbridge and is being dubbed 'The Eton of the East End'. In Brent, the dissident teacher Katherine Birbalsingh – who in days gone by may have rendered herself unemployable by 'coming out' at the Conservative party conference – is setting up a strictly academic secondary school. Arguments over the merits of traditional versus progressive education will only ever achieve so much on paper, but Free Schools and academies can win such arguments through the sheer weight of demonstration. If they achieve their promise, they may finally offer inescapable evidence of alternative approaches to the progressive orthodoxy, which mainstream schools will feel compelled to follow.

In 1967, the Californian psychologist Carl Rogers wrote one of the defining texts of child-centred education: *Freedom to Learn*. His work betrays the essentially anti-teaching nature of progressive education, as Rogers wrote: 'teaching, in my estimation, is a vastly over-rated function'. In place of teaching, he recommended teachers reconceptualise their role as 'facilitators of learning'.

Rogers outlined a series of general principles about how pupils, once granted freedom from the teacher's direction, will greatly improve their ability to learn:

> Human beings have a natural potentiality for learning… Significant learning takes place when the subject matter is perceived by the student as having relevance for his own purposes… Much significant learning is acquired through doing… Learning is facilitated when the student participates responsibly in the learning process… Self-initiated learning which involves the whole person of the learner – feelings as well as intellect – is the most lasting and pervasive.[3]

Almost fifty years of hindsight can show us that freedom to learn, once put into practice, becomes freedom to fail. During the 1960s and 1970s, the *Black Papers* argued this point persuasively, but had no real impact on schools. Similarly, the furore created by Melanie Phillips's criticism of British schools in the *Guardian* and later her book *All Must Have Prizes* changed the national debate around education, but little change was seen in the classroom. Today, there is high degree of intelligent debate about shortcomings of contemporary teaching methods, but to have any lasting legacy such debate must be translated into real action in schools.

The Coalition government's reforms are enabling teachers to make this a reality. By enabling groups and individuals to set up new schools outside of the education establishment, current reforms will allow fresh ideas finally to be injected into state education. This should not be seen as a question of partisan politics. There is a tendency to assume that traditional education is somehow 'right-wing', whilst progressive education belongs to the left. Such an assumption is nonsense. A more instructive distinction is that traditional education works, whilst progressive education has been proven to fail. There is little 'progressive' about an educational philosophy that prevents disadvantaged pupils from achieving and leads to a deepening of social inequality. As E. D. Hirsch has written, to be a political progressive, one has to be an educational conservative.

Progressive education has given us decades of chaotic schools, disenchanted teachers and pupil failure. Today, its legacy in Britain is an estimated seven million illiterate adults spanning the generations. The consequences for the economy, British society and our national culture are devastating. All involved in education need to realise that this is a national embarrassment for which poverty and inequality should never be used as an excuse. If schools are given the freedom to innovate they may yet stand the chance of correcting these past mistakes. If they do, we could finally hear progressive education's long, withdrawing roar.

Select Bibliography

Abbott, I. *et al.*, *Education Policy*, London: SAGE, 2012.

Adams, G. L., and Engelmann, S., *Research on Direct Instruction: 25 Years Beyond DISTAR*, Seattle: Education Achievement Systems, 1996.

Adonis, A., *Education, Education, Education: Reforming England's Schools*, London: Biteback, 2012.

Alexander, R., (et al), *'The Three Wise Men Report', Curriculum Organisation and Classroom Practice in Primary Schools: A discussion paper*, London: DES, 1992.

Alexander, R., *Primary Education in Leeds: Twelfth and final report from the Primary Needs Independent Evaluation Project*, Leeds: Leeds City Council Printing Unit, 1991.

Arendt, H., *Six Exercises in Political Thought*, London: Faber and Faber, 1961.

Arthur, J., *Education with Character: The moral economy of schooling*, London: Routledge, 2003.

Baker, K., *The Turbulent Years: My Life in Politics*, London: Faber and Faber, 1993.

Barber, M., *The Learning Game: Arguments for an Education Revolution*, London: Cassell Group, 1996.

Beere, J., *The Perfect Ofsted Lesson*, Carmarthen: Crown Publishing, 2010.

Benn, C., and Chitty, C., *Thirty Years On: Is Comprehensive Education Alive and Well or Struggling to Survive?*, London: Fulton, 1996.

Benn, C., and Simon, B., *Half Way There: Report on the British Comprehensive School Reform*, Harmondsworth: Penguin, 1972.

Bennett, N., *Teaching Styles and Pupil Progress*, London: Open Books, 1976.

Bennett, T., *Teacher Proof: Why research in education doesn't always mean what it claims, and what you can do about it*, London: Routledge, 2013.

Benson, A. C., *The Schoolmaster*, Woodbridge: Peridot Press, 2011.

Bentley, T., *Learning Beyond the Classroom: Education for a changing world*, London: Demos, 1998.

Berg, L., *Risinghill: Death of A Comprehensive School*, Harmondsworth: Penguin, 1968.

Birbalsingh, K., *To Miss With Love*, London: Penguin, 2011, p.33.

Bogdanor, V., *Standards in Schools*, London: Cranbourne Press, 1978.

Bowis, J., *ILEA: The Closing Chapter*, London: Conservative Political Centre, 1988.

Boyson, R., *Oversubscribed: The Story of Highbury Grove School*, London: Ward Lock Educational, 1974.

Brooks, D., *The Social Animal: The Hidden Sources of Love, Character, and Achievement*, New York: Random House, 2011.

Brooks, G. et al, *What Teachers in Training are Taught about Reading*, London: NFER, 1992.

Burkard, T., and Talbot Rice, S., *School Quangos: An agenda for abolition and reform*, London: Centre for Policy Studies, 2009.

Callaghan, D., *Conservative Party Education Policies*, Brighton: Sussex Academic Press, 2006.

Callaghan, J., *Time and Chance*, Glasgow: Collins, 1987.

Campbell, J., *Margaret Thatcher: Volume II: The Iron Lady*, London: Pimlico, 2004.

Cannadine, D. et al, *The Right Kind of History: Teaching the Past in the Twentieth Century*, Basingstoke: Palgrave McMillan, 2011

Capel, S., Leask, M., and Turner, T. (eds), *Learning to Teach in the Secondary School: A Companion to School Experience*, Abingdon: Routledge, 2009.

Caroll, C., *On the Edge*, Cheltenham: Monday Books, 2010.

Christodoulou, D., *Seven Myths about Education*, London: Routledge, 2013.

Clark, R. E., Kirschner, P. A., and Sweller, J., 'Putting Students on the Path to Learning: The Case for Fully Guided Instruction' in *American Education*, Spring, 2012.

Cox, B., *The Great Betrayal*, London: Chapmans, 1992.

Cox, C. B. and Dyson, A. E. (eds), *Black Paper 1: The Fight for Education*, London: Critical Quarterly Society, 1969.

Cox, C. B. and Dyson, A. E. (eds), *Black Paper 3: Goodbye Mr Short*, London: Critical Quarterly Society, 1970.

Cox, C. B., and Boyson, R. (eds), *Black Paper 4: The Fight for Education*, London: J. M. Dent & Sons, 1975.

Cox, C. B., and Boyson, R. (eds), *Black Paper 5*, London: Maurice Temple Smith, 1977.

Cox, C. B., and Dyson, A. E. (eds), *Black Paper 2: Crisis in Education*, London: Critical Quarterly Society, 1969.

Cox, C., and Marks, J., *The Right to Learn: Purpose, Professionalism and Accountability in State Education*, London: Centre for Policy Studies, 1982.

Crossland, S., *Tony Crossland*, London: Hodder & Stoughton, 1983.

Cunningham, P., *Curriculum Change in the Primary School since 1945: Dissemination of the Progressive Ideal*, London: Falmer, 1988.

Daunt, P. E., *Comprehensive Values*, London: Heinemann, 1975.

Davies, H., *The Creighton Report: A Year in the Life of A Comprehensive School*, Hamilton: Hamish, 1976.

de Waal, Anastasia, *Inspection, Inspection, Inspection: How Ofsted crushes independent schools and independent teachers*, London: Civitas, 2006.

Donoughue, B., *Downing Street Diary*, London: Jonathan Cape, 2008.

Donoughue, B., *The Heat of the Kitchen: An Autobiography*, London: Politico's, 2003.

Ecclestone, K., and Hayes, D., *The Dangerous Rise of Therapeutic Education*, Abingdon: Routledge, 2009.

Elton, R., *The Elton Report: Discipline in Schools*, London: Her Majesty's Stationery Office, 1989.

Furedi, F., *Wasted: Why Education Isn't Educating*, London: Continuum, 2009.

Graham, D., *A Lesson for us all: The making of the National Curriculum*, London: Routledge, 1993.

Halcrow, M., *Keith Joseph: A Single Mind*, London: Macmillan, 1989.

Hargreaves, D. H., *The Challenge for the Comprehensive School: Culture, Curriculum and Community*, London: Routledge and Kegan Paul, 1982.

Hattie, J., and Yates, G., *Visible Learning and the Science of How we Learn*, Abingdon: Routledge, 2013.

Hattie, J., *Visible Learning: A Synthesis of over 800 meta-analyses relating to achievement*, Abingdon: Routledge, 2009.

Hirsch, E. D., *Cultural Literacy: What Every American Needs to Know*, New York: Random House, 1988.

Hirsch, E. D., *The knowledge deficit: creating the shocking education gap for American children*, Boston: Houghton Mifflin, 2006.

Johnson, M., *Subject to Change: New Thinking on the Curriculum*, London: ATL, 2007.

Johnston, R. S., and Watson, J. E, *Insight 17: A Seven Year Study of the Effects of Synthetic Phonics Teaching on Reading and Spelling Attainment*, Edinburgh: Scottish Executive Education Department, 2005.

Kynaston, D., *Austerity Britain: 1945-51*, London: Bloomsbury, 2007.

Lawlor, S. (et al), *Teaching Matters: The Recruitment, Employment and Retention of Teachers*, London: Politea, 2007.

Lawlor, S., *Teachers Mistaught: Training in theories or education in subjects?*, London, Centre for Policy Studies, 1990.

Lowe, R., *The Death of Progressive Education: How teachers lost control of the classroom*, London: Routledge, 2007.

Lucas, H., *After Summerhill: What happened to the pupils of Britain's most radical school*, London: Herbert Adler, 2011.

Lupton, R., and Obolenskaya, P., 'Labour's Record on Education: Policy, Spending and Outcomes 1997-2010', *Social Policy in a Cold Climate Working Paper WP03*, London: CASE, 2013.

Macmillan, B., *Why Schoolchildren Can't Read*, London: Institute of Economic Ideas, 1996.

Marshall, P., (ed.), *The Tail: How England's Schools fail one child in five and what can be done*, London: Profile Books, 2013.

Marsland, D., and Seaton, N., *The Empire Strikes Back: The 'Creative Subversion' of the National Curriculum*, York: Campaign for Real Education, 1993.

Massey, A., *Best Behaviour: School discipline, intervention and exclusion*, London: Policy Exchange, 2011.

Mayer, R. E., 'Should There Be a Three-Strikes Rule Against Pure Discovery Learning? The Case for Guided Methods of Instruction', in *American Psychologist*, Vol. 59, No. 1, 2004.

Morris, J. M., *Reading in the Primary School*, London: Newnes, 1959.

Neill, A. S., *Summerhill*, Harmondsworth: Penguin, 1980.

North, J., (ed), *The GCSE: An Examination*, London: The Claridge Press, 1987.

O'Hear, A., *Father of Child-Centredness: John Dewey and the ideology of modern education*, London: Centre for Policy Studies, 1991.

Oakeshott, M., *The Voice of Liberal Learning*, Indianapolis: Liberty Fund, 1989.

Palmer, J. A. (ed.), *Fifty Modern Thinkers on Education: From Piaget to the Present*, Abingdon: Routledge, 2001.

Pedley, R., *The Comprehensive School*, Harmondsworth: Penguin, 1967.

Perkins, D.N., *Smart schools: From training memories to educating minds*, New York: The Free Press, 1992.

Peters, R. S. (ed.), *Perspectives on Plowden*, London: Routledge & Kegan Paul.

Phillips, M., *All Must Have Prizes*, London: Little Brown, 1996.

Plaskow, M., *Life and Death of the Schools Council*, Lewes: Flamer Press, 1985.

Plowden, B., *The Plowden Report: Children and their Primary Schools, A Report of the Central Advisory Council for Education*, London: Her Majesty's Stationery Office, 1967.

Pollard, S., *David Blunkett*, London: Hodder and Stoughton, 2005.

Rashid, S., and Brooks, G., *The levels of attainment in literacy and numeracy of 13- to 19-year-olds in England, 1948–2009*, London: NRDC, 2010.

Ravitch, D., *Left Back: A Century of Battles over School Reform*, New York: Simon & Schuster, 2001.

Raynor, J., and Harris, E., *Schooling in the City*, London: Open University Press, 1977.

Riley, K. A., *Whose School is it Anyway?*, London: Falmer, 1998.

Rogers, C., Freedom to Learn, Columbus: Charles E. Merrill Publishing Company, 1969.

Rose, J., *Intellectual Life of the British Working Classes*, London: Yale University Press, 2001.

Sandbrook, D., *Seasons in the Sun: The Fight for Britain, 1974-79*, London: Allen Lane, 2012.

Sealey L. G. W. and Gibbon, V., *Communication and Learning in the Primary School*, New York: Schocken, 1972.

Seltzer, K., and Bentley, T., *The Creative Age: Knowledge and skills for the new economy*, London: Demos, 1999.

Skidelsky, R., *English Progressive Schools*, Harmondsworth: Penguin, 1969.

Smith, J., *The Lazy Teacher's Handbook: How Your Students Learn More When You Teach Less*, Bancyfelin: Crown House, 2010.

Start, K. B., and Wells, B. K., *The Trend of Reading Standards*, Slough, NFER, 1972.

Steer, A. (et al), *Learning Behaviour: The Report of the Practitioners' Group on School Behaviour and Discipline*, Nottingham: DfES Publications, 2005.

Thornbury, R., *The Changing Urban School*, London: Methuen, 1978.

Timmins, N., *The Five Giants: A Biography of the Welfare State*, London: HarperCollins, 1995.

Tough, P., *How Children Succeed: Grit, Curiosity and the Hidden Power of Character*, London: Random House, 2012.

Trenaman, N., *Review of the Schools Council*, London: Department of Education and Science, 1981.

Vaughan, M. (ed.), *Summerhill and A. S. Neill*, Maidenhead: Open University Press, 2006.

Watts, J. (ed.), *The Countesthorpe Experience: The First Five Years*, London: George Allen & Unwin, 1977.

Weeks, A., *Comprehensive Schools: Past, Present and Future*, Methuen: London, 1986.

Whitman, D., *Sweating the Small Stuff: Inner-City Schools and the New Paternalism*, Washington DC: Thomas B. Fordham Institute, 2008.

Willingham, D. T., *Why Don't Students Like School?*, San Francisco: Wiley, 2009.

Wilson, J., *Discipline and Moral Education*, Windsor: NFER, 1981.

Wolf, A., *Review of Vocational Education: The Wolf Report*, London: DfE, 2011.

Woodhead, C., *A Desolation of Learning: Is this the education our children deserve?*, Chippenham: Pencil Sharp Publishing, 2009.

Woodhead, C., *Class War: The State of British Education*, London: Little, Brown, 2002.

Young, M., *Knowledge and Control: New Directions for the Sociology of Education*, London: Collier-Macmillan, 1971.

Notes

Introduction

1 *Times Educational Supplement*, 4 October 1996
2 Lupton, R., and Obolenskaya, P., 'Labour's Record on Education: Policy, Spending and Outcomes 1997-2010', *Social Policy in a Cold Climate Working Paper WP03*, London: CASE, 2013, pp.16-17
3 OECD, *Country Note: United Kingdom*, OECD Publishing, 2013, p.1
4 OECD, *OECD Skills Outlook 2013: First Results From the Survey of Adult Skills*, OECD Publishing, 2013, p.107
5 *Changing the pace: CBI/Pearson education and skills survey*, CBI, 2013, p.39
6 Marshall, P., (ed.), *The Tail: How England's Schools fail one child in five and what can be done*, London: Profile Books, 2013, p.16
7 Massey, A., *Best Behaviour: School discipline, intervention and exclusion*, London: Policy Exchange, 2011, p.5
8 House of Commons Education Committee, *Great teachers: attracting, training and retaining the best*, London: The Stationery Office Limited, 2012, p.35
9 *Degrees of Success: University Chances by Individual School*, London: The Sutton Trust, 2011, p.9
10 Rashid, S., and Brooks, G., *The levels of attainment in literacy and numeracy of 13- to 19-year-olds in England, 1948–2009*, London: NRDC, 2010, pp.33-34
11 Crawford, R., Emmerson, C., and Tetlow, G., *A Survey of Public Spending in the UK*, London: Institute for Fiscal Studies, 2009, p.22
12 Gove, M., 'The Progressive Betrayal', speech to the Social Market Foundation, 5 February 2013
13 Leading Article, 'Education Reform: Some good school work, but must do better', *Observer*, 9 February 2013

1 Radicalism: 1960-1967

1 Neill, A. S., *Summerhill*, Harmondsworth: Penguin, 1980, and Skidelsky, R., *English Progressive Schools*, Harmondsworth: Penguin, 1969
2 Vaughan, M. (ed.), *Summerhill and A. S. Neill*, Maidenhead: Open University Press, 2006, p.vii
3 *The Teacher*, January 2008, p.18
4 Brighouse, T., 'Introduction' in Vaughan, *Summerhill and A. S. Neill*, p.1

5 Vaughan, *Summerhill*, p.45
6 Lucas, H., *After Summerhill: What happened to the pupils of Britain's most radical school*, London: Herbert Adler, 2011, p.19
7 Rousseau, J. J., *Emile*, transl. Foxley, B., London: Everyman, 1911, p.57
8 O'Hear, A., *Father of Child-Centredness: John Dewey and the ideology of modern education*, London: Centre for Policy Studies, 1991
9 Ravitch, D., *Left Back: A Century of Battles over School Reform*, New York: Simon & Schuster, 2001, p.288
10 Skidelsy, *English Progressive Schools*, p.13
11 Hinshelwood, R., 'Susan Isaacs' in Palmer, J. A. (ed.), *Fifty Modern Thinkers on Education: From Piaget to the Present*, Abingdon: Routledge, 2001, p.6
12 Gross, M., 'An Experimental Education', *Standpoint*, May 2011
13 Hughes, C., 'Dartington to close after scandals and bad publicity', *The Times*, 17 April 1986
14 Wilby, P., 'Summerhill school: these days surprisingly strict', *Guardian*, 27 May 2013
15 *Hadow Report: The Primary School*, London: HM Stationery Office, 1931, p.139
16 *Hadow Report: Infant and Nursery Schools*, London: HM Stationery Office, 1933, p.185
17 Froome, S., 'Reading and the School Handicap' in Cox, C. B., and Boyson, R. (eds), *Black Paper 4: The Fight for Education*, London: J. M. Dent & Sons, 1975, p.11
18 Morris, J. M., *Reading in the Primary School*, London: Newnes, 1959, p.53
19 Cox and Dyson, *Black Paper 4*, p.9
20 Thornbury, R., *The Changing Urban School*, London: Methuen, 1978, p.130
21 Quoted in Cox, C. B., and Dyson, A. E. (eds), *Black Paper 2: Crisis in Education*, London: Critical Quarterly Society, 1969, p.10
22 Cox and Dyson, *Black Paper 2*, p.87
23 Start, K. B., and Wells, B. K., *The Trend of Reading Standards*, Slough, NFER, 1972, p.70
24 Start and Wells, *The Trend of Reading Standards*, pp.23-30
25 *I do, and I understand*, London: Nuffield Foundation, 1967, inside cover
26 Mansfield, D. E., *Mathematical Forum: An anthology of the first five issues of the Bulletin of the Nuffield Mathematics Teaching Project*, London: Butler and Tanner, 1966, p.2
27 Lowe, R., *The Death of Progressive Education: How teachers lost control of the classroom*, London: Routledge, 2007, pp.43-46

28 Sealey L. G. W. and Gibbon, V., *Communication and Learning in the Primary School*, New York: Schocken, 1972, p.128
29 Cunningham, P., *Curriculum Change in the Primary School since 1945: Dissemination of the Progressive Ideal*, London: Falmer, 1988, p.81
30 'Obituary: Lady Plowden' in *Guardian*, 3 October 2000
31 Plowden, B., *The Plowden Report: Children and their Primary Schools, A Report of the Central Advisery Council for Education*, Vol. I, London: Her Majesty's Stationery Office, 1967, p.9
32 Bernstein, B., and Davies, B., 'Some Sociological Comments on Plowden' in Peters, R. S. (ed.), *Perspectives on Plowden*, London: Routledge & Kegan Paul, p.56
33 Plowden, *The Plowden Report*, Vol. I
34 Riley, K. A., *Whose School is it Anyway?*, London: Falmer, 1998, p.13
35 Plowden, *The Plowden Report*, Vol. II, p.225
36 Peters, *Perspectives on Plowden*, pp.8; 12
37 M. Kogan, 'The Plowden Report Twenty Years on' in *Oxford Review of Education*, Vol. 13 No. 1, 1987, p.16
38 Cunningham, *Curriculum Change in the Primary School since 1945*, p.156
39 *Times Educational Supplement*, 10th January 1969
40 Cunningham, *Curriculum Change in the Primary School since 1945*, pp.31; 69
41 Pedley, R., *The Comprehensive School*, Harmondsworth: Penguin, 1967, p.59
42 Berg, L., *Risinghill: Death of A Comprehensive School*, Harmondsworth: Penguin, 1968, p.130
43 'Risinghill school to close', *The Times*, 4 June 1965
44 Lowe, *The Death of Progressive Education*, p.47
45 Partridge, R. W., 'Letters to the Editor', *The Times* 10 July 1969
46 Bogdanor, V., *Standards in Schools*, London: Cranbourne Press, 1978, p.6
47 Cunningham, *Curriculum Change in the Primary School since 1945*, p.87
48 Kynaston, D., *Austerity Britain: 1945-51*, London: Bloomsbury, 2007, p.575
49 Timmins, N., *The Five Giants: A Biography of the Welfare State*, London: HarperCollins, 1995, p.100
50 Davies, H., *The Creighton Report: A Year in the Life of A Comprehensive School*, Hamilton: Hamish, 1976, p.31
51 Crossland, S., *Tony Crossland*, London: Hodder & Stoughton, 1983, p.148

52 Weeks, A., *Comprehensive Schools: Past, Present and Future*, Methuen: London, 1986, p.8
53 Simon, B., 'Robin Pedley 1914-1988: Comprehensive Pioneer', *Education for Tomorrow*, No. 67, Autumn 2000
54 Pedley, *The Comprehensive School*, pp.32; 109; 161
55 Pedley, R., *The Comprehensive School*, Harmondsworth: Penguin, 1978, p.103
56 Benn, C., and Chitty, C., *Thirty Years On: Is Comprehensive Education Alive and Well or Struggling to Survive?*, London: Fulton, 1996, p.249
57 Quoted in Benn and Chitty, *Thirty Years On* p.251
58 Benn, C., and Simon, B., *Half Way There: Report on the British Comprehensive School Reform*, Harmondsworth: Penguin, 1972, p.230
59 Pedley, *The Comprehensive School* (1978), p.105
60 Benn and Chitty, *Thirty Years On*, pp.259-60
61 Benn and Simon, *Half Way There*, p.218
62 Quoted in Benn and Chitty, *Thirty Years On*, p.229
63 Boyson, R., *Oversubscribed: The Story of Highbury Grove School*, London: Ward Lock Educational, 1974, pp.10; 32
64 Foot, P., 'Boyson's Old School Ties', *Daily Mirror*, November 14 1979
65 Benn and Simon, *Half Way There*, p.371
66 Cox, B., *The Great Betrayal*, London: Chapmans, 1992, pp.143; 151
67 Johnson, C. M., 'Freedom in Junior Schools', in Cox, C. B. and Dyson, A. E. (eds), *Black Paper 1: The Fight for Education*, London: Critical Quarterly Society, 1969, pp.48-50
68 Raymond, J., *The Sunday Times* 16 March 1969
69 Gould, J., 'Culture and anti-culture', *Observer*, 23 March 1969
70 Cox, *The Great Betrayal*, p.5
71 Crawford, G. W. J., 'The Primary School: A Balanced View' in Cox and Dyson, *Black Paper 2*, p.100
72 Pedley, *The Comprehensive School* (1967), p.198

2 Riot: 1967-1979

1 Davies, H., *The Creighton Report: A Year in the Life of A Comprehensive School*, Hamilton: Hamish, 1976
2 Daunt, P. E., *Comprehensive Values*, London: Heinemann, 1975, p.108
3 Wilkinson, M., 'Stop these trendies before they ruin ALL our children', *Daily Mail*, 16 October 1973

4 Quoted in Sandbrook, D., *Seasons in the Sun: The Fight for Britain, 1974-79*, London: Allen Lane, 2012, pp.212-213
5 Watkins, A., 'From Tawney to Tameside', *Observer,* 8 August 1976
6 Thornbury, *The Changing Urban School*, p.5
7 Documentary can be viewed online: http://www.youtube.com/watch?v=JY7ThNFtf68 [accessed January 2014]
8 Butt, R., 'A sorry tale of two conflicting cultures in the country's classrooms', *The Times,* 18 July 1974
9 Butt, R., 'Politics and Education' in Cox and Boyson, *Black Paper 4,* p.43
10 Little, A., 'Declining pupil performance and the urban environment', in Raynor, J., and Harris, E., *Schooling in the City,* London: Open University Press, 1977, p.35
11 Quoted in Cox and Boyson, *Black Paper 4,* p.62
12 Riley, *Whose School is it Anyway,* p.27
13 Walker, D., 'William Tyndale' in Cox, C. B., and Boyson, R. (eds), *Black Paper 5,* London: Maurice Temple Smith, 1977, p.39
14 Sandbrook, *Seasons in the Sun,* pp.210; 208
15 Cox and Boyson, *Black Paper 5,* p.38
16 Abbott, I. et al., *Education Policy,* London: SAGE, 2012, p.32
17 Thornbury, *The Changing Urban School,* p.113; and Trenaman, N., *Review of the Schools Council,* London: Department of Education and Science, 1981, p.28
18 Plaskow, M., *Life and Death of the Schools Council,* Lewes: Flamer Press, 1985, p.4
19 Cannadine, D. et al, *The Right Kind of History: Teaching the Past in the Twentieth Century,* Basingstoke: Palgrave McMillan, 2011, p.160
20 Interview with Chris Culpin from 'History in Education Project', http://sas-space.sas.ac.uk/3149/ [accessed January 2014]
21 Thornbury, *The Changing Urban School,* pp.110; 123
22 Quoted in Cunningham, *Curriculum Change in the Primary School since 1945,* p.225
23 Cox and Boyson, *Black Paper 5,* p.17
24 Woodhead, C., *Class War: The State of British Education,* London: Little, Brown, 2002, p.33
25 Green, K., 'Why Comprehensives Fail' in Cox and Boyson, *Black Paper 4,* p.24
26 Bremner, M., 'Why do the critics so furiously rage together… and imagine a vain thing?' in Cox, C. B. and Dyson, A. E. (eds), *Black Paper 3: Goodbye Mr Short,* London: Critical Quarterly Society, 1970, p.126
27 Benn and Simon, *Half Way There,* p.354

28 Watts, J. (ed.), *The Countesthorpe Experience: The First Five Years*, London: George Allen & Unwin, 1977
29 Brian Simon, 'Countesthorpe in the Context of Comprehensive Development' in Watts, *The Countesthorpe Experience*, p.26
30 *Times Educational Supplement*, 28 January 2000
31 Watts, *The Countesthorpe Experience*, p.144
32 Pedley, *The Comprehensive School* (1978), p.105
33 NUT, *Teachers Talking*, London: Victoria House, 1978, p.7
34 Galton, M., Simon, B. and Croll., P., *Inside the Primary Classroom*, London: Routledge & Keegan Paul, 1980, p.140
35 Bennett, N., *Teaching Styles and Pupil Progress*, London: Open Books, 1976, p.152
36 Leading article, 'Progressive is not progressive', *The Times*, 26 April 1976
37 Quoted in *Cox and Boyson, Black Paper 5*, p.13
38 Leading article, 'Progressive is not progressive', *The Times*, 1 May 1976
39 Quoted in Bogdanor, *Standards in Schools*, London: Cranbourne Press, 1978, p.2
40 Simon, B., *Education and the Social Order*, London: Lawrence & Wishart, 1991, p.444
41 Cox and Boyson, *Black Paper 5*, p.16
42 Crawford et al, *A Survey of Public Spending in the UK*, p.22
43 Quoted in Riley, *Whose School is it Anyway?*, p.17
44 http://news.bbc.co.uk/1/hi/magazine/7021797.stm [accessed January 2014]
45 Young, M., *Knowledge and Control: New Directions for the Sociology of Education*, London: Collier-Macmillan, 1971, p.3
46 Kelly, A. V., *The Curriculum: Theory and Practice*, London: Sage, 2009, p.40
47 Cox and Dyson, *Black Paper 3*, p.67
48 *The Times Educational Supplement*, 8 May 1976
49 *The Times Educational Supplement*, 7 June 1974
50 Cited in Rose, J., *Intellectual Life of the British Working Classes*, London: Yale University Press, 2001, p.366
51 Quoted in Cox and Boyson, *Black Paper 5*, p.84
52 Watkins, A., 'From Tawney to Tameside', *Observer*, 8 August 1976
53 Murdoch, I., 'Socialism and Selection' in Cox and Boyson, *Black Paper 4*, p.9
54 Bernstein, B., 'Education cannot compensate for society', New Society, 26 February 1970, 344-47
55 Weeks, *Comprehensive Schools*, p.98
56 Cox and Boyson, *Black Paper 4*, p.9

57 Rose, *Intellectual Life of the British Working Classes*, p.373
58 Cox and Boyson, *Black Paper 5*, p.38
59 Quoted in Sandbrook, *Seasons in the Sun*, p.213
60 Cox and Dyson, *Black Paper 4*, p.4
61 Donoughue, B., *The Heat of the Kitchen: An Autobiography*, London: Politico's, 2003, p.240
62 Riley, *Whose School is it Anyway?*, pp.58-59
63 Callaghan, J., *Time and Chance*, Glasgow: Collins, 1987, p.409
64 Quoted in Lowe, *The Death of Progressive Education*, p.72
65 Donoughue, B., *Downing Street Diary*, London: Jonathan Cape, 2008, p.84
66 Cleland, I. D., 'Letters to the Editor', *The Times*, 22 October 1976
67 Callaghan, *Time and Chance*, p.410
68 *Education in Schools: A Consultative Document*, London: Her Majesty's Stationery Office, 1977, p.8
69 Lowe, *The Death of Progressive Education*, p.76

3 Reform: 1979-1986

1 Callaghan, D., *Conservative Party Education Policies*, Brighton: Sussex Academic Press, 2006, p.25
2 Simon, *Education and the Social Order*, pp.477; 500
3 Callaghan, *Conservative Party Education Policies*, p.45
4 Halcrow, M., *Keith Joseph: A Single Mind*, London: Macmillan, 1989, p.168
5 Elton, R., *The Elton Report: Discipline in Schools*, London: Her Majesty's Stationery Office, 1989, p.81
6 Simon, *Education and the Social Order*, pp.509-512
7 Halcrow, *Keith Joseph*, p.187
8 Elizabeth Cottrell, 'The Two Nations in Education' in Cox, C., and Marks, J., *The Right to Learn: Purpose, Professionalism and Accountability in State Education*, London: Centre for Policy Studies, 1982
9 HMI, *Primary education in England: A survey by HM Inspectors of Schools*, London: Her Majesty's Stationery Office, 1978, p.27
10 Quoted in Cox, *The Great Betrayal*, p.216-217
11 Butt, R., 'Schools: the battle has only just begun', *The Times*, 27 June 1985
12 Hillgate Group, *Learning to Teach*, London: The Claridge Press, 1989, p.7
13 Hargreaves, D. H., *The Challenge for the Comprehensive School: Culture, Curriculum and Community*, London: Routledge and Kegan Paul, 1982

14 Lawlor, S., *Teachers Mistaught: Training in theories or education in subjects?*, London, Centre for Policy Studies, 1990, p.28
15 Hillgate Group, *Learning to Teach*, pp.5; 29
16 HMI, The New Teacher in School, London: Her Majesty's Stationery Office, 1982, p.37
17 Lawlor, *Teachers Mistaught*, p.17
18 Wilson, J., *Discipline and Moral Education*, Windsor: NFER, 1981, p.46
19 Pilkington, E., 'Battle for the minds of new teachers', *Guardian*, 4 December 1990
20 Rowlands, C., 'Why don't they just let us teach?', *Daily Mail*, 12 May 1983
21 Phelps, P., 'The Battle of St Jude's', *Daily Mail*, 8 October, 1986; Lee-Potter, L., 'My warning to every headmaster in Britain', *Daily Mail*, 26 November 1986
22 Bowis, J., *ILEA: The Closing Chapter*, London: Conservative Political Centre, 1988
23 Quoted in Cox, *The Great Betrayal*, p.6
24 Cox and Marks, *The Right to Learn*, p.13
25 Alexander, R., *Primary Education in Leeds: Twelfth and final report from the Primary Needs Independent Evaluation Project*, Leeds: Leeds City Council Printing Unit, 1991, p.8
26 Cox, *The Great Betrayal*, p.265
27 Cox, *The Great Betrayal*, pp.28; 137
28 Elton, *The Elton Report*, p.58
29 Kilroy-Silk, R., 'Well schooled in violence', *The Times*, 28 October 1988
30 Kilroy-Silk, 'Rising toll of the classroom war', *The Times*, 5 December 1987
31 Figures can be accessed online at http://www.britsocat.com/ [accessed January 2014]
32 'Children favour school discipline, survey says', *The Times*, 1 December 1977
33 McCarthy, M., 'Four million – the truant constituents', *The Times*, 3 September 1986
34 Elton, *The Elton Report*, p.86
35 Thompson, S., 'Concern at teachers quitting 'burn-out' careers', *The Times*, 1 June 1988
36 Macmillan, B., *Why Schoolchildren Can't Read*, London: Institute of Economic Ideas, 1996, p.53
37 Brooks, G. et al, *What Teachers in Training are Taught about Reading*, London: NFER, 1992
38 Macmillan, *Why Schoolchildren Can't Read*, p.99

39 Smith, F., *Reading*, Cambridge: Cambridge University Press, 1985, p.5
40 *Times Educational Supplement*, 19 November 2004
41 Meek, M., *Learning to Read*, London: The Bodley Head, 1982, p.22
42 Meek, M., *How Texts Teach What Readers Learn*, Stroud: Thimble Press, 1988, p.8
43 Waterland, L., *Read With Me: An Apprenticeship Approach to Reading*, Stroud: Thimble Press, 1985, pp.9-10
44 Beard, R., and Oakhill, J., *Reading by Apprenticeship*, Slough: NFER, 1994, pp.16-21; 34
45 Macmillan, *Why Schoolchildren Can't Read*, pp.161-165
46 Martin Turner, 'Foreword: Educating the Educators' in Macmillan, *Why Schoolchildren Can't Read*, p.9
47 Turner, M., *Sponsored Reading Failure*, Oxford: the Education Unit, 1990, p.10
48 Macmillan, *Why Schoolchildren Can't Read*, p.75
49 Brooks et al, *What Teachers in Training are Taught about Reading*, pp.90; 56
50 Macmillan, *Why Schoolchildren Can't Read*, p.32
51 Benedict, P., 'A-plus is for the alphabet', *Guardian*, 20 March 1990
52 Bald, J., 'The great literacy cover-up', *Guardian* 5 October 1993
53 Caseby, R., and Abrams, F., 'Pupils find old-fashioned way of reading as simple as ABC', *The Sunday Times* 1 July 1990
54 Turner, *Sponsored Reading Failure*, p.21
55 Phillips, M., *All Must Have Prizes*, London: Little Brown, 1996, pp.75-80
56 Cato, V., and Whetton, C., *An Enquiry into LEA Evidence on Standards of Reading of Seven Year Old Children*, Slough: NFER, 1991
57 Gorman, T., and Fernandes, C., *Reading in Recession*, Slough: NFER, 1992, p.6
58 Macmillan, *Why Schoolchildren Can't Read*, p.97
59 North, J., (ed), *The GCSE: An Examination*, London: The Claridge Press, 1987, p.119
60 DES, *GCSE: The National Criteria*, London: Her Majesty's Stationery Office, 1985, p.3
61 Mobley, M., (et al), *All About GCSE: A Clear and Concise Summary of all the basic information about GCSE*, London: Heinemann, 1986
62 Phillips, M., 'A modern history lesson to gag on', *Guardian*, 29 June 1990. For a full account, see Phillips, *All Must Have Prizes*, pp.133-134

63 Cox, C., and Marks, J., *The Insolence of Office: Education and the Civil Servants*, London: The Claridge Press, 1988

64 Trenaman, *Review of the Schools Council*, p.33

65 Halcrow, *Keith Joseph*, p.169

66 Quoted in Phillips, *All Must Have Prizes*, p.3

67 Hill, G., 'Spectrum: What they do not know', *The Times*, 18 February 1988

68 http://www.britsocat.com/ [accessed January, 2014]

4 Reform: 1986-1997

1 Marsland, D., and Seaton, N., *The Empire Strikes Back: The 'Creative Subversion' of the National Curriculum*, York: Campaign for Real Education, 1993, p.1

2 Campbell, J., *Margaret Thatcher: Volume II: The Iron Lady*, London: Pimlico, 2004, p.542

3 Callaghan, *Conservative Party Education Policies*, p.86

4 HMI, *The Curriculum from 5 to 16: HMI Series: Curriculum Matters No. 2*, London: Her Majesty's Stationery Office 1985, p.16

5 Baker, K., *The Turbulent Years: My Life in Politics*, London: Faber and Faber, 1993, pp.168; 201

6 Graham, D., *A Lesson for us all: The making of the National Curriculum*, London: Routledge, 1993, pp.26-30

7 Baker, *The Turbulent Years*, p.203

8 Graham, *A Lesson for us all*, p.105

9 Cox, *The Great Betrayal*, p.248

10 Phillips, *All Must Have Prizes*, p.151

11 Baker, *The Turbulent Years*, p.201

12 Phillips, *All Must Have Prizes*, p.149

13 Lowe, *The Death of Progressive Education*, p.108

14 Graham, *A Lesson for us all*, p.1

15 *Times Educational Supplement*, 1 July 1988

16 Phillips, *All Must Have Prizes*, p.143

17 Baker, *The Turbulent Years*, p.198

18 Marsland and Seaton, *The Empire Strikes Back*, p.9

19 Callaghan, *Conservative Party Education Policies*, p.90

20 Black, P., *National Curriculum Task Group on Assessment and Testing: A Report*, London: Department of Education and Science and the Welsh Office, 1988

21 Phillips, *All Must Have Prizes*, p.182

22 Chaudhary, V., 'Charles's criticisms split educationists', *Guardian*, 25 March 1991

23 Skidelsky, R., and McGovern, R., 'Top marks for wasting time and money', *Guardian*, 16 April 1991

24 Lowe, *The Death of Progressive Education*, p.104
25 Meikie, J., 'Curriculum start 'will cost £2.8 billion'', *Guardian*, 20 March 1992
26 Graham, *A Lesson for us all*, p.102
27 Callaghan, *Conservative Party Education Policies*, pp.97; 102-113
28 Balen, M., *Kenneth Clarke*, London: Fourth Estate, 1994, p.221
29 Callaghan, *Conservative Party Education Policies*, p.120
30 Major, J., *John Major: the autobiography*, London: Harper Collins, 2000, p.212
31 Quoted in Lowe, *The Death of Progressive Education*, p.121
32 Callaghan, *Conservative Party Education Policies*, p.150-157
33 Leading Article, 'Classroom Confusion', *The Times*, 16 April 1990
34 Phillips, All Must Have Prizes, p.159
35 Quoted in Mcnee, M., and Coleman, A., *The Great Reading Disaster*, Exeter: Imprint Academic, 2007, p.181
36 Woodhead, *Class War*, pp.176; 3
37 Engel, M., 'Hard cheese and chalk', *Guardian*, 11 November 1996
38 Alexander, R., (et al), *'The Three Wise Men Report', Curriculum Organisation and Classroom Practice in Primary Schools: A discussion paper*, London: DES, 1992
39 Charter, D., 'Teachers bring back traditional classes for primary tests', *The Times*, 14 October 1996.
40 Alexander (et al), *The Three Wise Men Report'*, p.5
41 Lawlor, S., *Inspecting the School Inspectors: New Plans, old ills* (London: Centre for Policy Studies, 1993), p.7
42 Clare, J., 'Spectrum: The schools that must try harder', *The Times*, 16 January 1987
43 Preston, B., 'School inspectors to concentrate on improving three Rs', *The Times*, 15 February 1995.
44 Woodhead, *Class War*, p.21
45 Quoted in Phillips, *All Must Have Prizes*, p.55
46 O'Leary, J., 'Who will train the teachers', *The Times*, 2 May 1994
47 Phillips, *All Must Have Prizes*, p.39
48 Barber, M., 'Left and right kept behind after school', *Guardian*, 12 September 1996
49 Gray, J., 'Grasping the nettle', *Guardian*, 14 September 1996
50 Carvel, J., 'Left and right unite over education 'meltdown'', *Observer*, 13 September 1996
51 Turner, A. W., *A Classless Society: Britain in the 1990s*, London: Arum Press, 2014, p.179
52 Bevins, A., 'Blair takes tough love into the classroom', *Guardian*, 18 June 1995
53 Blunkett, D., *On A Clear Day*, London: Michael O'Mara, 2002, p.52

54 Pollard, S., *David Blunkett*, London: Hodder and Stoughton, 2005, p.170

55 Bevins, A., 'Blair takes tough love into the classroom', *Guardian*, 18 June, 1995

56 Tope, G., 'Curiouser and curiouser', *Observer*, 18 February 1997

57 Scott-Clark, C., Wark, P., 'Flagship school that sank', *The Sunday Times* 3 March 1996

58 Donoughue, *The Heat of the Kitchen*, p.241

5 Reform: 1997-2010

1 Bangs, J., et al, *Reinventing Schools, Reforming Teaching*, London: Routledge, 2011, p.11

2 DfEE, *White Paper: Excellence in Schools*, London: Her Majesty's Stationery Office, p.11

3 'Grice, A., 'Blunkett to push teaching back to basics', *The Sunday Times* 22 June 1997; 'School Blitz as Blunkett Goes Back to Basics', *The Express*, 8 July 1997

4 Lupton and Obolenskaya, 'Labour's Record on Education', p.35

5 Lowe, *The Death of Progressive Education*, pp.152; 157

6 HMI, *Excellence in Cities and Education Action Zones: Management and Impact*, London: Ofsted Publications Centre, 2003

7 Kendall, L. et al, *Excellence in Cities: The National Evaluation of a Policy to Raise Standards in Urban Schools 2000-20003*, London: Her Majesty's Stationery Office, 2005

8 Pollard, *David Blunkett*, p.233; 227

9 Burkard, T., and Talbot Rice, S., *School Quangos: An agenda for abolition and reform*, London: Centre for Policy Studies, 2009, p.4

10 Hargreaves, D., *The Mosaic of Learning*, London: Demos, 1994, p.43

11 Hargreaves, D., *A New Shape for Schooling*, London: Specialists Schools and Academies Trust, 2006, p.16

12 Wilby, P., 'Intellectual guru seeks 'system redesign' of secondary education, *Guardian*, 22 September 2009; Abbott et al., *Education Policy*, p.155

13 NCSL, *Learning-centred Leadership: Towards personalised learning-centred leadership*, Nottingham: NCSL, 2005, p.16

14 Woodhead, C., *A Desolation of Learning: Is this the education our children deserve?*, Chippenham, Pencil Sharp Publishing, 2009, p.123

15 DfES, *14-19 Curriculum and Qualifications Reform: Final Report of the Working Group on 14-19 Reform*, Annesley: DfES Publications, 2004

16 Taylor, M., 'Radical shift, says minister', *Guardian*, 24 February 2005
17 Pollard, *David Blunkett*, p.213
18 Blunkett, D., *The Blunkett Tapes: My Life in the Bear Pit*, London: Bloomsbury, 2008, p.619
19 Barber, M., *The Learning Game: Arguments for an Education Revolution*, London: Cassell Group, 1996, pp.170-171
20 Bennett, T., *Teacher Proof: Why research in education doesn't always mean what it claims, and what you can do about it*, London: Routledge, 2013, pp.66; 143
21 Brooks, G., *Sound sense: the phonics element of the National Literacy Strategy*, London: DfES, 2003, p.6
22 Revell, P., 'Each to their own', *Guardian*, 31 May 2005
23 Hastings, 'Learning styles', *Times Educational Supplement*, 4 November 2005
24 Willingham, D. T., *Why Don't Students Like School?*, San Francisco: Wiley, 2009, p.148
25 Hattie, J., and Yates, G., *Visible Learning and the Science of How we Learn*, Abingdon: Routledge, 2014, p.182
26 Bennett, *Teacher Proof*, pp.146-9
27 Miliband, D., *Choice and Voice in Personalised Learning*, speech given on 18 May 2004
28 Gilbert, C., *2020 Vision: Report of the Teaching and Learning in 2020 Review Group*, Nottingham: DFES Publications, 2006, p.6
29 Baker, M., 'Let's not get personal', http://news.bbc.co.uk/1/hi/education/7741943.stm [accessed January, 2014]
30 Christodoulou, D., *Seven Myths about Education*, London: Routledge, 2013, pp.50-53
31 Quoted in Furedi, F., *Wasted: Why Education Isn't Educating*, London: Continuum, 2009, p.23
32 Lightfoot, L., Grimston, J., 'Schools slump after teachers rebranded as 'progress leaders', *The Sunday Times*, 19 February 2012; Turner, B., 'Knowsley flagship Christ the King school to close within months', *Liverpool Echo*, 19 April 2013
33 *Newsletter: Campaign for Real Education*, Spring 2006
34 Johnson, M., *Subject to Change: New Thinking on the Curriculum*, London: ATL, 2007
35 QCA, *The National Curriculum*, London: QCA, 2007
36 Smithers, R., 'Birdwatching and cookery on personalised school timetable', *Guardian*, 6 February 2007
37 Hensher, P., 'Does anyone really understand the National Curriculum?', *Independent*, 3 April 2009
38 Wilby, P., 'Mick Waters, curriculum guru, takes stock', *The*

Guardian, 7 September 2010
39 de Waal, Anastasia, *Inspection, Inspection, Inspection: How Ofsted crushes independent schools and independent teachers*, London: Civitas, 2006, p.46
40 Woodhead, *Class War*, p.110
41 Beere, J., *The Perfect Ofsted Lesson*, Carmarthen: Crown Publishing, 2010
42 Birbalsingh, K., *To Miss With Love*, London: Penguin, 2011, pp.33-36
43 Christodoulou, *Seven Myths about Education*, pp.34; 103
44 http://teachingbattleground.wordpress.com/2013/02/16/what-ofsted-actually-want/ [accessed January, 2014]
45 *The Teacher*, January 2008, p.18
46 Taken from Adonis, A., *Education, Education, Education: Reforming England's Schools*, London: Biteback, 2012; and 'Strictly Come Learning', *New Statesman*, 14 October 2011
47 http://www.arkschools.org/secondary [accessed January 2014]
48 Memorandum submitted by New Line Learning to the Select Committee on Education and Skills, quoted in *Newsletter: Campaign for Real Education*, Spring 2007
49 Marley, D., 'Sole searching', *Times Educational Supplement*, 12 May 2008
50 Garner, R., 'Revealed: the school where 1 in four play truant', *The Independent*, 13 January 2010; Francis, P., 'Worry over schools' big number of vacancies', *Kent Messenger*, 21 January 2013
51 Adonis, *Education, Education, Education*, p.134
52 Carroll, C., *On the Edge*, Cheltenham: Monday Books, 2010, p.93
53 Bartholomew, J., *The Welfare State We're In*, Bury St Edmunds: Politico, 2004, p.216
54 Lawlor, S. (et al), *Teaching Matters: The Recruitment, Employment and Retention of Teachers*, London: Politea, 2007, pp.23; 12
55 McVeigh, T., 'It's all in a day's work', *Observer*, 21 January 2001
56 Steer, A. (et al), *Learning Behaviour: The Report of the Practitioners' Group on School Behaviour and Discipline*, Nottingham: DfES Publications, 2005, pp.10; 2; 16
57 Massey and Groves, *Best Behaviour*, p.14
58 Balls, E., 'Old Tories in disguise', *Guardian*, 26 August 2009
59 Coe, R., 'Improving Education: A triumph of hope over experience', Inaugural Lecture to Durham Unviersity, 18 June 2013, available at http://www.cem.org/attachments/publications/ImprovingEducation2013.pdf [accessed January, 2014]

60 Paton, G, 'GCSEs 'devalued by grade inflation' over the last decade', *The Daily Telegraph*, 16 August 2013
61 http://www.youtube.com/watch?v=XekkQ3HG2lg [accessed January, 2014]
62 Wolf, A., *Review of Vocational Education: The Wolf Report*, London: DfE, 2011, p.39
63 Paton, G., 'A-levels 'now two grades easier than 20 years ago'', *The Daily Telegraph*, 11 August 2008
64 *Newsletter: Campaign for Real Education*, Spring 2005
65 Woodhead, *A Desolation of Learning*, p.34
66 Wolf, *Review of Vocational Education*, pp.7; 141
67 Burkard, T., *The End of Illiteracy: The Holy Grail of Clackmannanshire?*, London: Centre for Policy Studies, 1999, pp.1-10
68 Burkard, T., *After the Literacy Hour: May the Best Plan Win!*, London: Centre for Policy Studies, 2004, p.3
69 Burkard, *The End of Illiteracy*, p.17
70 Johnston, R. S., and Watson, J. E, *Insight 17: A Seven Year Study of the Effects of Synthetic Phonics Teaching on Reading and Spelling Attainment*, Edinburgh: Scottish Executive Education Department, 2005, p.5
71 Marrin, M., 'Spelling out why black schoolboys fail', *The Sunday Times*, 5 June 2005
72 Marrin, M., 'Read my lips, I can fix our schools', *The Sunday Times* 21, October 2007
73 Benford, M., 'Phonics myopia is poor prescription'. *Times Educational Supplement*, 7 April 2006; Wadsworth, J., 'Don't buy this phonics snake oil', *Times Educational Supplement*, 3 March 2006
74 *The Daily Telegraph*, 19 January 2006
75 Curtis, P., 'Ken Boston's resignation accepted as delayed primary tables are published', *Guardian*, 1 April 2009
76 Burkard and Talbot Rice, *School Quangos*, p.2
77 Lupton and Obolenskaya, 'Labour's Record on Education', pp.16-17
78 Adonis, *Education, Education, Education*, p.72
79 Merits of Statutory Instruments Committee, *The cumulative impact of statutory instruments on schools*, London: The Stationery Office Limited, 2009, p.10
80 OECD, *Country Note: United Kingdom*, p.1
81 OECD, *OECD Skills Outlook 2013*, p.107
82 Smithers, R., 'Keep pupils in at lunch, minister tells schools', *Guardian*, 27 March 2004

6 The Child-centred Orthodoxy

1 Plowden, The Plowden Report, Vol. I, p.460

2 Ofsted, *Transforming Religious Education: Religious education in schools 2006-09*, Ofsted, 2010, p.45

3 Ofsted, *Mathematics: made to measure*, Ofsted, 2012, p.24

4 Ofsted, *Geography Survey Visits: Generic grade descriptors and supplementary subject-specific guidance for inspectors on making judgements during visits to schools*, Ofsted, 2013, p.3

5 Ofsted, *English Survey Visits: Generic grade descriptors and supplementary subject-specific guidance for inspectors on making judgements during visits to schools*, Ofsted, 2013, p.4

6 Mayer, R. E., 'Should There Be a Three-Strikes Rule Against Pure Discovery Learning? The Case for Guided Methods of Instruction', in *American Psychologist*, Vol. 59, No. 1, 2004, pp.14-19

7 Skidelsky, *English Progressive Schools*, p.27

8 Quoted in Feinberg, E., and Feinberg, W., 'Carl Rogers', in Palmer, *Fifty Modern Thinkers on Education*, p.49

9 Evans, D., 'He's not the messiah…', *Times Educational Supplement*, 14 September 2012

10 Hattie, J., *Visible Learning: A Synthesis of over 800 meta-analyses relating to achievement*, Abingdon: Routledge, 2009

11 Adams, G. L., and Engelmann, S., *Research on Direct Instruction: 25 Years Beyond DISTAR*, Seattle: Education Achievement Systems, 1996

12 Capel, S., Leask, M., and Turner, T., (eds), *Learning to Teach in the Secondary School: A Companion to School Experience*, Abingdon: Routledge, 2009, p.267

13 Clark, R. E., Kirschner, P. A., and Sweller, J., 'Putting Students on the Path to Learning: The Case for Fully Guided Instruction' in *American Education*, Spring, 2012, pp.6-11

14 Willingham, *Why Don't Students Like School?*, pp.53; 107

15 Kornell, N., Hays, M. J., & Bjork, R. A., 'Unsuccessful retrieval attempts enhance subsequent learning' in *Journal of Experimental Psychology: Learning, Memory, and Cognition*, Vol 35, July 2009, pp.989-998

16 Hattie and Yates, *Visible Learning and the Science of How we Learn*, p.76

17 Alexander, R., (et al), 'The Three Wise Men Report', p.9

18 Smith, J., *The Lazy Teacher's Handbook: How Your Students Learn More When You Teach Less*, Bancyfelin: Crown House, 2010

19 Marshall, *The Tail*, p.16

20 Oakeshott, M., *The Voice of Liberal Learning*, Indianapolis: Liberty Fund, 1989, p.71

21 Judt, T., *The Memory Chalet* (St Ives: Random House, 2010), pp.87-88

7 Empty Vessels and the Neglect of Knowledge

1 Quoted in Christodoulou, *Seven Myths About Education*, p.72
2 Seltzer, K., and Bentley, T., *The Creative Age: Knowledge and skills for the new economy*, London: Demos, 1999, p.19
3 Benn and Chitty, *Thirty Years On*, pp.259-60
4 Christodoulou, *Seven Myths About Education*, p.129
5 Hardy, G. H., *Ramanujan: twelve lectures on subjects suggested by his life and work*, Providence: AMS, 1940, p.12
6 Hirsch, E. D., *Cultural Literacy: What Every American Needs to Know*, New York: Random House, 1988, p.61
7 Willingham, *Why Don't Students Like School?*, p.28
8 Perkins, D.N., *Smart schools: From training memories to educating minds*, New York: The Free Press, 1992, p.8
9 QCA, *A framework of personal, learning and thinking skills*, QCA, 2007, p.2
10 Clare, J., 'Why study when you can surf?', *The Daily Telegraph*, 5 February 2003
11 See AQA English/English Language papers from 2011-2012, http://www.aqa.org.uk/subjects/english/gcse/english-language-4705/past-papers-and-mark-schemes [accessed January, 2014]
12 Hirsch, *Cultural Literacy*, pp.41-7
13 Hirsch, E. D., *The knowledge deficit: creating the shocking education gap for American children*, Boston: Houghton Mifflin, 2006, p.75
14 Smithers, R., 'Clarke dismisses medieval historians', *Guardian*, 9 May 2003
15 Bentley, T., *Learning Beyond the Classroom: Education for a changing world*, London: Demos, 1998, p.19
16 Hirsch, *The knowledge deficit*, p.47
17 Christodoulou, *Seven Myths About Education*, p.60
18 Benson, A. C., *The Schoolmaster*, Woodbridge: Peridot Press, 2011, p.30
19 Gilbert, *2020 Vision*, p.20
20 Kingsley Amis, 'Pernicious Participation', *Black Paper 1: The Fight for Education*, pp.9-10
21 Oakeshott, *The Voice of Liberal Learning*, p.103

8 Discipline, Character and Moral Education

1 Hunter, M., 'Chaotic Legacy of the Classroom Radicals', *Standpoint*, March 2012

2 Massey, *Best Behaviour*, p.5

3 Berliner, W., 'Guardian survey finds teachers want to be treated as professionals', *Guardian*, 3 October 2011

4 Massey, *Best Behaviour*, pp.25-26

5 Ross, T., 'UK riots: anarchy shames our 'failing' schools, says Dr Rowan Williams', *The Daily Telegraph*, 12 August 2011

6 Seldon, A., 'We need to fix Britain's character flaws', *The Daily Telegraph*, 15 May 2012

7 Middleton, C., 'The school that beat the rioters', *The Daily Telegraph*, 16 August 2011

8 House of Commons Education Committee, *Great teachers: attracting, training and retaining the best*, London: The Stationery Office Limited, 2012, p.35

9 Carroll, *On the Edge*, p.153

10 Berliner, W., 'Guardian survey finds teachers want to be treated as professionals', Guardian, 3 October 2011

11 Freedman, S., Lipson, B., and Hargreaves, D., *More Good Teachers*, London: Policy Exchange, 2008, p.15

12 Hobson, A. J., et al., *Becoming a Teacher: Teachers' Experiences of Initial Teacher Training, Induction and Early Professional Development*, Nottingham: DCSF, 2009, p.26

13 Quoted in Hobson, P., 'A. S. Neill', in Palmer, Fifty Modern Thinkers on Education, p.1

14 Quoted in Phillips, *All Must Have Prizes*, p.221

15 Bentley, *Learning Beyond the Classroom*, p.188

16 Steer (et al), *Learning Behaviour*, p.15

17 Shackle, S., 'Strictly come learning', *New Statesman*, 14 October 2011

18 See Bennett, *Teacher Proof*, pp.90-105; and Ecclestone, K., and Hayes, D., *The Dangerous Rise of Therapeutic Education*, Abingdon: Routledge, 2009

19 Humphrey, N., Lendrum, A., and Wigelsworth, M., *Social and emotional aspects of learning (SEAL) programme in secondary schools: national evaluation*, Manchester: DFE, 2010, p.3

20 Haidt, J., *The Righteous Mind: Why Good People are Divided by Politics and Religion*, London: Allen Lane, 2010, pp.7-8

21 Capel, Leask and Turner (eds.), *Learning to Teach in the Secondary School*, p.221

22 Phillips, *All Must Have Prizes*, p.215

23 DiCenso, A., Guyatt, G., Willan, A., and Griffith, L., 'Interventions To Reduce Unintended Pregnancies Among Adolescents: Systematic Review Of Randomised Controlled Trials', in *British Medical Journal*, Vol. 324, No. 7351 (Jun. 15,

2002), pp.1426-1430

24 Haidt, *The Righteous Mind*, pp.28; 66

25 Heffer, S., *High Minds: The Victorians and the Birth of Modern Britain*, London: Random House, 2013, p.456

26 Wats, R., 'Eton to give state schools advice on building character', *The Daily Telegraph*, 3 February 2013

27 Arthur, J., *Education with Character: The moral economy of schooling*, London: Routledge, 2003, p.20

28 Neill, *Summerhill*, p.221

29 Duhigg, C., *The power of habit: why we do what we do and how to change*, London: William Heinemann, 2012, p.133

30 Whitman, D., *Sweating the Small Stuff: Inner-City Schools and the New Paternalism*, Thomas B. Fordham Institute, 2008

31 Tough, P., *How Children Succeed: Grit, Curiosity and the Hidden Power of Character*, London: Random House, 2012, p.57

32 Brooks, D., *The Social Animal: The Hidden Sources of Love, Character, and Achievement*, New York: Random House, 2011, pp.288-289

33 James Q. Wilson, *The Moral Sense*, New York: The Free Press, 1993, p.250

34 Lawrence, D. H., *The Rainbow*, London: Methuen & Co., 1915, p.358

35 Exley, S., 'Sir Michael Wilshaw vows to crack down on bad behaviour as he launches Ofsted annual report', *Times Educational Supplement*, 11 December 2013

9 The Soft Bigotry of Low Expectations

1 Quoted in Gordon, P. (ed), *The Study of Education: A Collection of Inaugural Lectures*, London: Woburn Press, 1980, p.53

2 White, J., 'What schools are for and why', *Impact No. 14*, London: Philosophy of Education Society of Great Britain, 2007, pp.7-8

3 Quoted in Burkard, T., *Inside the Secret Garden: The Progressive Decay of Liberal Education*, Buckingham: The University of Buckingham Press, 2007, p.175

4 Barker, B., *The Pendulum Swings: Transforming School Reform*, Stoke on Trent: Trentham Books Limited, 2010, p.19

5 Milne, J., 'Return of the gala queen', *Times Educational Supplement*, 11 May 2007

6 Wilby, P., 'Dear Tristram Hunt… advice for combating Michael Gove', *Guardian*, 15 October 2015

7 Fowler, R., 'Michael Wilshaw takes over at Ofsted', *The Daily Telegraph*, 2 November 2011

8 Patel-Carstairs, S., 'Rich pupils 'twice as likely to attend a top university'', *The Daily Telegraph*, 23 July 2013

9 Sutton Trust, *Responding to the new landscape for university access,* December 2010, p.2
10 Marshall, *The Tail,* p.10
11 Mongon, D., *Educational Attainment: White British students from low income background,* London: Ofsted, 2013, p.8
12 Gove, M., 'Speech to Brighton College', 10 May 2012
13 Davies, N., *The School Report: Why Britain's Schools are Failing,* Vintage: London, 2000, pp.x; 17
14 NUT, PISA Results press release, 3 December 2013. http://www.teachers.org.uk/node/20039 [accessed January, 2014]
15 OECD, *PISA 2012 Results: What Students Know and Can Do – student performance in mathematics, reading and science* (volume I), OECD, 2013, p.341
16 Adamson, P., *Measuring Child Poverty: New League tables of child poverty in the world's rich countries,* Florence: UNICEF, 2013, p.3
17 OECD, *PISA 2012 Results: What Makes Schools Successful? Resources, Policies and Practices* (Volume IV), p.313
18 Welham, H., 'Coping with 'requires improvement', exam myths and giving feedback', *Guardian,* 7 February 2014
19 Taylor, M., 'It's official: class matters', *Guardian,* 28 February 2006
20 Sutton Trust, *Improving the Impact of Teachers on Pupil Advancement in the UK,* September 2011, p.2
21 Marzal, A., 'The 100 most improved primaries in England', *The Daily Telegraph,* 13 December 2012
22 BBC, *Analysis: Do Schools Make a Difference? Transcript of a recorded documentary,* London: BBC, 2012
23 Taylor, R., 'Blair urges headmasters to defeat 'forces of conservatism'', *The Guardian,* 21 October 1999
24 Quoted in Cox and Boyson, *Black Paper 5,* p.84
25 Johnson, *Subject to Change*
26 White, 'What schools are for and why', p.28
27 Quoted in Phillips, *All Must Have Prizes,* pp.175-176
28 Conway, D., *Liberal Education and the National Curriculum,* London: Civitas, 2010, p.80
29 Arnold, M., Collini, S. (ed), *Culture and Anarchy and Other Writings,* Cambridge: Cambridge University Press, 1993, p.79
30 Rose, *Intellectual Life of the British Working Classes,* pp.150; 186
31 Quoted in Conway, *Liberal Education and the National Curriculum,* p.50
32 Rose, *Intellectual Life of the British Working Classes,* pp.42; 162-163
33 Johns, L., Speech to the Conservative Party Conference, 1 October 2013, http://www.conservativepartyconference.org.uk/Speeches/2013_Lindsay_Johns.aspx [accessed January, 2014]

Conclusion

1 Arendt, H., *Six Exercises in Political Thought*, London: Faber and Faber, 1961, pp.178-179; 195
2 *Newsletter: Campaign for Real Education*, Winter 2005
3 Rogers, C., *Freedom to Learn*, Columbus: Charles E. Merrill Publishing Company, 1969, pp.103; 157-164

Index